DATE DUE

OCT 0 2 2006			

Myth

Myth

A Handbook

William G. Doty

Greenwood Folklore Handbooks

GREENWOOD PRESS
Westport, Connecticut • London

Library of Congress Cataloging-in-Publication Data

Doty, William G., 1939–
  Myth : a handbook / William G. Doty.
     p. cm.—(Greenwood folklore handbooks, ISSN 1549–733X)
    Includes bibliographical references.
    ISBN 0–313–32696–7 (alk. paper)
    1. Myth. I. Title. II. Series
  BL304.D577   2004
  201'.3—dc22   2004007989

British Library Cataloguing in Publication Data is available.

Library of Congress Catalog Card Number: 2004007989
ISBN: 0–313–32696–7
ISSN: 1549–733X

First published in 2004

Greenwood Press, 88 Post Road West, Westport, CT 06881
An imprint of Greenwood Publishing Group, Inc.
www.greenwood.com

Printed in the United States of America

Copyright Acknowledgments

    The author and publisher gratefully acknowledge permission to excerpt passages from the following sources:

Excerpts from personal communication from Liz Locke, 1991, are reprinted by permission of Liz Locke.

Excerpts from *Creation and Procreation: Feminist Reflections on Mythologies of Cosmogony and Parturition* by Marta Weigle, © 1989, are reprinted by permission of the University of Pennsylvania Press.

Excerpts from *God: Myths of the Male Divine* by David Leeming and Jake Page, © 1996, are used by permission of Oxford University Press, Inc.

Excerpts from *Goddess: Myths of the Female Divine* by David Leeming and Jake Page, © 1994, are used by permission of Oxford University Press, Inc.

Excerpts from Donna Rosenberg, *World Mythology*. New York: McGraw Hill, 1994. Used with permission of the McGraw Hill Companies.

Excerpts from Michael Jordan, *Myths of the World: A Thematic Encyclopedia*. London: Kyle Cathie Limited. 1993 © Michael Jordan. Used by permission of Kyle Cathie Limited.

Excerpts from *Entropy* by Jeremy Rifkin, with Ted Howard, © 1980 by Foundation on Economic Trends. Used by permission of Viking Penguin, a division of Penguin Group (USA) Inc.

Excerpts from *Book of the Hopi* by Frank Waters, © 1963 by Frank Waters. Used by permission of Viking Penguin, a division of Penguin Group (USA) Inc.

Excerpts from Snorri Sturluson, *Prose Edda of Snorri Sturluson*. Edited and translated by Jean Young. Copyright (c) 1964 The Regents of the University of California. Used with permission.

Every reasonable effort has been made to trace the owners of copyright materials in this book, but in some instances this has proven impossible. The author and publisher will be glad to receive information leading to more complete acknowledgments in subsequent printings of the book and in the meantime extend their apologies for any omissions.

Contents

Preface

I have enjoyed working on this volume, which reflects some of my monster book, *Mythography: The Study of Myths and Rituals* (2000), and several other writings on myth and ritual, but also takes into account about 150 publications that have come my way since finishing that thorough revision of a volume first published in 1986. This book should provide a more accessible introduction to the study of myth, with many fewer scholarly references or details.

For three of the longer chapters and for general stylistic grooming, I have once again had the assistance of my doctoral student and friend, Jon Berry, Project Editor at the University of Alabama Press. It is always amazing how we can improve each other's writing.

In-text bibliographic references lead to full citations in the Works Cited at the end of each chapter. The volume bibliography in the back matter is selective rather than inclusive. The 75-page bibliography in *Mythography* and a selected introductory bibliography there is broken into 23 annotated topics that provide hundreds of references. Several subtopics reappear in other chapters, in order to facilitate comprehension for users who access chapters in a nonsequential reading.

One
Introduction

Myth is regarded variously across a wide spectrum of opinions spanning several centuries. Introducing a recent issue of the journal *Folklore Forum* on "Myth," the guest editor began by noting "the variety inherent in our understanding of myth as we near the end of the twentieth century," and she named as "problematic terms" most of the characteristics myth research had become comfortable with: narrative, genre, sacred, belief, performance, ritual, interpretation, context, production, document, coding, and evidence. "Even taking the definition wars of the past century or so into consideration, whose arguments centered largely on descriptions of folklore's long-acknowledged genres of legend, saga, epic, ballad, and folktale," Liz Locke noted, "it must be admitted that such a state of semantic disarray and/or ambiguity is truly extraordinary" (1998: 1).

Terms can be defined according to their linguistic or semantic derivation, for which one utilizes an etymological dictionary, or according to their historical usage. For the latter, one needs something like the *Oxford English Dictionary*, which in its first edition was titled *A New English Dictionary on Historical Principles*, and which documents as closely as possible the ways in which English words were actually used at specific dates. Here we combine both perspectives, noting first that "mythos" meant "plot" to Aristotle, whose *Poetics* scientifically organized dramatic narratives into the sequence of beginning/middle/end. His teacher Plato worried about the influence of old wives' tales in the education of the elite citizens of his idealized "republic." Out of the rulers' control, such materials—and the poets' elaborations of them—were to be excluded because they were unphilosophized and unrationalized.

Aristotle's *Poetics* scientifically organized dramatic narratives into the sequence beginning, middle, and end. Courtesy of Thoemmes.

But at the same time Plato created his own mythic stories to elucidate points in his own philosophical agendas, some of which, like his narrative of The Cave (*Republic* 514a–521b) have remained important allegories for several thousand years (Luc Brisson's exhaustive account of *Plato the Mythmaker* [1998] amplifies fully these brief remarks). Aspects of *The Matrix* movie trilogy doubtless owe something to this story of persons chained for years in such a way as to see only shadows of real images who then, when released, are unable to tolerate life in the open air.

MYTHS IN SOCIETIES

Myths serve as stand-ins for serious truths of Western civilization, even while other similar stories have been laughed at as mindless fictions. Fictions

Aspects of *The Matrix* trilogy doubtless owe something to the story of persons who are chained for years in such a way as to see only shadows of real images, and then, when released, are unable to tolerate life in the open air. Courtesy of Photofest.

(from the Latin word for forming, fabricating, cognate with factory) imply arbitrary codings or interpretations of human cultural significances, so that myths may be understood less as preaching than as poetic revisionings of the everyday. Myths are seldom fantasy constructions; more frequently they are the backbones of practical ways of living realistically. Yet even though mythic patterns of heroines and heroes appear to be almost beyond daily comprehension, careful attention reveals that their contents touch less on fantasy than on everyday questioning of quite realistic developmental issues: When should the adolescent separate from parents? Where do individual goals augment or expand communal goals? Should communal or parental guidelines always be respected or sometimes challenged? What is the role of fate in human decision making? And is it passed along by heredity?

The study of mythologies reflects the ways our society has answered such questions. We find reflected in the study of myths many issues of what a culture considers to be appropriate behaviors and models of selfhood, as well as models of social and political ways of existing. Considering myths as purely fictional or imaginative projections of social well-being, therefore, short-circuits important mythical potentials for social evolution and individual and cultural development.

Myths convey knowledge accrued over generations. Hence mythologies are "conservative" in the sense of protecting such knowledge, as well as in

Psyche brought to life by Eros' kiss, marble sculpture, 1793 (detail). © The Art Archive / Musée du Louvre Paris / Dagli Orti.

terms of proscribing behaviors—think how one learns from the story of King Midas not to be too greedy, from the story of Psyche and Cupid (Eros) not to be too curious about a divine gift. Contemporary approaches emphasize the need to look for the ways in which traditional myths can be resources for "thinking outside the box" today, rather than merely limiting consciousness to classical models of values—the term *classical* has dropped in value to *outdated* in many parts of contemporary "Do it now!" culture.

Although these are "folk" materials, this means little more than that they are not just restricted to upper-class, elitist literature. A bias in that direction probably stems from the fact that when educated classes started to be aware of the huge extent of folk materials, they sought to control it by the usual political and academic tyrannies: folk meant popular, and from their perspective that meant inferior. Today disciplines such as gender studies, American studies, cultural studies, and even pop culture studies bear more democratized aspects: pop culture simply *is* the culture most of us are surrounded by every day, and it is certainly the arena in which the vast bulk of money is spent. Hence a study such as Georges-Claude Guilbert's *Madonna as Postmodern Myth* (2002) makes immediate sense; its subtitle is *How One Star's Self-Construction Rewrites Sex, Gender, Hollywood, and the American Dream.* Glitz in style threatens to replace historically established values that previous generations considered divinely inspired and essential to "culture."

And other biases are likewise giving way to new perspectives, such as the long-established use of *literary* distinctions within folkloristics. According to that custom, myths have to do with fabulous realms, deities, abnormal natural powers; legends are stories that have some basis in the historical career of someone; and fairy or folk tales no one "believes" in, partly because they have lost their earlier well-established place as adult pastimes to become primarily of interest to children. Other distinctions have been made, but today (with some exceptions: Alan Dundes [1984] restricts myth to "sacred narratives," a restriction discussed later), folklorists emphasize that the literary markers are less important than *audience reception* within a particular sociohistorical context. The same story can be a "legend" to someone who believes its subject to have been a historical figure, but merely pious fantasy to a nonreligious reader; a rap star earning millions of dollars a year may still be considered beneath contempt by parents and teachers.

Because folklore studies is one of the primary places where mythologies have been analyzed seriously, we will look more closely at that field in a subsequent chapter. But it is important to remember that myths are studied in many branches of knowledge: classes in American Studies departments look primarily at historical models of the Western Frontier, for instance, or at the American superhero in contemporary mass media. Religious Studies faculty treat myth as particularly "marked" within religious associations: either negatively, when it refers to what outsiders, others, believe, or positively, when it is seen as providing symbols and metaphors for the language of the faith.

Anthropologists and ethnologists were some of the first to recognize how certain cultural stories recurred across time, and they learned right away that many such myths are surrounded with social stipulations. Particular myths should be related only in the winter, for instance, or are shared only when the adolescent has been initiated at a certain age. Classicists and historians of antiquity focus upon myths of a selected period such as classical Greek and Rome or sagas such as the *Gilgamesh* epic from the Ancient Near East. Because of the ongoing significance of the classical languages in the West, Greek and Latin mythologies are among the most familiar, and terms in our every-day language often derive directly from them: *martial, narcissistic, Herculean task,* and *mercurial temperament.* Isaac Asimov gives a nice sample: "a police car's signal is a siren and a sea cow is a sirenian. A circus organ is a calliope; a jelly-fish is a medusa; and an Australian anteater is an echidna. We call out in a stentorian voice; listen to a kindly mentor or a bearded nestor; despise a hec-toring bully" (1961: 5).

Much interpretation today accords a great deal of importance to the recog-nition of the *contexts* in which myths originate and are transmitted, a recog-nition that realizes that the same myth may function at one time in a society in many different contexts: just think how shocking it might be to a fervent lover of Shakespeare to spot a leatherbound collector's edition of his plays and poetry propping open a ventilating window in the basement! (or for a fervent Christian, a crucifix used for the same purpose).

Homer, blind Greek poet, singing to sailors. Clas-sicists and historians of antiquity focus upon myths of a selected period, such as classical Greek and Rome. © Mary Evans Picture Library.

MYTH AND "THE REAL TRUTH"

One philosophical issue in our approach to the roles and functions of myths in societies is much like that driving *The Matrix* trilogy, namely *the nature of reality.* You have to watch certain cues in the Wachowski brothers' movies—a green tint is the artificial Matrix world and a blue tint the supposedly real-time world—to interpret its meanings. And contemporary philosophy has become quite sophisticated about devising methods of determining how knowledge is produced (epistemology) as well as how meanings are conveyed, so that interpretations can be made (hermeneutics, phenomenology). I mention philosophy because the question of "the real" is also the question of "the truth," and ever since Plato, the "truth" was thought to exist in ideals (archetypes) located "somewhere else."

Late Greek distinctions between myth *(mythos)* and reason *(logos)*—originally, in actual usage, they might both refer to the same piece of language—and a particular manner in which mythic figures were allegorized to mean just about anything led to a situation whereby Latin chose to avoid a form of the Greek term *mythos* and used in its place a still-neutral word, *fabula,* which just to complicate matters was translated into English as *fable* where it referred to a story about a talking burro or whatever.

For much of Western history, the logos-ical (logical) ruled the mythical. In Enlightenment rationalism the logical/rational became considered the Truth machine, and myth was associated with falsity or fiction. Even in Romanticism, when myths of many cultures other than Greece and Rome and Israel began to be discovered and collected, myths had the connotation of "outside the normal course of language," bearing inspiring meanings, perhaps, but not to be trusted with the bank book.

But what goes around comes around, and in much contemporary philosophical thought, the notion that there is a transcendent, timeless Truth somewhere has mostly vanished (especially in postmodernist thinkers). It is, rather, a matter of perspective, something affirmed as such by a particular community of interpreters (earlier generations sought timeless, "universal," or "absolute" affirmations of "truth" and often ignored the socially constructed nature of what any particular society comes to consider ultimate).

Interpretation is very much a matter of managing, selecting, and assigning meanings considered important within specific historical periods or social classes, and the same story can be read very differently by successive generations. Every telling is a retelling, a new version for a particular occasion, as noted earlier. Hence we can now suggest that "myth is a way of making meanings" within a particular tradition (McCutcheon 2000: 201–7). And simply transmitting, adapting, adopting for one's own use a mythical unit means that we should not speak too quickly about "secondary myth" but recognize that it is all secondary with respect to prototypes that become unattainable the first time they are passed along.

Later we'll discuss how something can be said to have "mythical" qualities (mythicity)—even if the subject has none of the characteristics we usually associate with most myths in a Freshman 101 literature course.

NAVIGATING THIS VOLUME

This book, like others in this Greenwood series, is laid out simply and designed to be used by starting at the beginning and working through the pages, *or* to be useful when first accessed at any particular chapter. Chapter 2 provides a number of definitions of myth and mythology—we will see that the type of definition is determined by the intentions of the definer!—and we canvass some of the various types of myths, motifs, and themes (such as heroine stories or accounts of the first beginning of things) as well as traces in language and artistic imagery.

Myths are above all (but not exclusively) *narrative,* and that means we have to consider what happens when oral materials become written down, and hence subject to canonization (restriction to only a certain number of "true" stories). They are *poetic* in the sense of being richer language than what may be found in a newspaper, but they are also *performative*—that is, it is important to respect the ideal context in which they are *spoken or enacted* in rituals (even the reading of a myth in a classroom or around a campfire can ritualize the story).

Chapter 3 provides examples of myths with some minimal commentary, first within the English-speaking world (Britain, the United States, and now as the international world language) and then in a few non-English speaking contexts (antiquity, Africa, the Far East, and India) and concludes with a discussion of "comparative mythology," as the engine that has driven most of the World Mythologies collections available in any library or bookstore.

My taking up the term *mythography,* which early on referred to collecting myths, for *the study of myths and rituals,* in the first edition of my *Mythography: The Study of Myths and Rituals* (1986; 2nd entirely revised ed. 2000), has now become standard among most academics. Chapter 4 provides a mini-mythographic history of the concepts and treatments of myth. It also treats attitudes toward myth in various divisions of the educational curriculum, especially within literary studies—where folklore is often taught today—and some branches of psychology.

The fifth chapter comes back to the issue of transmission and metamorphosis of mythological images and stories. It also relates myth to religion, ideology, and politics, and it is here that it will become evident that mythology is not just about matters of the ancient world but is also very much a matter of popular culture and the arts today. The Disney empire has come to dominate retellings of so many favorite myths and tales today—precisely by rewriting traditional stories in ways that shred and discard them before substituting pious, massively patriarchal versions that a vast market chooses as replacements for earlier standard views (see discussions in Zipes 1994: chap. 3, "Breaking the Disney Spell," and Lawrence and Jewett 2002: chap. 9).

The bibliography in the back matter provides recommended readings. Other back matter resources include a guide to Internet resources on the World Wide Web and other electronic resources; a glossary of terms, leading interpreters, and other technical items; and an extensive index.

WORKS CITED

Asimov, Isaac. 1961. *Words from the Myths.* New York: New American Library.

Brisson, Luc. 1998 [1982]. *Plato the Myth Maker.* Ed. and trans. Gerard Naddaf. Chicago: U of Chicago P.

Doty, William G. 2000. *Mythography: The Study of Myths and Rituals.* Revised 2nd ed. Tuscaloosa: U of Alabama P.

Dundes, Alan, ed. 1984. *Sacred Narrative: Readings in the Theory of Myth.* Berkeley: U of California P.

Guilbert, Georges-Claude. 2002. *Madonna as Postmodern Myth: How One Star's Self-Construction Rewrites Sex, Gender, Hollywood, and the American Dream.* Jefferson, NC: McFarland.

Lawrence, John Shelton, and Robert Jewett. 2002. *The Myth of the American Superhero.* Grand Rapids, MI: Eerdmans.

Locke, Liz, guest ed. 1998. "Myth" issue, *Folklore Forum* 29 (2).

McCutcheon, Russell T. 2000. "Myth." In *Guide to the Study of Religion,* eds. Willi Braun and Russell T. McCutcheon, 190–208. New York: Cassell.

Zipes, Jack. 1994. *Fairy Tale as Myth, Myth as Fairy Tale.* The Thomas Clark Lectures, 1993. Lexington: UP of Kentucky.

Two
Definitions and Classifications

Simple matters call for simple definitions. Unfortunately, some of the most important topics in our culture cannot be treated adequately by a simple definition. With respect to defining *myth,* a very handy Web site by Elizabeth Holtze, for her class ENG 3430, Classical Mythology (at Metropolitan State College of Denver), provides some 27 definitions or definitional comments. Earlier, for my own courses and publications, I gathered about 45, but I could easily double or triple that number.

THE COMPLEXITY OF DEFINING MYTH

Now if all the definitions agreed, we would be home free, but they do not. In fact, there is a wide range, from "outright lie" to "most important underlying source of cultural life." We do not have sufficient definitions (although after a while one does find many duplications) to allow two or three to carry the production of future knowledge. Because myths—however defined—are culturally important in a foundational manner, the process is not similar to defining what alphabet blocks are, but demands a reexamination of some of our oldest and richest cultural inheritances. Hence this chapter touches on important *interpretive* perspectives: for instance, what is the long-term significance of being shackled to the trivializing and ignorant use of *myth* in the sense of "deception, false presentation" or of "primitive science in primitive societies"? How problematic is it that a society usually refers to another culture's sacred narratives as "merely myths"?

Northrop Frye emphasizes the importance of the context of a definition: "The word *myth* is used in such a bewildering variety of contexts that anyone talking about it has to say first of all what his chosen context is" (1990: 3). Or as I have written elsewhere, "Myths can be made to mean whatever the myth teller wants them to mean, and their rhetorical power can be subjected to the prevailing modes of discourse of a particular era or power elite" (2000: 25). I have suggested that "*Myth* is a term with no singular historical usage; rather, it has carried and does carry a wide range of defining features, although individual writers tend to stress features most amenable to their own philosophical view of language, history, the human imagination, and presumed correlations with ritual" (30).

My academic colleague Liz Locke scanned a year's (1991) issues of *Time* magazine in order to see what a mass media sample of American usage might disclose for the term *myth*. She found six broad categories:

1. Greater or more relevant reality: mythicized phenomenon of celebrity; strange, mythicized American phenomenon; the Horatio Alger story is a myth.
2. Traditional fictions/stories: the myths of these tribes; many cultures possess a form of this myth; democracies that lack such myths.
3. Misconceived belief/untruth: another myth holds that incest occurs only if such and such occur; our reaction against the myth of Columbus; one of TV's most enduring myths, that the legal system has a warm side.
4. Personal organizing principle: the poet, the generator of her own myth; a mythology that Keith Moon would envy; the myth honors your suffering.
5. Collective organizing principle: American Express's almost mythic reputation; haunted by racial and sexual myths; the scale of California's mythology.
6. Metaphor/symbol: as the California myth gains circulation; a constitutional monarch supplies the mythic dimension; in American mythology, Pearl Harbor still represents.... (Locke, personal communication, summarized and cited by permission).

Both at the popular and the scholarly level, it ought to be obvious, therefore, how Manfred Frank can assert that "The correct definition of myth exists as little as that of the correct definition of human being itself" (quoted in Doty 2000: 32). And I find that applies to the classic equation of myth with *narrative* or *story,* a distinction already based in Aristotle's treatment in the *Poetics* of *mythos* as "plot." Of course, the narrativizing of a story is important: to create a narrative is to organize events into a chronological series of events, with (classically, in Aristotle's study of drama) beginning, middle, and end.

Professor of Classics and Folklore at Indiana University William F. Hansen reminds us that *mythos* was used by the Greeks "for all kinds of narratives, including the Aesopic fables" (1998: 91). To be sure, classicists are a bit less likely than folklorists to apply the strict genre distinctions most of us learned in high school: myth concerns the sacred, legend has some historical kernel. In fact, Hansen also suggests with respect to understanding the Greek attitude toward myth as being somehow "sacred" that there is "no real evidence that I can see that the Greeks regarded myths as 'sacred stories,' unless you take 'sacred' in a very watered-down sense. Narratives were not held by the same kinds of conventions and rules as, say 'sacred space'—the sanctuary or temple, for instance, of a god or goddess" (92).

A position of special status was not required to tell myths, nor was the telling restricted to a special time or place. "You could call them 'sacred' in the sense that they have to do with gods [and heroes, which he has just mentioned—WGD], but I don't think that's what people mean when they talk about 'sacred stories' any more than that's what they mean when they refer to 'sacred space.' They're qualitatively different in the Greek case. So if you build in 'sacred' as one of your [definitional] criteria—and that certainly is a very common criterion in defining 'myth'—you'd run into trouble right away with the Greek materials" (92).

Hansen also suggests that we need to step back from our great reverence for certain myths (I would include "scriptural" myths) and realize that in the Hellenistic period when the collectors of mythology were active, "literature" had become less elevated than in the Classical period. The collectors were interested in a range of materials—including myths—that were passed around as freely as "literature" is on our television channels (105). Certainly one of the most compendious collections, the *Bibliotheca/Library* of Apollodorus (1976; he lived 180–120 B.C.E.), had no "sacred" overtones, because it was used primarily in adolescent schoolrooms!

On the other hand, myths are *complex narratives,* not simple folktales or song-texts, "by which human cultures stabilize and encode their deepest ambiguities" (Robinson 1993: 136). They are "deep stories" of a culture (Wagner and Lundeen 1998: 3) that reflect the human tendency to organize its representation of the past, present, and future according to specific emphases and moral highlights. Indeed, the "narrative quality of existence" posited frequently, especially in a movement within the academic field of religious studies several years ago entitled "religion as story" or "narrative theology," refers to the vast importance of the fact that a culture can be understood by the way it tells its own stories and which stories it chooses to tell (cf. Wiggins 1975).

University of Chicago scholar Bruce Lincoln suggests that we look not only at the types of narrative included, but also at how a particular type, myth, may have been regarded as "in-spired," literally "breathed into":

Who speaks in myth? It is possible—and useful—to consider myth not as a *content,* but a *style* of narration. To take a convenient example, Hesiod begins his *Theogony* by invoking the Muses and goes on to tell how they made him a poet not only by teaching him, but by placing their breath inside him, where it literally supplied the substance of his speech. [...H]is poem legitimates itself by insisting that we do not just hear Hesiod's voice, but that of the goddesses mediated through him. In the moment that an audience accepts his claim, the *Theogony* constitutes itself as myth: a narrative with more-than-human status. (1998: 86)

Lincoln adds a nuance to "sacred" that does not entail the religious meanings it usually does in our culture: "Analysts ought to take seriously the claim that the ultimate authors of myth transcend the human, at least in the sense that they stand beyond the living members of the community. With rare exceptions, myths are not the creation of individual authors, but collective products elaborated over relatively long periods of time" (87). It is in this sense, notes Donald Mills, that "myths are a cultural inheritance, a tradition handed down from one generation to another, and therefore invested with communal values. This explains the close association between a community and its mythology" (2002: 4).

In such cases we must consider who is telling the myth and whose diction is allowed to be heard. Whose authority is so weak the person's words are totally discounted? Eliott Oring observes with respect to myth, legend, and tale that "these terms do not refer to the forms of narrative so much as *the attitudes of the community toward them*. Thus, myth is a term used for a narrative generally regarded by the community in which it is told as both sacred and true. Consequently, myths tend to be core narratives in larger ideological systems" (1986: 124, my emphasis, cited in Trubshaw 2002: 55).

And in fact they can become as common as images on coins. Oring notes, "There are few, if any folk narratives in our own society which could be readily categorized as myths according to our [usual] definition. Those narratives which deal with ultimate truths are generally safeguarded through a written, indeed printed, tradition" (124). Hence, of course, the leather-bound-with-gilt-edges and zippered editions of religious scriptures and the conservative's reluctance to pay attention to critical biblical (or in another context, legal) studies. Studies of "urban folklore" and other contemporary phenomena such as the mythological aspects of *Star Wars* or *The Lord of the Rings* have begun to challenge such traditional positions.

In opposition to seeing mythic materials as entirely bound up with preliterary or literary expressions, we ought to recognize that they are not just sung, told, and scribed; they also appear in the visual arts, particularly sculpture, mosaics, and painting. *Because* they are complex and foundational, their

Studies of contemporary phenomena, such as the mythological aspects of *The Lord of the Rings*, have begun to challenge such traditional positions about myth as narrative. Courtesy of Photofest.

traces are everywhere. As Nicole Loraux aptly notes with respect to life in classical Athens (1986: 345), "anyone wanting to take a walk without everywhere encountering the city presented through its myths would probably have to go outside the walls" of the city, although even in the countryside, "myths speak everywhere to citizens." Further, classicists John Scheid and Jesper Svenbro (1996: 3) also suggest that restricting Greek myth to narratives is short-sighted: "Mythology [...] cannot be confined to the domain of stories." The bias against the nonliterary or narrative "texts" is only now being challenged adequately as part of the recent emphasis upon visual culture, pop culture, and artistic embodiment of mythic perspectives generally.

Many times, indeed, mythological scenes in art (on vases, mosaics, wall paintings) represent materials no longer (if they ever were) available in written form. Hence the importance of bringing the archaeological record alongside the written collections—as Timothy Gantz has accomplished in *Early Greek Myth: A Guide to Literary and Artistic Sources* (1993) and as illustrated in the many volumes of the *Lexicon Iconographicum Mythologiae Classicae*

Greek bathing and hunting scene from *Painted Vases of the Leiden Museum* by Roulez, 1854. In many instances, mythological scenes in art, such as Greek vases, represent materials no longer (if they ever were) available in written form. © The Art Archive / Bibliothèque des Arts Décoratifs Paris / Dagli Orti (A).

(1984– ;The Lexicon of Classical Mythological Iconography—an internationally supported project).

Nor is "myth" *narrative* in some absolute, almost scriptural sense. Indeed it can be and has been distinguished from many other sorts of narrative: the *legend* that has some historical core; the *saga,* an elaborated account of heroic figures, often engaged in war; the *epic* narrative usually focused around a single dominating hero. Robert Graves (1955: 10) clarifies the nature of Greek myth (usually taken as the prototype of all subsequent Western mythology, although it was already influenced by pre-Greek myth) by differentiating it from

- Philosophical allegory (as in Hesiod's *Theogony*)
- Etiological (tracing the origins) explanation
- Satire or parody

- Sentimental fable (Ovid's Narcissus and Echo)
- Political propaganda (rhetorical speeches in general)
- Moral legend; theatrical melodrama (more common in Latin literature)
- Heroic saga (the *Iliad*)
- Realistic fantasy (Odysseus's visit to the Phaecians, a fantasy people Odysseus encountered on a fictionalized version of Corfu)
- Other types of literature

What seems essential is not the specific type of narrative that myth represents so much as finding some way to name what is mythic about a particular narrative myth. Michael McGuire (1997: 2) points to the fact that the

Front cover of Adolf Hitler's *Mein Kampf.* Anyone who reads the book even today is immediately aware of an underlying mythic scenario that its author had in mind. © Topham / The Image Works.

strange "narrative" of Adolf Hitler, *Mein Kampf,* makes little sense in terms of its awkward textual structures—yet anyone who reads it even today is immediately aware of an underlying mythic scenario that its author had in mind.

And in addition to this quality of "mythicity," it is probably important to recognize myth as *a type of communicative speech* (not necessarily oral, but represented as discourse directed at an audience). Roland Barthes refers to it as "a mode of signification, a form" (1972: 109). Hence it can be defined as a way or pattern of *signifying,* something semiotic in nature, to be interpreted hermeneutically; that is to say, not within positivistic science frameworks, but with a sort of interpretive poetics.

And perhaps it is not the form ("narrative" of a particular type), which we should add to our always-elusive definition, so much as *the way myth utters its message.* Certainly myth is not simple discourse because it often operates by means of irony (Ryan 1999: 13 n. 1), as do many political cartoons. Neither is it a type of protoscientific expression, almost mathematical in nature, nor does it display a strict philosophical rationality (see Brisson [1998] and essays in Buxton [2001]).

Lincoln has recently revisited the mythos versus logos distinctions that have been dominant within much of the mythological and philosophical research for the last 150 years. Based on very close readings of the earlier Greek literature as a whole, he suggests that myth is "speech that is raw and crude, but forceful and true" (in Hesiod's *Theogony*). It "denotes a blunt and aggressive act of plain-speaking: a hardboiled speech of intimidation" (in Homer's *Iliad*); and "highly male gendered, it is an act of speech that in its operation establishes the speaker's domination of interlocutor and audience alike" (1996: 3–5; see now his 1999 vol., which draws out his observations from early Greek usage).

Hence myth is not, in this early context, material that is considered "spacey" or "fictitious," but rather action oriented, the sort of thing the macho Greek leader ought to be able to wield like a sword. Michael McGuire's reading of the myth of Hitler's *Mein Kampf* likewise considers it a highly rhetorical genre that has particular *social functions* (2): it makes strong claims and arguments about real life as actually lived, not just about supernatural realms or powers.

Typically, *myths provide symbolic representations of cultural priorities, beliefs, and prejudices.* They dramatize and make abstractions concrete (Girling 1993: 14); perhaps we might say that they *embody* important sociocultural notions in such ways that they produce *charters* (Bronislaw Malinowski's term) for social formation and development. They can be referred to not as equivalent to fairy tales and fantasy literature, but as enacted (performantial) narratives, that is to say, *as language that does something,* namely legitimizing and establishing the social realities that form real life.

Mythic expression is never about trivial matters; it involves instead perspectives, behaviors, and attitudes that a society considers central and essential. These are foundational, "originary," a term identifying the ongoing fruitfulness of some early materials, rather than arguing that such and such is "the earliest" formulation of something now held dear. It is clearly the sort of expression that presents dramatic embodiments of ideals and values and models of the heroic and supreme. Even through the watering down of Disney productions, one has a sense that there is something *powerful* in a truly mythological story.

I am less convinced that the traditional evaluation of myths as DayGlo arrows pointing to gods or goddesses is appropriate, or at least we ought to consider what the epic figures are doing in all those horrendous slaughters on the battlefields. (As I commuted to teach for a year at another campus, I listened to audiotapes of a reading of Homer's *Iliad,* and I learned quickly to be mindful that the battle rage of the epic not get translated into road rage on the Alabama highways.)

Although myths are often said to be "religious" or to have reference to "the sacred," a more neutral analytical observation would be that they are *primary, foundational* materials of a social group. Reference to transcendent religious deities may be present in some, but think of all the myths about male and female heroes who have no such reference. It seems enough to observe that mythical accounts "embody ideas of wholeness, of order replacing chaos" (Doty 2000: 60)—something of a Modernist concept, but still valuable— and that a large number of traditional myths have related hierarchies of divine beings to the experienced conditions of human existence.

In the founding period for a large part of Western culture, however, they remained beings *born on the planet,* whose home, while elevated on some place like Mt. Olympus, was yet rooted in the same soil that the farmer plowed. They left footprints that could be clearly seen, and they had marital quarrels; they fell in love and got furious from time to time (see Sissa and Detienne [2000], *The Daily Life of the Greek Gods*). In this regard, we need to look as often as it is feasible at early versions of myths in epic and poetry because the later collectors leave out such real-world details or, as in Pindar, eliminate such mortal touches as not befitting the "divine" models.

What does seem to remain valid from earlier definitions is the suggestion that important myths appear on the scene not as authored by individuals, but derived from collaborative social experience over a period of time. I suggest that *myths coalesce social values or projections that have been found worthy of rep-*

View of Olympus, home of the gods, fresco in the Room of the Giants. A large number of traditional myths related hierarchies of divine beings to the experienced conditions of human existence. © The Art Archive / Palazzo del Te Mantua / Dagli Orti (A).

etition and replication. Like archetypes, they display guiding models for modes of attitudes and behaviors that can be helpful—or correspondingly, harmful.

I like such a definition better than I like Northrop Frye's suggestion that myths provide "a verbal *temenos* [a marked out sacred space, such as a temple] drawn around the sacred or numinous area" (Frye 1990: 238). As I have argued already in *Mythography,* I no longer find the traditional "religious" definitions of myth as being of much use (see "Intervention of Suprahuman Entities," 2000: 74–77). William Padden (2000: 340) refers to *superhuman agency.* Even more to my liking is the indirection of Philip Wheelright (in Vickery 1966: 59–66, at p. 65) in his reference to "a belief in a penumbral reality, something extending beyond yet interpenetrating with the affairs of mortal men." That seems to me to avoid some of the excessive "personalizing" of religious figures in recent Christian teaching—I often imagine that the ancients would consider contemporaries who sing or talk about "walking in the Garden alone with Jesus" as absolutely crazy. Their divine figures were not chummy, but awesome; even the awareness of the presence of Eros, a personification of the erotic energies of life, could be terrifying.

Nor do I swing around to the opposite end of the spectrum and suggest that mythology is all about personal self-fulfillment. Although I like the suggestion (in spite of my hesitations about prioritizing "narrative" in the definition of myth) that the sorts of materials that myths relate represent "quintessential story" (Doty 2000: 37), I think many present-day myth appropriations are narcissistic and individualized at an extreme so that they ignore the ways myths have operated traditionally. What I have called *the individual mythostory* (19, 44, 56) can refer to much of what is cultivated in the New Age circles of the later 1990s as "finding and living your *own* myth," or *automythological* self-help instructions for a more fulfilling life, but such an approach only skims the surface of the depths.

I hope to provide here a historical as well as a contemporary-culture account, and it is important to recognize just how myths have reverberated in the past (and are perhaps still functioning in many aspects of contemporary mass-mediated experiences). Clearly mythological materials have *functioned* and probably still do function, even though now named "religious" perspectives, as a way of sharing communal cultural values and identities and as impartings of social identity and solidarity (Girling 1993: ix, 33, 47). They represent a practice of encoding deep human ambivalences that need to be identified and lifted up into consciousness by means of mythic stories and theatrical renditions. Claude Lévi-Strauss famously tracks the way in which systems of myths continuously resolve conflicts between dualistic values such as raw and cooked (by introducing something braised) or life and death (in which a third entity portrays a sort of semilife)—Shakespeare is serious, it seems, not Disney's trivializations.

Myths are not like cotton candy at a circus that disappears with the first lick, but they graph fundamental psychological realities of everyday life: the family, sibling rivalry, male or female hero worship, or the respect or disrespect a society affords the aging. Or in more elevated contexts: the Queen's Annual Address to Parliament; the mythological shaping of George Washington's career by Pastor Weems; the "First Thanksgiving"; the institution of the Olympic Games by the Greek hero Pelops after Poseidon helped him win the hand of Hippodameia in a chariot race.

Much contemporary focus upon myth brings out psychological dimensions and functions. It is, of course, obvious how influential theorists such as Carl G. Jung, Mircea Eliade, and Joseph Campbell have been in this respect.

Andrew Von Hendy points out how scholars such as Campbell and those influenced by him fail to recognize the essentially Romantic myth theory they cultivate. Such writers see myth as "the vehicle of insight into a timeless realm of transcendental values" (2002: xii), what Robert Ellwood refers to as "the stylistic and imagistic calling forth of a romantic sense of wonder associated with archaic religion" (1999: 112).

It was precisely the sort of "domestication of the hero" and turning mythology into self-quest literature represented by these figures that led to much of the New Age ahistorical regard for shamanism, storytelling in general, and mythologies no longer situated in their actual sociohistorical contexts (where they often had meanings very different from what these later interpreters sought to make of them). But certainly across the history of myth studies, myth has been understood less as providing deep psychological insight than as a source of cosmology, the explanation of the nature of the world and its creation. In that respect, however, it is striking that the majority of the reference works I have consulted that treat "cosmology" now refer solely to contemporary astronomical theories, ignoring completely the historical use of the term.

TYPES OF MYTHS

To say what comprises the types of myth predominant in a specific culture is not difficult. But to name the types as a whole is a different story because different cultures ascribe more or less power to natural forces, patterns of lifestyle and career, importance of the self and the community, hierarchies and powers of transhuman beings, and many other matters. A glance at several collections of world mythology will disclose the ways the collectors have found to have some uniformity in the cultures surveyed, even while allowing for emphases particular to each (the table of contents in Willis 1993 provides a good example; further discussion of how one can do "comparative mythology" appears in chapter 3, and typological issues are discussed in Doty 2004).

The entry "Myth and Mythology" in *The New Encyclopedia Britannica* (Bolle et al. 1993: 715–32), in a section titled "Major types of myth" (723–26), provides for several types that deal with the construction of the world (its origins and organization) and of eventual entropy or destruction or millenarian prospects. It also includes myths of time and eternity; culture heroes; rebirth and renewal (seasons, stages of life); "myths of high beings and celestial gods" and those of religious founders, kings, and other important social figures; and finally myths of transformation—of particular features of the world or of developmental changes in the human life cycle.

Certainly the Christian dominance of Western religion has created a climate that expects a culture's mythical accounts to begin—as does Genesis (a segment edited and revised quite *late* in terms of the formation of ancient Israelite literature)—with narratives concerning the First Events. Such accounts are not necessarily those featured in all mythologies, notably not in Greek mythology, for instance, where the creation of the order of things is indeed related in Hesiod and the Orphic theologians but does not seem to have been of interest to, say, the Homeric tradition. Appropriately enough, for instance, *Cassell's Dictionary of Classical Mythology* (March 1998: 222) provides at "Creation" only a reference to the fairly extensive entry for a personification, namely Gaia, the primordial goddess of the Earth, if not indeed the Earth itself (324–26).

The extensive appendix ("Selected Texts of Creation and Procreation") to Marta Weigle's *Creation and Procreation: Feminist Reflections on Mythologies of Cosmogony and Parturition* (1989) provides an excellent balance to creation myths featuring primarily *male* creators. She points out how gender bias recurs in many cultures, where the idea of women doing what they famously do in every culture—giving birth—is ignored and devalued. Instead, she suggests,

> there is need for a way of thinking strongly about birth, whether actual, ritual, or imaginative. The mothers, midwives, and gossips who think and act strongly about childbirth must be counted among the enablers of powerful symbolic processes. Emergence myths must be included in mythology as paradigms of creation that empower in the same way as so-called true cosmogonies. All are expressions of pro/creation and renewal. (145)

What many myths struggle with is not so much "how" something began in terms of the natural sciences but rather with what it signifies, its meaning, and of course, how the human race is to be related to it, either as a source of proper behavior or as revealing which powers (divine or otherwise) are to be respected and in which order they are to be approached (as with respect to the ranking of the nine gods of the Egyptian Ennead), and in what manner the human self and the society are influenced and developed by the apparently cosmic characters: the stories of the labors of Herakles (Hercules), overwrought and overdetermined as they seem to be, convey tons of instruction about human social interaction (almost totally lacking in the Disney version of 1997, *Hercules*). Likewise, trickster myths often convey social norms precisely by describing behaviors taught to be just the opposite of proper living.

The universe may be considered to have been created out of the bodily components of a protohuman such as the Chinese P'an Ku/Coiled Antiquity

(Birrell 1993: 11, 30). Or the food grains derive from a primordial cow, in Iranian mythology (Lincoln 1999: 162). In India such provenance comes from Purusha, whose sacrificed body produces all the entities of the universe. Other myths elsewhere establish the creation of the constellations from the bodies of earth-beings honored and commemorated by being transported into the stars.

Myths certainly teach about love and sexuality; their heroines or heroes often learn proper behavior the hard way. And they teach about the physical landscape: tracking on a map the points mentioned in central Navajo myths, for instance, demonstrates that mythological accounts often function as an atlas or gazetteer. The blood from a primordial monster is said to have hardened into ridges on the landscape that look suspiciously like lava flows! Or elsewhere a series of small lakes were said to have been formed when a primeval giant plonked down his size E sandals as he crossed the countryside.

Mythical battles graph perspectives upon how power is exercised by deities or heroes or sky-beings. Figures of superhuman wisdom as well as vast foolhardiness provide mythical models; stories of the origins of funerals or marriages contribute proper social sanctions. Relationships between human beings and forest beings (or those of the steppes or the depths of the ocean) are fleshed out and honored; encounters with barbarians, witches, and evil magicians provide caution about trusting outsiders. The "other" or "different" is—may we never forget—also "distinctive" or outstanding in some important aspect, but myths tend to be solicitous primarily of the perspectives of their originators.

The origins of death are attributed to mistakes made by primordial mythological characters. Memorial customs are founded on the death of some protohistorical figure. And life after death is copiously myth-ed out in several cultures, so that myths detail not just beginnings, but also contemporary and future realities.

The reason for farming or hunting in a certain manner is narrated: special magical apples or coconuts give birth to insight or to material possessions (the Hainuwele myth, in Indonesia). A magical ash tree at the very axis of the world (Yggdrasil in Norse mythology) connects heaven and earth, its roots reaching deeply into the place of the dead. In Iroquois myth, due to breaking of certain taboos, the uprooting of a huge celestial tree of corn leads to Earth Woman (Atahensic) being kicked down from the sky. She falls onto the backs of loons or ducks and then creates the Earth (known as Turtle Island), spreading dirt on the backs of turtles until it becomes solid. Too much water marks any number of flood myths; in the Mayan *Popol-Vuh,* a flood erases the early mistake of the creator in making human beings—the few human survivors are said to be the ancestors of the monkeys!

The tree Yggdrasil is the world tree, the world as it was imagined with Asgård on top. The gods lived in Asgård, "Midgård" was the human world, and "Jotunheim" was the giants' world. © Topham Picturepoint / Sjoberg Classic / The Image Works.

SECONDARY AND OTHER ELABORATIONS

Myths can be regarded within a society in a variety of ways, and a single myth may fall into higher or lower favor repeatedly. What we might call the myth of the American Frontier or the Wild West, for instance, has enormously influenced our narratives (including Western movies and television serials, of course). It is so popular that at the Wal-Mart where I shop, a DVD featuring 11 full-length John Wayne movies sells for only $6.00. As I write, however, influences of the Hong Kong kung fu and cyberpunk films break out in *The Matrix, Crouching Tiger, Hidden Dragon,* and *12 Monkeys,* and the Western movie influence is clearly in the shadows (note also the popularity of the Harry Potter films and *The Lord of the Rings* series).

It is important to try to establish the level of functional vitality of a myth, its relative influence, and derivations of its basic plot. We ought to recognize

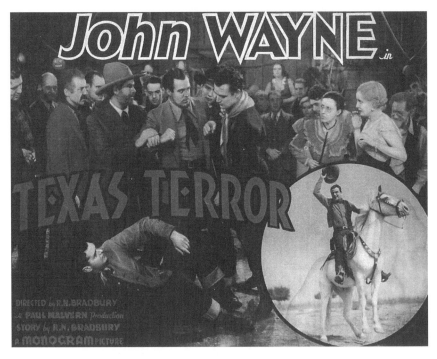

A poster for a John Wayne movie, showing him as a cowboy on horseback. The myth of the American Frontier or Wild West has enormously influenced our narratives, including Western movies and television serials. Courtesy of the Library of Congress.

just where in the social context it is most revered: Is it a myth appealing primarily to children or to adults? Can you talk about it in school or church? Who gets upset if you tell it? Why? What competes with it?

Furthermore, we must always remember that people are the most unaware of the myths that they live out every day. It seldom takes much work, however, before even a superficial glance at the daily newspaper reveals implicit (albeit consciously forgotten) references to mythic stories and figures (as I mentioned earlier, Asimov 1961 is a revealing scan of such materials, but many myth handbooks also show how many terms and concepts are myth driven; the *Etymological Dictionary of Classical Mythology* posted by Elizabeth Wallis Kraemer [1998] has an informative resume).

Much of pop culture (advertising, romance novels) certainly is myth driven, and many of the behavioral patterns of gender display are also. Masculinity and femininity are idealized from a perspective that ignores the ways many members of a society are unconscious of the influences on current feminine and masculine ideals. "Gender" became a contested discourse late in the twentieth century— something to be negotiated, rather than understood as a "natural" category determined for all time by something like biblical or philosophical images.

Another example would be the determination of attitudes toward and repressive treatment of Native American Indians, rather soon after contact with the immigrant Europeans. The white European settlers simply could not "see" the natives as settled, peaceable farmers, even in the cases where they were, because of their own cultural model of "savages" as rapacious hunters. Even today Native Americans are conceptualized (and acted out in movies) as befeathered, half-naked warriors riding bareback after bison—yet the model for such an image, the Plains hunter, existed for barely a century of Native American history and is atypical of most American Indian nation-societies.

The issues are largely attitudinal: a member of a society has to be *taught* attitudes. In contemporary jargon, societies are said to be *socially constructed.* Hence the importance of learning which mythic patterns have influenced one's own society and the mostly indirect manner in which such influences takes place—usually unconsciously and innocently. It was not for nothing that Plato wanted to control the stories children's nurses passed along; he was quite aware of the poetic power of such narratives, the affective ways in which stories become the bases of the ways we interpret our environment and make our moral choices, how we relate to groups and to individuals in a positive or negative manner.

Myths may have various meanings to different members of a society at this or that particular period, as suggested earlier. The term *polysemy* refers to their characteristic ability to seed different interpretations (the -*semy* refers to semiotics, the discipline that shows how signs—such as myths—convey meanings) in their ongoing influences. There is, in fact, a sort of ethics to mythography, one that involves the analyst's dedication to accuracy, her or his insistence on thinking through the possible influences (entailments) that particular kinds of stories may exert.

Two exemplary studies in this respect are Lawrence and Jewett (2002), *The Myth of the American Superhero,* and Jewett and Lawrence (2003), *Captain America and the Crusade against Evil.* Both demonstrate how extensively some of the ideals such as that of the Western Frontier Hero have been influential upon countless literary and cinematic productions. In a valuable way, these authors critique such materials as mindless repetitions of older models that have become not only useless today, but also dysfunctional in terms of confronting the complexities of contemporary social patterns—often shaped entirely by international commerce and politics.

When my students first read the studies of Jewett and Lawrence, they are initially suspicious, but after a week or two they come back to me and state how amazingly enough they have recognized precisely the heroic models these authors chart in some television programs, films, and novels they have just experienced. *Captain America* is especially sharp in disclosing how recent militaristic American politics derive precisely from the "superhero acting against the bad guys all on his own" model that so many twentieth-century films incorporated.

There are several accounts of the way in which the Nazi regime reshaped traditional Teutonic mythical heroes toward stimulating a national realm of great terror and eventually death to Jews, homosexuals, and Gypsies. Two well-illustrated volumes, Sam Keen's *Faces of the Enemy* (1986) and Kinser and Kleinman's *The Dream That Was No More a Dream* (1969), help flesh out the adaptations of mythological materials—Keen on the part of both Nazi and Axis sides, to formulate effective propaganda, Kinser and Kleinman illustrating the capture of traditional Teutonic images to construct idealistic images of the heroicized Nazi state.

If we regard attitudes as a sort of essential knowledge for living as a member of a particular society, it becomes clear that they convey crucial psychological and developmental learning skills. Myths model possibilities (both positive and negative) for the roles its citizens will enact. Again we understand the concern of Plato in *The Republic* for ensuring that only healthy myths reach children's minds, not what he considered to be the silly nonsense of unlettered nursemaids.

And it is also clear why the influential historian of religion Mircea Eliade repeatedly emphasized how origin myths, in fact most cosmogonic myths, set exemplary models for societies. He proposed that humans understand themselves in mythological terms of having been constituted by events that happened in the primal times; by reenacting them in religious rituals participants become transported back to the special time of the beginnings once again, and when they return to the nonritual realm, they bear the strong and healthy qualities of the mythical prototypes (for a selection of Eliade's statements of these theme, see Beane and Doty 1975: chap. 1).

This makes some sense—the first step in medical healing, for instance, is to track the causes (the etiology) of the problem; even in psychoanalysis, the first work is compiling the personal history as far back as possible. Eliade saw operative here a sort of special mythico-ideological perspective: "Knowing the origin of an object, an animal, a plant, and so on is equivalent to acquiring a magical power over them by which they can be controlled, multiplied, or reproduced at will" (in Beane and Doty 1975: 5). We may not talk much about "magical power" today, but we do indeed have a sense that knowing something's (or someone's) origins means a certain power of comprehension of it: Where did you get it? How much did it cost? And of course most scholarly works begin with a survey of the available literature, often from its earliest point to the present. Even the technician fixing my computer asks: When did you first start noticing the problem?

Nonetheless, contemporary myth scholars feel Eliade's emphasis on the "unique time" of the beginnings was overly influenced by his Christian theological perspectives. They have suggested that many *other* types of myth have to be taken into account as well. The *New Encyclopedia Britannica,* for instance (Bolle et al. 1993), features "Myths of eschatology [last things] and destruction" immediately after the first topic, "Myths of origin," and suggests that

> Even the term origin should be used with caution for cosmogonic events (as well as for other myths purporting to describe the beginning of things), because the origin of the world hardly ever seems the focal point of a mythological narrative—as a mythological narrative is not a matter of inquiry into the first cause of things. Instead, cosmogonic myths are concerned with origins in the sense of the foundation or validity of the world as it is. (Bolle et al. 1993: 723)

I am much in sympathy with this point: such myths do not operate as a sort of proto- or pseudoscience. As is the case with many biblical myths, the intention is not to document specific factual happenings (a worldwide flood, a fateful specific separation of agriculture and hunting lifestyles—Cain and Abel) but to code the ways in which the world is considered to have specific meanings that other peoples might not posit.

Myths develop into symbolic languages used to make social statements that are useful or not, healthy or not, important or not. They provide a society and its individuals with possible projected models, with creative ways of seeing the "deep" significance of apparently insignificant events and images, and with the knowledge that grounds value structures that provide foundations for a better future. Far from being—in much of popular parlance—unreal "fictions" or mindless stereotypes, there is a mythic knowledge that conveys what a culture considers important above all else. Hence it is always important to ask of any particular myth what the consequences of adopting its vision would be—and today some of those "particular myths" might include The Stock Market, The Economy, America as the World Superpower, or the almost mythical assumption that life can only have value when one has a toned body, a gas-guzzling SUV automobile, and a cell phone.

Myth is not spacey talk about never-never lands. It is grounded in pragmatic, realistic encounters with others and with important aspects of the natural and cultural worlds in which we dwell. Robert Neville refers to the projection of mythic values in the symbolic codes that get embedded in the stories we favor: "symbols within the myth or story refer to other symbols within the myth or story, and when people are 'thinking mythically' they are interpreting things, perhaps even the meanings of their own lives, within the coded contours of the narrative; they take themselves to inhabit the myth with nowhere else to stand" (1996: 39). Sissa and Detienne (2000: 167–68) note that for both the ancient Greeks and Romans, myth and religion—what was ritually due the gods—functioned as a *nomos,* or code of good conduct.

A mythical position is a "religious" position when it guides the way a society codes what it regards as supernatural or natural, false or true, effective or ineffective. It locates such codings within the framework of values that interact to enable a society to have an identity and a way of operating with other societies. Myths, then, contain *a superplus of meaning,* which is doubtless why they need to engage the imagination in ways that leave indelible impressions upon our minds of the tragic defeat of Oedipus, the foolish reliance of one knight upon another, or Faust's terrible contract with Mephistopheles.

Recognizing the superplus or surplus of meanings can remind us of the importance of careful training in mythical analysis and interpretation because interpretations and applications can emphasize and develop several different aspects. At the "beginnings" (i.e., the mythical first-times), apparently some citizens can find powerful energy for driving a social order and giving it lasting meaning. We circle back to the origins of literature for a revelation of extraordinarily energy-rich sources of our symbolism; a myth may become a resource of "archetypal" significance. Much of poetic and religious expression

Oedipus, blind after plucking out his eyes, with his daughter Antigone during the plague in Thebes. © The Art Archive / Musée des Beaux Arts Orléans / Dagli Orti (A).

seeks to renew the power of the mythical models that have long pedigrees as important to a culture: "renewal" may mean metamorphosis, development, and change. A culture's most powerful myths are thought to live on despite being remade in each revisioning.

ARCHETYPES IN MYTHS

Archetypal analysis has been developed in the psychological teachings of Carl G. Jung and his followers—a school that has been a powerful resource with respect to reviving interest in matters mythical in the latter half of the twentieth century. It has also been a feature of the myth criticism of the Canadian literary scholar Northrop Frye, who suggests that the archetypes of the seasons can be correlated with four major types of literary expression (see especially Frye 1957).

But my own take on the concept is that archetypes best explain *retrospectively* how certain repeatedly expressed figures and themes have made it into the big leagues; if literary genres teach us what to expect in a type of literature, a knowledge of mythologems or archetypes can help us understand the more interior contents and characters. Clearly mythic narratives are "special"; I suggest that that special quality comes from addressing not trivial but vital issues and situations in the human experience.

Archetypal issues are those faced in every generation (although they will be shaped differently in various chronological and social contexts). They have little to do with what to wear at the prom, but a lot to do with how a state considers its leadership role among the nations. A survey of the various archetypal situations and figures assists one in understanding particular narratives or films. Because they recur in so many different cultures with quite different individual manifestations, they approach the quality of *universals,* transpersonal and transhistorical influences that are remarkably stable at their core, for all their differences in manifestation from one to another culture.

The Mother, the Wise Old Man, the Trickster, the Innocent Child, the Spirit, the Heroine, the Bowery Bum, the Jock: these are organizing principles for novels or works of art. Like dreams, they seem to speak a language transcending any personal biographical experience or story. Such transcendence suggests that ultimately, no narrative can express everything, or the depth of anything, that there is a mystery to myth (the two terms are etymologically related through the root *my-*) that cannot be specified without killing the messenger. I like Eric Gould's suggestion that the archetypal or "universal may well be only that which is always open to interpretation" (1981: 85), that is to say, not simplified into Disney-like trivializations, reduced as they usually are to the cheapest versions of any of our most rightwing politicians.

Rather, existentially global, archetypal figurations represent experiences encountered across human cultures expressed in the infinitely varied garb of human personality. They are part of the imagery of the social web or context that binds a community together (see suggested readings, Doty 2000: 208). They are the stories that most effectively open up, rather than close down, human imagination and creativity (see Mackey-Kallis 2001: chap. 9). They are often psychologically affective: you read Hemingway's *The Old Man and the Sea,* and you feel touched; you watch an episode of *Star Wars,* and you know that something within an ancient heroic myth has energized you; you read about Mother Teresa, and you understand that the Great Mother is not an abstraction.

In this sense archetypal aspects of myths may provide for a reorienting of emotional states. Poets and artists throughout the ages have found new inspi-

The Heroine of Monmouth, published by Currier & Ives, c1876. Archetypal figures represent experiences encountered across human cultures and are part of the imagery of the social web or context that binds a community together. Courtesy of the Library of Congress.

rations for their work in plumbing the mythical resources of their tradition (I suggest Collette Astier's "Oedipus," 1996, for an excellent tracking of a mythical figure throughout several thousands of years of reinterpretation). Archetypes, repeated themes in mythological materials, are ways of understanding the depth dimensions of everyday life; they give breadth to any particular story by reminding us that elsewhere, the same image was interpreted differently, asking whether we need to work against the other realizations or take them further.

When reading stories about Mother Teresa, we understand that the Great Mother archetype is not an abstraction. Here are President and Mrs. Ronald Reagan presenting Mother Teresa with the Medal of Freedom at a White House Ceremony. © Ronald Reagan Library.

They also ask whether we can swallow our pride and admit that we are no different from countless others in the world's existence who have needed to say "we, our," rather than merely "I, mine." This involves accepting and appreciating that our mythic universes often overlap, that the cultural richness of the past deserves reexploring constantly, lest the noise of the merely technological contemporary drowns out lasting cultural significance forever.

Our time is a time rich in scientific and technological expertise. Medical and other advances astonish us daily. And yet those whose lifelong dedication has been to the humane tradition, to the humanities, discover repeatedly that schools are apparently unable to convey great stretches of the massive accomplishments in human thought and the arts. Increasingly what is not conveyed is a comprehension of the history of human cultures and appreciation of the very large areas of human existence that are not addressed in the natural or economic sciences, and those include the realm of mythological means of addressing ongoing human problems and issues.

Doubtless part of this situation is caused by the discrepancy between economic awards to the science and technology vectors of our society and those doled out sometimes grudgingly to artists, philosophers, and the helping professions. But it is also caused by the recurrent modern emphasis upon having grown "beyond myth" itself. Here, of course, we confront the association of myth with so-called primitive stages of the development of human civilizations. What has had to be relearned over and over again is that myth is not premodern or prescientific, but a resource for imaginative creativity like nothing else in our cultural production.

Infatuated with scientific and technological advances, we generally preach the myth of mythlessness (i.e., a "myth" in which the term means only "falsehood, deceit"). Any even elementary exposure to the history of science discloses how repeatedly scientists have claimed to be "beyond myth," only to discover that strictly values-oriented matters—the province of religion, philosophy, and indeed mythology—have structured the "neutral" inquiries and experiments all along. Ask what the Department of Defense budgets have meant for the development of science programs at colleges and universities over the last century, and you will have some idea what I have in mind.

The *myth of mythlessness* presupposes that mythic levels of understanding and expression are only levels to be gotten beyond, into pure technology and science. The expression also identifies that a "myth," that is to say, a particular set of interpretations about reality, has ruled the sci-tech world just as completely as any other part of our existence (the classic text in this respect is Thomas Kuhn's *The Structure of Scientific Revolutions*).

WORKS CITED

Apollodorus, of Athens. 1976. *Gods and Heroes of the Greeks: The* Library *of Apollodorus.* Trans., intro., notes by Michael Simpson. Amherst: U of Massachusetts P.

Asimov, Isaac. 1961. *Words from the Myths.* New York: New American Library.

Astier, Colette. 1996. "Oedipus." In *Companion to Literary Myths, Heroes, and Archetypes,* ed. Pierre Brunel, trans. Wendy Allatson, Judith Hayward, and Trista Selous, 903–11. New York: Routledge.

Barthes, Roland. 1972. *Mythologies.* Trans. Annette Lavers. New York: Hill and Wang.

Beane, Wendell C., and William G. Doty, eds. 1975. *Myths, Rites, Symbols: A Mircea Eliade Reader.* 2 vols. New York: Harper and Row.

Birrell, Anne. 1993. *Chinese Mythology: An Introduction.* Baltimore: Johns Hopkins UP.

Bolle, Kees W., Richard G. A. Buxton, and Jonathan Z. Smith. 1993. "Myth and Mythology." *The New Encyclopedia Britannica* 24: 715–32.

Brisson, Luc. 1998 [1982]. *Plato the Myth Maker.* Ed. and trans. Gerard Naddaf. Chicago: U of Chicago P.

Buxton, R.G.A., ed. 2001. *From Myth to Reason? Studies in the Development of Greek Thought.* New York: Oxford UP.

Doty, William G. 2000. *Mythography: The Study of Myths and Rituals.* Revised 2nd ed. Tuscaloosa: U of Alabama P.

———. 2004. "What's a Myth? Nomological, Topological, and Taxonomic Explorations." *Soundings: An Interdisciplinary Journal* 86 (3/4).

Ellwood, Robert. 1999. *The Politics of Myth: A Study of C. G. Jung, Mircea Eliade, and Joseph Campbell.* Issues in the Study of Religion. Albany: SUNY P.

Frye, Northrop. 1957. *Anatomy of Criticism: Four Essays.* Princeton, NJ: Princeton UP.

———. 1990. *Myth and Metaphor: Selected Essays, 1974–1988.* Ed. Robert D. Denham. Charlottesville: UP of Virginia.

Gantz, Timothy. 1993. *Early Greek Myth: A Guide to Literary and Artistic Sources.* Baltimore: Johns Hopkins UP.

Girling, John. 1993. *Myths and Politics in Western Societies: Evaluating the Crisis of Modernity in the United States, Germany, and Great Britain.* New Brunswick, NJ: Transaction.

Gould, Eric. 1981. *Mythical Intentions in Modern Literature.* Princeton, NJ: Princeton UP.

Graves, Robert. 1955. *The Greek Myths.* 2 vols. Rev. ed. Harmondsworth: Penguin.

Hansen, William F. 1998. Forum Interview, by Stephen Gencarella Olbrys. *Folklore Forum* 29 (2): 91–108.

Holtze, Elizabeth. n.d. "ENG 340 Definitions." http://clem.mscd.edu/~holtzee/3430/page2.htm (accessed 6/28/01).

Jewett, Robert, and John Shelton Lawrence. 2003. *Captain America and the Crusade against Evil.* Grand Rapids, MI: Eerdmans.

Keen, Sam. 1986. *Faces of the Enemy.* San Francisco: HarperCollins.

Kinser, Bill, and Neil Kleinman. 1969. *The Dream That Was No More a Dream: A Search for Aesthetic Reality in Germany, 1890–1945.* New York: Harper and Row.

Kraemer, Elizabeth Wallis. 1998. "An Etymological Dictionary of Classical Mythology." http://www.kl.oakland.edu/kraemer/edcm/.

Kuhn, Thomas S. 1970 [1962]. *The Structure of Scientific Revolutions.* 2nd ed. Chicago: U of Chicago P.

Lawrence, John Shelton, and Robert Jewett. 2002. *The Myth of the American Superhero.* Grand Rapids, MI: Eerdmans.

Lexicon Iconographicum Mythologiae Classicae. 1981– . Zürich: Artemis.

Lincoln, Bruce. 1996. "Gendered Discourses: The Early History of *Mythos* and *Logos*." *History of Religion* 36 (1): 1–12.

———. 1998. Contribution to PERSPECTIVES feature, What Is Myth?. *Folklore Forum* 29 (2): 86–88.

———. 1999. *Theorizing Myth: Narrative, Ideology, and Scholarship.* Chicago: U of Chicago P.

Loraux, Nicole. 1986. *The Invention of Athens: The Funeral Oration in the Classical City.* Trans. Alan Sheridan. Cambridge: Harvard UP.

Mackey-Kallis, Susan. 2001. *The Hero and the Perennial Journey Home in American Film.* Philadelphia: U of Pennsylvania P.

March, Jenny. 1998. *Cassell's Dictionary of Classical Mythology.* New York: Cassell.

McGuire, Michael. 1997. "Mythic Rhetoric in *Mein Kampf:* A Structuralist Critique." *The Quarterly Journal of Speech* 63 (1): 1–13.

Mills, Donald H. 2002. *The Hero and the Sea: Patterns of Chaos in Ancient Myth.* Wauconda, IL: Bolchazy-Carducci.

Neville, Robert Cummings. 1996. *The Truth of Broken Symbols.* SUNY Series in Religious Studies. Albany: SUNY P.

Oring, Eliott, ed. 1986. *Folk Groups and Folklore Genres: An Introduction.* Logan: Utah State P.

Padden, William E. 2000. "World." In *Guide to the Study of Religion,* ed. Willi Braun and Russell T. McCutcheon, 334–47. New York: Cassell.

Robinson, Maryanne. 1993. "Hear Silence: Western Myth Reconsidered (In the Thoreau Tradition)." In *The True Subject: Writers on Life and Craft,* ed. Kurt Brown, 135–51. St. Paul, MN: Graywolf P.

Ryan, Allan J. 1999. *Trickster Shift: Humor and Irony in Contemporary Native Art.* Vancouver: U of British Columbia P and Seattle: U of Washington P.

Scheid, John, and Jesper Svenbro. 1996. *The Craft of Zeus: Myths of Weaving and Fabric.* Trans. Carol Volk. Cambridge: Harvard UP.

Sissa, Giulia, and Marcel Detienne. 2000. *The Daily Lives of the Greek Gods.* Mestizo Spaces/Espaces Métisse. Trans. Janet Lloyd. Stanford, CA: Stanford UP.

Trubshaw, Bob. 2002. *Explore Folklore.* Wymeswold, UK: Heart of Albion.

Vickery, John B., ed. 1966. *Myth and Literature: Contemporary Theory and Practice.* Lincoln: U of Nebraska P.

Von Hendy, Andrew. 2002. *The Modern Construction of Myth.* Bloomington: Indiana UP.

Wagner, Jon, and Jan Lundeen. 1998. *Deep Space and Sacred Time:* Star Trek *in the American Ethos.* Westport, CT: Praeger-Greenwood.

Weigle, Marta. 1989. *Creation and Procreation: Feminist Reflections on Mythologies of Cosmogony and Parturition.* Philadelphia: U of Pennsylvania P.

Wiggins, James B., ed. 1975. *Religion as Story.* New York: Harper and Row.

Willis, Roy, gen. ed. 1993. *World Mythology.* New York: Holt.

Three
Examples and Texts

The materials in this chapter represent a certain bias, that of contemporary Western mythological perspectives. It would be impossible to canvass all the various types and themes of mythological materials of the world in such a short volume, and even books collecting "world mythology" can only present selections from the various cultures represented. It is worthwhile to examine a few books on *another* mythology, just to see how cultures vary in the issues their mythologies engage.

DESCRIPTIVE EXAMPLES OF MYTHIC MATERIALS/TYPES/THEMES

As an example, in many ways Chinese mythology is quite foreign to the Westerner, not least of all because myth as such was greatly discounted in importance by the learned scholars who treated mythology there. In many ways the study of Chinese mythology has just begun, in both the East and the West. *Chinese Mythology: An Introduction,* by a Cambridge University professor, Anne Birrell, presents an account of the situation and surveys the myths. Her *Chinese Myths* provides additional information about the situation:

Ancient China has no Hesiod, Homer, or Ovid to retell the mythic oral tales at length. Instead, Chinese writers introduced fragmentary passages of mythic stories into their works of philosophy and history to illustrate their arguments and give authority to their statements. Chinese myth thus exists as an amorphous, diffuse variety of anonymous archaic expression that is preserved in the contexts of philosophical, literary, and historical writings. They are brief, disjointed, and enigmatic. These mythic fragments incorporated into miscellaneous classical texts vary in their narration, and authors often adapted myth according to their own point of view. The result is that Chinese myth survives in numerous versions, the content of which is broadly consistent, but which shows significant variation in the details. Whereas the reshaping of archaic oral Greek and Roman myth into an artistic form of narrative literature implies the loss of the authentic oral voice, the Chinese method of recording mythic fragments in a wealth of untidy, variable stories is a rare survival of primitive authenticity. (2000: 13–14)

The "numerous versions" include not one, but six story lines of the creation of the world and four flood stories. And when I made a list of the types of myths that Birrell treats (16 primary types in 1993, but I found 43 additional types mentioned in her index), it was clear that East and West do indeed both share common interests and have others that are quite different. Chinese categories include, for instance, the theriomorphic (animal or beast having human features) and vegetal (plants that can point out a false flatterer at the royal court, for instance; 2000: 54).

With this proviso about being unable to treat the full range of world mythological traditions, I provide first a number of examples of several categories. Part 2 reproduces a small collection of actual myth texts, some highly condensed and some full length, before Part 3 examines just a few of the common themes that are to be found relatively frequently and looks briefly at the sorts of "comparativism" that have been influential in determining just which themes, examples, and myths ought to be compared and in what dimensions.

- Archetypes: as suggested earlier, literary archetypes are patterns that seem to structure various modes of literary expression (as canvassed especially in the work of Northrop Frye and the earlier myth-literature critics); for Jungian thought, they represent culture-spanning common characterizations (Stevens 1998); and generally speaking they simply refer to repeated or perhaps universal figures. Examples include the mother-daughter pair, the twins, female and male heroes, the healer, the wise old man, the young child, and the bride.

- Dreamtime or the Dreaming is represented primarily by the Australian *Alcheringa*, an ancient, even primordial time when various ancestor beings made their ways across land and sea, making all the species that live on the land today, and establishing the important symbolic geographic features, as well as ritual procedures.

- Female and male heroes appear as figures somehow larger than usual life forms, with special physical abilities, intuitive powers, and especially stamina to complete the hero quest for selfhood: one of the most self-evident portrayals of that cycle may be found in various episodes of *Star Wars*. A wide range of examples will be found in Leeming (1973 or 1998) or in Campbell (1968).

- Life cycle; initiation: although now studied in the modern period as a matter of developmental psychology, life cycle (or life crisis) stages have been ritualized across several cultures. Initiation is particularly the time when the neophyte is fully accepted into society, often with a new name, and told the secret myths that have been previously tabooed. An important step toward adult maturation, many persons have recently felt that they never achieved full social status when such rites were not performed because their culture felt they were no longer relevant in contemporary society.

- Rebirth and renewal, resurrection: an example from Greek myth is the mock re-birthing of Herakles—whom Zeus had decided to take into the pantheon of the Twelve Olympians—by having the goddess Hera appear to undergo birth, then producing the grown Herakles from under her skirts. When the Hittite god Telipinu gets furious, he disappears and the earth becomes barren—he is coaxed back with magical drinks and food, and ameliorated, he brings back the vegetation. The resurrection of Jesus of Nazareth as the Christ of Christian faith is celebrated every Easter.

In the movie *Star Wars*, female and male heroes appear as figures somehow larger than usual life forms, with special physical abilities, intuitive powers, and stamina to complete the hero quest for selfhood. Courtesy of Photofest.

- Death, scapegoat: the hero is often terminated by some violent means such as dismemberment, castration, or hanging; lamentations follow and barrenness of the land, but the mythological promise is usually "life out of death" or renewal. Hence the death of the hero is the death of the scapegoat, whose sacrifice cleanses the community of overweening pride (hybris) or some other fault.

- Miraculous conception/birth of child: "divine child" traditions include virgin birth or protective angel sorts of stories—basically the idea is utopian, expressing the hope that life as usual can be transcended onto a new plane of fresh creativity; the moment of birth is a moment of tremendous significance for the entire universe: "the instant the future Buddha was conceived in the womb of his mother, all the ten thousand worlds suddenly quaked, quivered, and shook" (Leeming 1998: 17).

- Trickster: a figure familiar especially in Africa and in Native American mythologies: Ananse the Spider in Africa, Grandmother Spider in America; Raven or Coyote in America; or Legba in Africa and Haiti. These figures challenge the ordinary realms of reality, suggesting that there are more things in our waking world than we can imagine, most of them challenging the "ordinary realms" and proposing to turn them on their heads. (See Hynes and Doty 1993, Erdoes and Ortiz 1998, Reesman 2001.)

SOME SAMPLE TEXTS

Origin Myths

Singing Creation   (Weigle 1989: 181) (Northern California, Round Valley Yuki Indians) Weigle compares this creator figure to the *Deus faber* (god the creator) who divides the primeval waters by means of words on the second day of creation in Genesis 1.6–8, or the God who asks Job (38.4) where he was "when I laid the foundation of the earth?"

There was only water, and over it a fog. On the water was foam. The foam moved round and round continually, and from it came a voice. After a time there issued from the foam a person in human form. He had wing feathers of the eagle on his head. This was Taikó-mol [Solitary Walker]. He floated on the water and sang. He stood on the foam, which still revolved. There was no light. He walked on the water as if it were land. He made a rope and laid it from north to south, and he walked along it, revolving his hands one about the other, and behind him the earth was heaped up along the rope. But the water overwhelmed it. Again he did this, and again the water prevailed. Four times this was done.

Taikó-mol was constantly talking to himself. "I think we had better do it this way. I think we had better try it that way." So now he talked to himself

The raven as Trickster is a familiar figure in Native American mythology. © Mary Evans Picture Library.

and he made a new plan. He made four *lilkae* [stone markers], and planted one in the north and others in the south, west, and east. Then he stretched them out until they were continuous lines crossing the world in the center. He spoke a word, and the earth appeared. Then he went along the edge and lined it with whale-hide, so that the ocean could not wash away the earth. He shook the earth to see if it was solid, and he still makes this test, causing earthquakes.

An Emergence   (Jordan 1993: 54) (Mandan Sioux) Much more elaborate accounts of the people emerging from a series of underworlds are common among the American Southwestern Native Americans.

In the beginning the Sioux nation live in an underground village on the shores of a huge lake. Some of the tribe climb up a gigantic grape vine whose roots penetrate their subterranean land, to catch sight of the upper world which they discover to be airy and sunny and plentifully stocked with plants and animals. They bring back such enthusiastic reports that the whole tribe sets out to climb the grape vine. Only half of them manage to climb up the stem, however, because a very fat lady brings it crashing down.

Procreation and Creation (Weigle 1989: 228–31; extensively paraphrased and condensed by WGD) (Northeastern Siberia Chukchee) Here a male creator competes with a female creator (*creatrix*). She brings the people into being, he provides them with an organized world to live in and foods to eat.

The self-created Ku'urkil (Raven) and his wife live together where there are no humans, nor any other living creature—no reindeer, walrus, whale, seal, fish, or human being. The woman says to Ku'urkil that he should go and try to create the earth. He complains that he cannot create the earth, and she says that she would try to create companions for them. She goes to sleep, Raven watching over her, and marveling as her black feathers and talons become human and fingers. Try as he might, Raven could not change his own body.

The wife's abdomen enlarges, and when Raven looks at her again he finds that she has created three human beings before she awakes from her sleep. All three have bodies like ours, only Raven has the same bird's body and black feathers. The children laugh at Raven, and ask the mother, "Mamma, what is that?"

"It is the father."

"Oh, the father! Indeed! Ha, ha, ha!" They come nearer and push him with their feet. He flies off, crying, "Qa, qa!" They laugh again, until the mother admonishes them to cease.

Raven said, "There, you have created humans! Now I shall go and try to create the earth." He flew away and asked all the benevolent Beings for advice, but nobody gave it. He asked the Dawn, Sunset, Evening, Mid-day, and Zenith—but received no answer and no advice. At last he came to the place where the sky meets the horizon. There he saw a tent full of men, who were making a great noise.

Ku'urkil, the self-created one, learns that these people have been created from the dust resulting from the friction of the sky meeting the ground. They are to multiply and become the first seed of all the peoples upon the earth. But there is no organized earth. They ask Raven to create the earth for them, and he agrees to try. He flies and defecates: every piece of excrement falls upon water, grows quickly, and becomes land. Then he began to pass water: where a single drop falls, it becomes a lake; where a jet falls, it becomes a river. After that he began to defecate a very hard substance: large pieces of that excrement became mountains, smaller pieces became hills, and the whole earth became as it is now.

When the people complained that they needed food, Raven, the good fellow, flew off and found many kinds of trees—birch, pine, poplar, aspen, willow, stone-pine, and oak. He took his hatchet and began to chop, throwing the chips into the water, which carried them into the sea. When he hewed pine, and threw the chips into the water, they became mere walrus; when he hewed oak, the chips became seals. From the other types of wood chips came polar bears, whales, fish, crabs, worms, and every kind of beings living in the sea; then, moreover, wild reindeer, foxes, bears, and all the game of the land. He created them all, and then he said, "Now you have food! hm!" His children became men, and they separated and went in various directions.

The males could not multiply, for there were no women yet. Raven began to think, "What is to be done?" A small Spider-Woman (Kurgu-ne'ut) descends from above on a very slender thread. She announces her intention to bring females, even though she is so tiny. And indeed, her abdomen soon enlarged, and she gave birth to four daughters. They grew fast and became women. One of the males took away one woman as a companion.

The next day Raven went to visit them, made a hole in the tent-cover, and peeped through. "Oh," says he, "they are sleeping separately in opposite corners of the sleeping-room! Oh, that is bad! How can they multiply?" Raven calls a woman to him and treats her to sexual intercourse, which she finds quite pleasant, and soon she teaches the man how to multiply their kind. Therefore girls understand earlier than boys how to copulate. In this manner humankind multiplied.

Brother and Sister Creators   (Weigle 1989: 203–5, who has extensive discussion of the contexts, 202–3) (Californian Luiseño Indian) Primordial incest as the source of procreation is by no means unusual in the mythologies of the world.

In the beginning all was empty space. Ké-vish-a-ták-vish was the only being. This period was called Óm-ai-yá-mai signifying emptiness, nobody there. Then came the time called Há-ruh-rúy, upheaval, things coming into shape. Then a time called Chu-tu-taí, the falling of things downward; and after this, Yu-vai-to-vaf, things working in darkness without the light of sun or moon. Then came the period Tul-múl Pu-shún, signifying that deep down in the heart or core of earth things were working together.

Then came Why-yaí Pee-vaí, a gray glimmering like the whiteness of hoar frost; and then, Mit-aí Kwai-raí, the dimness of twilight. Then came a period of cessation, Na-kaí Ho-wai-yaí, meaning things at a standstill.

Then Ké-vish-a-ták-vish made a man, Túk-mit, the Sky; and a woman, To-maí-yo-vit, the Earth. There was no light, but in the darkness these two became conscious of each other.

"Who are you?" asked the man.

"I am To-maí-yo-vit. And you?"

"I am Túk-mit."

"Then you are my brother."

"You are my sister."

By her brother the Sky the Earth conceived and became the Mother of all things. Her first-born children were, in the order of their birth, See-vat and P-ve-ut, Ush-la and Pik-la, Ná-na-chel and Patch'-ha-yel, Tópal and Tam'-yush.

Then came forth all other things, people, animals, trees, rocks, and rivers, but not as we see them now. All things then were people.

But at first they were heavy and helpless and could not move about, and they were in darkness, for there was no light. But when the Sun was born he gave a tremendous light which struck the people into unconsciousness, or caused them to roll upon the ground in agony; so that the Earth-Mother, seeing this, caught him up and hid him away for a season; so then there was darkness again.

After the Sun was born there came forth another being called Chun-itch'-nish, a being of power, whose voice sounded as soon as he was born, while all the others rolled helplessly upon the ground, unable to utter a word. The others were so terrified by his appearance that the Earth-Mother hid him away, and ever since he has remained invisible.

The rattlesnake was born at this time, a monster without arms or legs.

When all her children were born, the Earth-Mother left the place and went to Ech'-a-mo Nóy-a-mo. The people rolled, for like newborn babies they could not walk. They began then to crawl on hands and knees, and they talked this way: Chák-o-lá-le, Wá-wa, Tá-ta. This was all that they could say. For food they ate clay. From there they moved to Kak-wé-mai Po-lá-la, then to Po-és-kak Po-lá-lak.

They were growing large now and began to recognize each other. Then the Earth-Mother made the sea so that her children could bathe in it, and so that the breeze from the sea might fill their lungs, for until this time they had not breathed.

Then they moved farther to a place called Na-ché-vo Po-mé-sa-vo, a sort of a canyon which was too small for their abiding-place; so they returned to a place called Tem-ech'-va Tem-eck'-o, and this place people now call Temecula, for the Mexicans changed the Indian name to that.

Here they settled while everything was still in darkness. All this time they had been traveling about without any light.

The Earth-Mother had kept the sun hidden away, but now that the people were grown large enough and could know each other she took the Sun out of his hiding-place, and immediately there was light. They could all see each other; and while the Sun was standing there among them they discussed the matter and decided that he must go east and west and give light all over the world; so all of them raised their arms to the sky three times, and three times cried out Cha-cha-cha, and he rose from among them and went up to his place in the sky.

After this they remained at Temecula, but the world was not big enough for them, and they talked about it and concluded that it must be made larger. So this was done, and they lived there as before.

The Big Bang   (Leeming and Page 1996: 185–86) (Contemporary Science) These authors introduce the text: "Scientific inquiry, indeed, is not generally taken as a means of exploring theological matters, or even matters that have a moral dimension. Scientists seek the ways nature *works,* not why it works. Yet astrophysicists and astronomers, armed with mathematics and other unimaginably powerful tools, do look back into the origin of things, the beginning of the universe. In the origins of this universe and in the death of stars that collapse into what are called black holes, some see the possibility of many other universes existing on what seem unimaginable planes—universes of energy and matter finally collapsing into infinitesimally small places called singularities and, possibly, vanishing only to emerge outside into another place of creation—another universe aborning. There is plenty of disagreement—the astrophysicists' tools are not omnipotent—but most agree on a general story of how this universe began." The following text is presented, then, not as commentary, but set out like the other myth texts in the volume, and not attributed to a specific author.

There is a singularity somewhere. It is infinitely small, and infinitely heavy, infinitely dense. It contains all the matter and energy a universe would require. And then, perhaps of its own accord, it explodes in a violent seizure too great to imagine, though some have tried to quantify it into whatever form of things existed before matter and energy, before dimension and time.

At any rate, it exploded, and in such tiny fractions of seconds that they can only be spoken of but never comprehended, the universe began to inflate, to grow, to change, to fall into an orderly evolution of elements and existence. It followed the rules which some mathematicians can nearly divine, becoming stars, galaxies, gases, things, continents, life, parrots, music, fast-food stores. It became temples, and weapons, and the human imagination, and every living and extinct creature that has ever dwelled here on the planet earth—itself a remote backwater in the exurbs of an unimportant galaxy in an unmeasured universe.

Or, perhaps, it is the most important corner of the universe, this earth—and for reasons we cannot ever fathom.

Certainly astrophysicists will never fathom the reasons, if they exist but they can and do, from time to time, wonder what lay before that Big Bang.

Before?

Nothing, for in it time, too, was created.

Well, then, *beyond* it somehow.

There are physicists who speculate that beyond or outside of the Big Bang there was what you might think of as an urge—an urge for some kind of creation and order, possibly a mathematical urge.

Which, of course, should sound familiar by now.

Human Origins

Khnum and the Creation of Mankind   (Jordan 1993: 52–53) (Egyptian: principally from hymns and calendar liturgies from the Temple of Khnum at Esna in Upper Egypt. Dating from the Greco-Roman period [circa 700 B.C.E.–395 C.E.], the concept probably originated in Egyptian antiquity)

The God Khnum on the sacred barque (perhaps representing the appearance of the sun during its sleep at night), fresco from Tomb of Ramses III, 1194–1163 B.C., Egyptian pharaoh, Valley of the Kings, Thebes, Egypt. © The Art Archive / Dagli Orti.

Khnum, a chthonic [underworld] god usually depicted in human form or with the head of a ram, is sitting before a potter's wheel creating human beings out of clay at the behest of the creator gods. His sacred animal, the ram, signifies the creativity of the natural world, and he also creates all the members of the animal kingdom.

He installs the respiratory and digestive systems, designs the reproductive organs, and supervises pregnancy and labor. He directs the flow of the circulatory system around the newly fashioned body, and puts skin on the bones.

In a more specific episode of the mythology, Khnum is directed by the creator god Amun to implant two clay figures that he has just made into the womb of Queen Mutemwiya. Amun has impregnated her in a sacred marriage, and she is destined to give birth to [Pharaoh] Amenhotep III. One of the figures in the Temple represents Amenhotep bodily, the other represents his *ka* or life force.

In addition to his role as the potter, Khnum controlled the Nile through his supervision of Hapy, the fertility god of the Nile flood, who lives in caverns adjacent to the cataracts. When Khnum allows the inundation to take place each year, it leaves behind a rich layer of silt on which the Egyptian harvest germinates.

> **Quetzalcoatl**   (Leeming and Page 1996: 103–6) (Mexico: Toltec, Aztec) The snake is not always seen as a positive creature, although it often is, because it spans the above- and the below-worlds and hence is doubly wise. The "Feathered Serpent" of ancient Mexico was a creator of cities and the founder of agriculture and the arts. Here he becomes a sacrifice that will lead to the revival of the human race.
>
> Snake-bird.
> Plumed serpent.
> God of the wind, the master craftsman of life.
> The civilizer, creator, patron of all the known arts.

This was Quetzalcoatl, god, founding king, and priest who taught men to sing of himself/herself: She of the star-studded dress, he who lights up all, mistress and lord of our flesh, who brings life to the world, maize and cotton, who sustains the earth.

Quetzalcoatl lived in a house of jade and quetzal plumes, the very home of the sun itself, and all of the succession of kings of the Toltecs, the master craftsmen, acted just as Quetzalcoatl did in the beginning. Indeed, they became Quetzalcoatl, seeking through prayer and meditation to see with a clarity of vision the two faces of the dual god they had come to be. They—he—presided over the Golden Age, the fabled time before the new ones came from the northeast—the necromancers bent on destruction.

Quetzalcoatl, the feathered serpent Aztec god, giving maize to the native Indians, 1961 fresco. © The Art Archive / Museo Ciudad Mexico / Dagli Orti.

One of these was Tezcatlipoca, a treacherous one, whom people saw entering the city one day, his bear face blackened and painted with stripes. They did not see him seduce the niece of Quetzalcoatl but soon became aware of the lawlessness and vice that resulted. The canny Tezcatlipoca danced with bells on his ankles and sang during a festival, and people lost their heads, imitating him, congregating in revelry on a bridge. But the bridge collapsed under their weight and they perished in the river. Others died, suffocated, when they looked upon the magical puppet dancing in the necromancer's hand.

The people who remained stoned him to death, but his body stank so horribly that some died. The rest dragged him out of town, hoping that was an end to it, but Tezcatlipoca revived and returned and entered the palace of the great god-king Quetzalcoatl.

There, he played a trick on the god, producing drink, and a mirror.

"I have come," the sorcerer said, "to show you your body."

"Welcome," Quetzalcoatl said. "Please explain yourself."

"Look in the mirror. That is you." And Quetzalcoatl saw himself, bearded, with a long and homely face, and he was frightened. If my people were to see me, they too would be frightened, he thought, and decided he would have to leave. For four days he lay in a stone box and, finally feeling ill, he rose up, sang a long and sad song, promising one day to return from the East, and left, accompanied by bright-colored birds.

When he reached the great sea to the East, some say, he went across the divine waters in a boat, one day to sail back. But that is not what happened.

Upon reaching the shore, he donned his green mask of jade and his multicolored plumes and, thus adorned, he set fire to himself. The ashes of the plumed serpent were immediately raised up, along with a great flight of birds of all hues, tinting the eastern sky. This is why he came to be known also as the Lord of the Dawn. After his death, the dawn did not come for four days, while Quetzalcoatl descended into the underworld. But again he arose in the morning, enthroned in the morning sky as a star.

Before appearing as the morning star, while still among the dead, Quetzalcoatl went to the Lord of the Dead and pointed out that the earth was not inhabited. He announced that he would take the bones that lay around in the Kingdom of the Dead and put them on earth. He gathered them up in two bundles—one the bones of a man, the other of a woman—and carried them upward. Once on earth, he ground them up and cast them on the ground and threw upon them some blood from his penis. Thus, it is said, did the earth come to be peopled.

And people—now the Aztecs—remembered Quetzalcoatl and recalled his promise to return. So they kept a watch on the easternmost shore of the land. But in his absence, they welcomed other gods, including Tezcatlipoca, the treacherous necromancer who was also the sun-giver of warmth for the crops, but also the edgy, unpredictable bestower of drought. To appease him, the Aztecs offered him the hearts torn from the chests of the handsomest prisoners of war.

One day, the sentries on the eastern perimeter of the land saw someone coming across the sea, glittering and shining. They ran to their emperor and pontiff, Montezuma, and gladly announced that Quetzalcoatl had returned. Montezuma sent presents including a snake mask adorned with turquoise and the plumes of the quetzal bird, an emblem of the god.

Of course, it was not Quetzalcoatl but the Spaniard named Cortés. Within a year, Cortés had destroyed the great city where people still remembered Quetzalcoatl. He sacked the great city and burned it, even setting fire to the aviaries that graced every home with color and song. The songs of the birds were silenced; the story ended, but people remain who still wonder if perhaps Quetzalcoatl will one day make good his promise and come home.

The Sun and the Moon and Humans   (Jordan 1993: 73) (Mexico, Aztec)
The following is drawn from materials known from pre-Columbian writings (codices) and details on stone carvings.

On the fifth day of the creation of the fifth, and present, world age, the gods sit in assembly to elect a new sun god. Tecciztecatl, the son of the rain god Tlaloc, and Nanahuatl, the son of the sun god Quetzalcoatl, are considered to be the main contenders, but the two youths are of contrasting character. Tecciztecatl possesses great wealth but is of cowardly disposition, while Nanahuatl, though impoverished and sickly, shows great courage. According to different traditions both either cremate themselves or are thrown into a sacrificial fire by their respective fathers as a sacrifice for the benefit of mankind. The heart of Nanahuatl, representing courage and light, ascends to become the new sun, Atl, while that of Tecciztecatl becomes the moon.

The creator goddess Cihuacoatl-Quilaztli employs a magical vessel in which she grinds the bone fragments obtained from previous world ages of mankind into a powder. The gods then collectively commit self-sacrifice, allowing their blood to drip into the vessel and from the resulting mix the human race of the fifth sun is formed.

From the Body of a Woman Creator   (Jordan 1993: 76–77) (Polynesian–Cook Islands and Hervey Islands) This account features a female creator *(creatrix)* whose story begins in the common mythological site of the world egg, who then gives birth from all parts of her body.

Vari-Ma-Te-Takere (woman in the very beginning) is the primordial female being who lives in the cramped space at the very bottom of the world coconut or egg which rests in the land of Te-Enua-Te-Ki (the land of eternal silence) in the depths of the primeval ocean. So restricted is her living space that she is obliged to sit with her knees touching her chin.

Vari-Ma-Te-Takere engenders six children from her own body, three of whom she plucks from her left side and three from her right. The first of these offspring is Avatea (Vatea), the first man on earth, who is also perceived as a moon god. The primordial mother plucks him from her left side and when he grows he divides vertically into a hybrid being; his left side is fish-like but his right side is human. Although he is born in the bottom of the world coconut

Avatea ascends and finds a place at the opening of the upper world where he is given the earth to live upon, a place called "Under the Bright Moon."

The second child, taken from the right side, is Tinirau, the younger brother of Avatea, who becomes the god responsible for fish. His home is immediately beneath that of Avatea, on the sacred island of Motu-Tapu, where he looks after all the different kinds of fish in great ponds. Like his older brother he develops in the form of a fish-man, his left side being in the form of a sprat.

The mother goddess's third child, plucked from her left side, is Tango, who lives in Enua-Kura, the land of the red parrot feather, immediately below that of Tinirau. The fourth, Tumuteanaoa (echo) comes from the right and lives in the land of hollow grey rocks, Te-Parai-Tea.

Vari-Ma-Te-Takere's fifth child, coming from the left of her body, is Raka (trouble), who makes his home in the deep ocean. His mother also gives him a birthday gift of a great bag containing the winds, which become his foster-children. Each of these is provided with a hole at the edge of the horizon through which it may blow. In spite of his name, Raka is also imbued with knowledge of things which help mankind and which he passes on to the people of the earth.

The sixth and last child, born from the right side, is Tu-Metua (stick-by-parent). He elects to stay with his mother in her confined space at the bottom of the world coconut where he lives, like her, in perpetual silence.

According to the Cook Island tradition, the second of the six offspring is the earth mother Papatuanuku, who becomes the consort of her brother Avatea.

The Origin of Specific Earth Features

Cosmic Beginnings and Structures   (Jordan 1993: 51–52) (Prasun Kafir, in the Hindu Kush mountains that stretch from northern Pakistan to northeast Afghanistan)

The universe is built of three components. The upper world of Urdesh is one in which there exist seven heavens (bisht), the highest of which is Il-Munj, and the rivers which bound these heavens are the stars, including the north star. The middle world, thought of either as a large disc or as a sleeping giant, is Michdesh, upon which all living things exist. The lowest world is Yurdesh, the underworld, which is a mixture of paradise and hell (zozuk). It is reached through one of several holes in the ground, the most significant of which is near the Prasun village of Kushteki. Those who look into the hole die and are immediately transported to the underworld.

In an alternative tradition the transition from earth to the realms of heaven is gradual. It begins deep in the valleys of the Hindu Kush with the rivers which represent the highway between middle, upper and underworlds. The river comes from the high places and it flows into the realm of the dead at the lowest point in the valley. Heaven begins where the mountain peaks and glaciers touch the sky and the homes of the gods are the sacred mountain lakes overlooked by trees which symbolize the presence of both gods and men.

In a third tradition there exist only an upper world and an underworld. The upper world, covered by a roof of sky, is a place where both gods and mortals move freely, but the real home of both gods and demons is the underworld from which the unborn emerge and to which humankind returns at the moment of death. The lakes are the doorways between worlds and anyone who jumps into a sacred lake makes the journey from one to the other.

In the beginning there exists nothing, neither sun nor moon, and the cosmos is ruled by the supreme god Imra, a deity endowed with great wisdom and cunning. He rules the world at the head of a trinity which also includes Mandi (Mon) as his youthful adjutant and the god of war, Gish. These three supreme gods are equaled in might by the supreme goddess Disani. One other deity occupies a position of high rank, Munjem Malik, the god of the earth who rules the mountain valleys and who also presides over the council of gods. His head appears above ground in the valley of Parun, where it emerges in the form of a vast boulder.

Beneath the highest level of the hierarchy exists a vast pantheon of gods who oversee all of nature. They include Sudrem, the weather god; Zuzum, the god of winter; Wushum, the god of law; Bagisht, the god of waters; and Maramalik, the underworld god of the dead. All the deities are in a permanent state of conflict with the army of demons, the yush and the wechi, who embody the harshness and dangers of the natural world. It is this endless battle which preoccupies the spirit world.

 Zuni Earth-Mother and Sky-Father   (Leeming and Page 1996: 120–21) (Zuni, Southwest America) An American variant of the worldwide theme of the primal parents having to be separated so that the children (human beings) could establish themselves. The cooperation between masculine and feminine creators is striking here.

In the fourfold womb of the world, all terrestrial life was conceived from the lying together of the Earth-Mother and Sky-Father upon the world waters. Soon, Earth-Mother grew large with so great a number of progeny. She pushed Sky-Father away from her and began to sink into the world waters, fearing that evil might befall her offspring, just as mothers always fear for their firstborn before they come forth.

Unnerved by this foreboding, she kept her offspring unborn within her and discussed her fears with Sky-Father. Together, they wondered how, even in the light of the Sun, these offspring would know one place for another. Changeable as are all surpassing beings, like smoke in the breeze, the couple took the form of a man and a woman.

Suddenly a great bowl filled with water appeared near at hand to Earth-Mother and she realized that each place in the world would be surrounded by mountains like the rim of the bowl. She spat in the water and, as foam formed, she said, "Look! It is from my bosom that they will find sustenance."

She blew her warm breath over the foam and some lifted upward, shattering, sending down mist and spray in great abundance. "So," Earth-Mother said. "Just so will clouds form at the rim of the world where the great waters are and be borne by the breath of the surpassing beings until your cold breath makes them shed, falling downward—the waters of life falling into my lap where our children will nestle and thrive, finding warmth in spite of your coldness."

"Wait," said Sky-Father and he spread his hand over the bowl, setting in its crevices what looked like yellow corn-grains gleaming in the dark of the early dawn of the world. He took seven of them up between his thumb and fingers and said, "When the Sun is not nearby and all is dark in the world, our children will be guided by these lights which will tell them the regions of space. And just as these grains shine up from the water to light the sky, so will numberless seedlings like them spring up from your bosom when my waters touch them, and our children will be fed."

In this way, and in many others, Earth-Mother and Sky-Father talked and provided for their progeny, the people and other creatures of the world.

Descriptions of Deities and Generations

The Ogdoad of Hermopolis   (Jordan 1993: 59–60) (ancient Egypt) Egypt is one of the cultures with several "creation" narratives; as in others, different temples celebrated one or another organization of the universe, promoting its own favored creator deity.

Eight primordial elements of chaos known as the Ogdoad exist before the creation of the sun god and, according to Hermopolis tradition, before the existence of the Heliopolis pantheon, the Ennead. The Ogdoad is divided into four pairs of entities who are personified as frogs (gods) and snakes (goddesses), creatures suitably equipped for life in the primeval ooze. They include

Nun and Naunet representing the primordial waters, Kek and Kauket representing darkness, Heh and Hauhet representing infinity, and Amun and Amaunet representing hidden power.

At one particular moment, the eight components of the Ogdoad interact to break the laws governing chaos and out of the new order they generate the primeval mound of silt on which the sun god, Amun, in a new role, is to be born from a cosmic egg. This mound later becomes Hermopolis.

The primordial couples, with one exception, now become redundant. Amun and Amaunet, however, continue to play a dominant creative role at Thebes when Heliopolis is deserted. Amun retains his snake symbolism at Thebes, but is also symbolized by the ram and the Nile goose. He is perceived as being hidden, but nonetheless as pervading the whole universe. He has a strongly ithyphallic form which enables him, as first-born of the gods, to impregnate his own mother.

The moon god Thoth plays a significant role in the Ogdoad mythology. The priest of the Ogdoad at the time of the transition from Hermopolis to Thebes in the fourth century B.C.E. was also the High Priest of Thoth, who thus became the tutelary god of Hermopolis and the new head of the Ogdoad, titled "Lord of Khemnu."

The cosmogony at Hermopolis takes an almost scientific slant when compared with the highly personal and physical method of creation at Heliopolis and the more cerebral or metaphysical process at Memphis.

The Hymn of Primal Man   (Jordan 1993: 66–67) (Vedic and Brahmanic Hindu, India) This late hymn from the *Rig Veda* follows an ancient notion of dismemberment leading to the creation of life.

The myth identifies a gigantic creator being, Purusa, with a thousand heads, a thousand eyes and a thousand feet. He is the immortal ruler, past, present and future, who pervades all matter. From him is engendered the active female principle of creation, Viraj, and paradoxically he is born by her. The great gods (it is not clear how they arise) engender Rudra, the god of sacred rites; Agni, the god of fire who fashions the semen of Purusa; and Vac, the goddess of speech. As he commits incest with his daughter, some of Purusa's semen falls upon the womb of the earth, the *yoni*, and becomes the Angirases, a class of beings who act as mediators between gods and men.

Through primordial sacrifice the creator being becomes the victim. The gods, the demi-gods and the sages dismember him and anoint him before spreading him upon the sacred grass and consigning him to the funeral pyre. From the fat of the sacrifice are created all living things, all inanimate things and all abstract things. From his mouth, arms, thighs and feet come the four *varnas* or classes of Vedic society.

The moon from his mind was born, and from his eyes the sun.
From his mouth came Indra and Agni,
From his breath was Vayu born.

As the gods and their attendants burn the being he becomes both the victim of sacrifice and the object of oblation. Thus is the first model laid down for ritual conduct.

The Brahmana texts elaborate further on the incest of Prajapati (Purusa) with his daughter Viraj (Rohini), introducing the primordial "lord of creatures" as a stag while she takes the form of a doe. The gods see what Prajapati has done and wish to punish him, but they are unable to find a champion to administer appropriate justice so they assemble all that is fearsome in the cosmos and from it create the malevolent storm god Rudra.

As the stag ejaculates, his semen becomes a lake and is surrounded by the protecting flames of the fire god, Agni. As the semen ignites, the first part of it becomes Aditya (probably here applied as an epithet of Surya, the sun god); the second part becomes Bhrgu, the "Crack of Fire"; and the third part becomes the six lesser sun gods, the Adityas. The charred wood becomes the black cattle and the red earth becomes the tawny cattle.

In another of the Brahmanas, it is the offspring of Prajapati who commit incest with one another to bring about the birth of Rudra.

Trivikrama, The Three Steps of Vishnu That Organize the Cosmos   (Jordan 1993: 75–76) (Vedic, Brahmanic and Puranic Hindu India)

Ten major incarnations, or *avataras,* of Vishnu are conventionally understood and each of these is explained by its own myth. In making three giant strides Vishnu is seen to be separating the realms of the cosmos by propping them apart. While the first two separate earth and sky the third step is regarded as symbolic of Vishnu himself, the embodiment of "all creatures."

Vishnu appears in his fifth incarnation as Vamana, a dwarf, symbolizing the puny state of mankind set against the vastness of the cosmos. He has taken this guise in order to trick Bali, the demonic son of the sun god Virocana, whose tyrannical dominion over the world has become a serious threat. To restore equilibrium Vamana requests of Bali a plot of land on which he may meditate. The area of ground is to be a modest one, three paces wide.

Bali is deceived, and grants the dwarf's request, upon which Vishnu returns to his full stature. With his first stride he demarcates and separates the earth and with his second the heaven. The third step separates the living world of creatures. An alternative tradition suggests that Vishnu resists taking a third step which would claim the underworld and, instead, binds Bali with ropes, sending him and his kind to be its rulers.

Romulus and Remus   (Rosenberg 1994: 110–13; edited and condensed by
WGD) (ancient Rome)

After Aeneas, Ascanius, and Aeneas' grandson, Silvius, died, the kingdom of
Alba Longa [the ancient pre-Roman city considered to be the birth place of
the twins] passed from father to son until the time of Numitor and Amulius,
who were brothers. The brothers agreed to divide their inheritance and to
choose their portions by lot. One would draw the kingdom of Alba Longa,
and the other would keep the Trojan wealth of gold, silver, and jewels that
had come down to them. Numitor drew the kingdom, but Amulius seized the
throne and exiled his brother from Alba Longa.

Amulius then murdered Numitor's sons and made his daughter a Vestal
Virgin in order to prevent her from marrying and having children who could
inherit the throne. She became pregnant anyway, and gave birth to twins,
claiming that Mars was their father. However, King Amulius nonetheless im-
prisoned his niece and ordered her infants drowned in the Tiber River.

Heavy rains had brought the Tiber over its banks, and servants entrusted
with drowning the infants decided to drown them in the flooded overflow
area instead of penetrating to the actual riverbed of the Tiber. They left the
twins in a basket. When the flood waters receded, the basket containing the
twins rested upon dry land. A wolf discovered them and mothered them by
giving them her own milk to suck.

The king's herdsman accidentally came upon the infants and found the
wolf there, tenderly licking the babes with her tongue. He brought the twins
back to his hut for his wife to nurse, and the couple reared the boys to be
good, strong, and courageous young men. They earned fame by attacking
robbers and sharing with their shepherd friends the goods they retrieved in
their raids.

The robbers retaliated by choosing a local holiday as the occasion for lay-
ing a trap for Romulus and Remus. Romulus defended himself successfully,
but the robbers caught Remus and brought him before his uncle, King
Amulius. They charged Remus and his brother with the crime of stealing Numitor's cattle. After King Amulius heard their accusation, he sent Remus to
Numitor for punishment.

The king's herdsman had always suspected that the boys he had reared
were of royal blood, and now he told Romulus of his suspicions. When the
robbers brought Remus before Numitor and announced that he was one of
twins, Numitor also guessed the truth. Remus' age and his noble bearing
made it likely that he was Numitor's grandson. Therefore, the king asked
Remus about himself and his parents. Remus explained that he had thought
his brother and himself to be the children of the king's herdsman, but that he

Sculpture of Romulus and Remus nursing from a wolf, in Capitoline Museum, Rome, Italy. Courtesy of the Library of Congress.

had heard strange tales of his infancy, involving danger by water and rescue by wolf and bird.

Aided by Numitor, Romulus and Remus each gathered a group of herdsmen, quietly met at the king's house, and killed Amulius in a surprise attack. Numitor then explained to the people how King Amulius had usurped the throne and had tried to kill anyone who would succeed him. Amulius had been an unpopular king, so the people of Alba were not saddened by his murder. They unanimously acclaimed Numitor their king.

Romulus and Remus then decided to found a town at the spot where, as infants, they had been left to drown. Since they were of the same age, they could not agree on which of them should rule the town. They decided to ask the gods of the countryside to reveal the answer. Romulus and his followers stood upon the Palatine hill, and Remus upon the Aventine hill. Remus saw the first sign, six vultures. Romulus then saw twelve vultures. Remus claimed the kingship because he had been given the first sign. Romulus claimed kingship because his sign was twice as strong as his brother's. Angry words led to death-dealing blows, and after Romulus killed Remus he proclaimed himself king of the new town and named it Rome after himself.

Romulus increased the population of Rome by opening the settlement to poor people, slaves, and banished men who wanted to begin a new life. However, they had few women. Neighboring communities refused to let their women intermarry with the Romans because they did not want their neighbor to become too powerful. They also felt socially superior to the inhabitants of Rome.

Romulus decided to hold a great celebration on a holiday sacred to the god Neptune. Hundreds of people from the neighboring communities took advantage of the occasion to visit the new town. At a prearranged signal, the Roman men suddenly seized all of the visiting young women, including the daughters of the powerful Sabines. The parents of all of these women were outraged, but they were forced to return home without their daughters. Romulus assured the young women that they would have loving husbands and many privileges in the Roman community. Their husbands lived up to that commitment, and the women accepted their new families and homes.

However, the Romans could not stop the relatives of these women from seeking revenge for their abduction, attacking Rome repeatedly. Finally, in order to acquire peace for themselves and their Roman families, the Sabine women took a stand against their relatives and forced them to come to peaceful terms with their own Roman husbands.

Through his military skill and strength, Romulus brought a forty-year period of peace to his city. He made good laws, and everyone appeared to love him: the common people, the army, and the senators. One day, Romulus was standing among his senators and reviewing his troops when a violent storm burst upon them. Dark clouds obscured the sun, making the day as black as night. Resounding thunder and crashing lightning sent many people scurrying for shelter. A thick cloud descended and completely enveloped Romulus so that no one could see him. When the storm blew over and the cloud disappeared, Romulus had disappeared also.

No one could say what had become of him. Most of the senators, soldiers, and townspeople decided that Romulus had become a god. After all, he was the son of Mars. But some suspected that a group of senators had secretly murdered him because he appeared to favor his army over the Senate. Eventually Romulus attained immortality and seemed a guarantee of the success of the great city of Rome.

Transformations, Metamorphoses

Krishna's Cosmic Mouth   (Jordan 1993: 104) (Puranic Hindu India)

Rama and Krishna are playing in the mud, occasionally returning to their mothers' breasts for comfort and reassurance. Krishna, in particular, gets up to all sorts of boyish pranks with the cattle of the village and other objects of amusement. Sometimes his behavior is more reprehensible, when he steals from neighbors or when he pees on their clean floors!

One day some of Krishna's playmates report to Yasoda, his foster mother, that he has been eating dirt and Yasoda scolds him severely. Krishna, however, asserts that the other boys are lying. Yasoda commands this infant incarnation of Vishnu to open his mouth. Inside she perceives, not dirt, but the whole universe—the heavens, the earth and all its features—and she becomes deeply confused, wondering if she is under some strange delusion or if she is indeed witnessing the power of a god. As soon as Yasoda understands the true nature of the vision before her, Vishnu removes all trace of the experience from her memory, but still she understands that Vishnu, in one of his multitude of aspects, has been made incarnate as her son.

Daphne's Escape from Apollo   (Ovid, *Metamorphoses,* 1.452–567) (Roman)

In one of two ancient stories about Daphne, the virgin huntress daughter of a river-god, Apollo made fun of the archery skills of the god Eros, and the love-god took revenge upon him by shooting him with a golden arrow that incited Apollo to fall violently in love with Daphne. Simultaneously he shot Daphne with a lead arrow that caused the victim to repel any overtures of love.

So, even though she had a raft of suitors, she chose to remain a virgin, and fled even from the handsome hunk Apollo. But not fast enough: he was just about to catch her near the banks of her father's river, the *Peneius.* She called to her father for help, and he acted immediately, causing her body to become numb and heavy, her curvaceous breasts to be covered with bark, her hair to turn to leaves, and her feet to begin growing down as roots into the ground.

Apollo remained unrequited, but in her honor, adopted the laurel tree and its branches and wood as his permanent tribute to her memory. The crown of laurel leaves became the prize for the victor at the Pythian Games in Apollo's honor, and now is a frequently-used symbol for "victory," but in the arts, the favorite representation of this story has always been that of the moments of transformation from beautiful young woman into the graceful laurel tree.

Shamanic Transformation

The theme of being completely infused with another spirit being is central to accounts of shamanic training and practice. The shaman is a figure who can enter the world of spirits easily because of the powers granted her or him by such beings. In such a state, she or he can locate missing animals, bring back ill souls (thought to be wandering too far from the fleshly body), or see into the future.

Apollo and Daphne (Daphne metamorphosing into a laurel tree while fleeing Apollo's amorous advances). © The Art Archive / National Gallery London / Eileen Tweedy.

Imagery in the art of shamans is frequently of a human transforming—walrus tusks jut out from the jawbone, for instance, or one side of the head is that of a frog. Perhaps the ultimate transformation takes place in the extended initiation by a seasoned shaman: the individual is deconstructed into many tiny pieces, or stripped of the flesh (skeletonization is frequently represented), or transformed into an animal like the badger. The basic underlying idea seems to be that having been wounded, torn into shreds, and reconstructed again, the healer can most effectively assist those who are now in pain or ill. They may determine, for instance, that some hostile sorcerer has shot "darts" into the patient, and with elaborate music, drumming, and drama, "suck out" the offending projectile and destroy it.

Hamatsa shaman possessed by a supernatural power after having spent several days in the woods as part of an initiation ritual. The shaman can enter the world of spirits easily because of the powers granted her or him by such beings. Courtesy of the Library of Congress.

In what is still a valuable introduction to the world of shamanic practice, Joan Halifax remarks:

> The communion between culture and nature occurs first in the realm of spirit. The shaman has died to the phenomenal world, the world of everyday reality. The ravenous spirits of the Underworld have dismembered and consumed the neophyte, thus releasing him or her to a higher order of existence where the cooked and the raw become one. In a state of surrender, the initiate is receptive to the teachings from the spirit

world. Bear, frog, raven, eland, seal, wolf, and mosquito instruct through the very act of destruction—a covenant forged in death *and* in spirit between the eater and the eaten. (1982: 78)

Flood

Yü Conquers the Flood   (Leeming 1990: 53–55) (Chinese) The flood theme is one of the very oldest in Chinese mythology. A flood myth from the *Shu ching* in the Chou Dynasty dates from as early as 1000 B.C.E.

"Everywhere the tremendous flood waters were wreaking destruction. Spreading afar, they embraced the mountains and rose above the hills. In a vast flow they swelled up to Heaven. The people below were groaning." In response to their appeals, a being who in the *Shu ching* is referred to simply as Ti, "Lord," rather reluctantly (because he had reservations about his ability) commanded Kun to deal with the flood. (By the commentators this "Lord" is equated with the sage ruler Yao; in all probability, however, he was none other than the supreme divinity, Shang Ti, the "Lord on High.")

For nine years Kun labored without success to dam up the waters. At the end of that time either Yao or his successor Shun (the texts differ) had Kun executed at the Feather Mountain (Yii-shan), and ordered Kun's son, Yü, to continue the task. The latter, instead of trying to dam up the waters in the manner of his father, adopted the new technique of channeling passages for them to drain off to the sea. In this way he eventually conquered the flood and made the land fit for habitation. As a reward, he was given the throne by Shun and became founder of the Hsia dynasty.

In contrast to this "historical" account, we can, by piecing together the fragments found both in Chou and Han literature, produce another version which is much more "mythological":

On being ordered to deal with the flood, Kun stole from the Lord the "swelling mold" (Asi *jang*)—a magical kind of soil which had the property of ever swelling in size. With this he tried to build dams which, through their swelling, would hold back the waters. When his efforts failed, the Lord, angered by his theft, had him executed at Feather Mountain, a sunless place in the extreme north. There his body remained for three years without decomposing, until somebody (unspecified) cut it open with a sword, whereupon Yü emerged from his father's belly. (One tradition says that Yii was born from a stone, which would apparently signify that Kun's body had turned to stone.) Following Yü's birth, Kun became transformed into an animal—variously said to be a yellow bear, black fish, three-legged turtle, or yellow dragon—and plunged into the Feather Gulf (Yu-yuan). A cryptic line in the *Tien wen* poem, however, suggests that he subsequently managed to get to the west, where he was restored to life by a shamanness.

Yü, we are told, "came down from on high" to continue his father's work. He was helped by a winged dragon which, going ahead of him, trailed its tail over the ground and thus marked the places where channels should be dug. For some eight or ten years Yü labored so intensely that, though several times passing the door of his home, he had no time to visit his family within. He wore the nails off his hands, the hair off his shanks, and developed a lameness giving him a peculiar gait which in later times came to be known as the "walk of Yü." Nonetheless, he eventually succeeded in draining the great rivers to the sea, expelling snakes and dragons from the marshlands, and making the terrain fit for cultivation. So great, indeed, were his achievements that the *Tso chuan* history, under the year 541 B.C., reports a noble as exclaiming: "Were it not for Yü, we would indeed be fish!"

Manu   (Jordan 1993: 55) (India) The story of Manu, who alone is saved from the great flood, must remind us of Utnapishtim in the Gilgamesh Epic and of Noah stories. Like the other flood heroes, Manu receives supernatural help and is saved by remaining in a ship until he is able to tie up on an Indian version of Mount Ararat.

1. In the morning they brought to Manu water for washing, just as now also they (are wont to) bring (water) for washing the hands. When he was washing himself, a fish came into his hands.

2. It spake to him the word, "Rear me, I will save thee!" "Where-from wilt thou save me?" "A flood will carry away all these creatures: from that I will save thee!" "How am I to rear thee?"

3. It said, "As long as we are small, there is great destruction for us: fish devours fish. Thou wilt first keep me in a jar. When I outgrow that, thou wilt dig a pit and keep me in it. When I outgrow that, thou wilt take me down to the sea, for then I shall be beyond destruction."

4. It soon became a *ghasha* (a great fish); for that grows largest (of all fish). Thereupon it said, "In such and such a year that flood will come. Thou shalt then attend to me (i.e. to my advice) by preparing a ship; and when the flood has risen thou shalt enter into the ship, and I will save thee from it."

5. After he had reared it in this way, he took it down to the sea. And in the same year which the fish had indicated to him, he attended to (the advice of the fish) by preparing a ship; and when the flood had risen, he entered into the ship. The fish then swam up to him, and to its horn he tied the rope of the ship, and by that means he passed swiftly up to yonder northern mountain.

6. It then said, "I have saved thee. Fasten the ship to a tree; but let not the water cut thee off whilst thou art on the mountain. As the water subsides, thou mayest

gradually descend!" Accordingly he gradually descended and hence that (slope) of the northern mountain is called "Manu's descent." The flood then swept away all these creatures, and Manu alone remained here.

Goddesses

The Goddess of the Universe and her Bad Brother   (Rosenberg 1994: 374–76; edited and condensed by WGD) (Shinto, Japan)

Amaterasu Omikami, goddess of the sun and of the universe, sent her brother and husband, the god of the moon, down to the reed plains to serve the goddess of food. As soon as the goddess saw him, she turned toward the land and spit boiled rice from her mouth. Next she turned toward the sea and spit all kinds of fish from her mouth. Finally, she turned toward the mountains and spit a variety of fur-coated animals from her mouth. She then prepared all of these as food and placed them upon 100 tables for the moon god to eat.

When the moon god saw what she had done, he was furious. "How dare you feed me with food that you have spit from your mouth!" he exclaimed, "You have made the food filthy and disgusting!" He drew his sword and killed the goddess. Then he returned to Amaterasu and told her of his deed.

To his surprise, Amaterasu exclaimed, "You are an evil god! I can no longer stand the sight of your face. Take yourself from my presence, and see to it that we do not meet face to face again!" So the sun and the moon lived apart from one another, separated by day and by night.

Amaterasu sent her messenger, the cloud spirit, down to the goddess of food. He found that the goddess was indeed dead. However, he also found that the ox and the horse had issued forth from her head, grain had grown from her forehead, silkworms had come forth from her eyebrows, cereal had emerged from her eyes, rice had grown from her stomach, and wheat and beans had grown from her abdomen. The cloud spirit collected all of these and returned to Amaterasu with them. The goddess of the sun was delighted with the variety of foods. "You have given me great cause for rejoicing!" she exclaimed to her messenger. "Human beings will be able to eat these foods and survive."

Not long thereafter, Izanagi and Izanami gave their son Susano-o-no-Mikoto the nether land to rule and banished him there, but first he decided to visit his shining sister. He was such a violent god that the mountains and hills groaned aloud and the sea frothed in tempestuous tumult as he made his way up to heaven. When she saw him coming, Amaterasu suspected his intentions, thinking he sought to have more than his allotted realm to rule.

The goddess bound up her hair in knots and tied her skirts into trousers as if she were a male. She placed two huge quivers of arrows upon her back, and girded herself with three long swords. In one hand, she carried her bow upright in shooting position, with an arrow ready on the bowstring; in her other hand, she firmly grasped one of her swords, supposing to intimidate her brother. "Why have you come to me?" she calmly asked him.

"You look as if you are expecting trouble!" Susano-o-no-Mikoto replied. "Certainly you should have no fear of me. I have never had a black heart, although our parents dislike me and have condemned me to rule the nether land. I simply wanted to see you before I left the world of light. I do not intend to stay long." Amaterasu, wishing to believe the best of her brother, put away her weapons. She welcomed him among the heavenly gods and hoped that his visit would be as brief as he had said.

But Susano-o-no-Mikoto stayed longer than he was wanted, and his behavior was very rude. He and Amaterasu each had three rice fields of their own. Whereas Amaterasu's fields thrived in spite of excessive rains or prolonged drought, Susano-o-no-Mikoto's rice fields were always barren. In times of drought, the soil was parched and cracked; in heavy rainfall, the soil washed away. Finally Susano-o-no-Mikoto became possessed by jealous anger. When the rice seeds were sown in the spring, he removed the divisions between the fields, filled up the channels, and destroyed the troughs and pipes. Amaterasu, wishing to believe the best of her brother, remained calm and tolerant.

In the autumn, when the grain was mature, Susano-o-no-Mikoto freed the heavenly colts and caused them to lie down in the middle of the rice fields. Again Amaterasu remained calm and tolerant. Then Susano-o-no-Mikoto spoiled the harvest feast of first-fruits by defiling the purity of the palace with disgusting filth. Again Amaterasu remained calm and tolerant.

Finally, while Amaterasu sat weaving cloth for the clothing of the gods in her sacred weaving hall, her evil brother silently removed some roof tiles in order to create a hole in the ceiling. Then he threw a colt of heaven into the room. Amaterasu was so startled that she pricked herself with her shuttle. This time the sun goddess could not forgive Susano-o-no-Mikoto. In great rage, she left the palace and entered the rock cave of heaven. She locked the door and remained there in isolation. Now that her brilliance no longer illuminated heaven and earth, day became as black as night. The universe was forced to exist in total, continuous darkness. Without the sun, plants could not grow. People everywhere stopped their activities, watching and waiting to see how long the deprivation would last.

All of the gods gathered along the banks of the Peaceful River of Heaven and discussed how to placate Amaterasu's wrath. They placed a statue of the sun goddess outside the rock cave and offered prayers to it. They also made many special offerings—including fine cloth, rich jewels, combs, and a mirror—which they hung upon a sakaki tree—and goddesses danced and chanted by the door.

Amaterasu heard the music and said to herself, "I hear both beautiful prayers of supplication addressed to me and the sounds of music and dance. Why are the gods so happy when my seclusion in this rock cave has brought constant darkness to the central land of fertile reed plains?" Her curiosity overcame her anger, and she opened the door a crack to look outside. This was just what the gods had hoped Amaterasu would do. Rejoicing in the return of the sun's brilliant rays, they took Amaterasu by the hand, had her among them, and convinced her to rejoin them.

The gods punished Susano-o-no-Mikoto by demanding from him 1,000 tables of offerings. They also plucked out his hair and the nails on his fingers and toes. Finally they said to him, "Your behavior has been intolerably rude and improper. From this time forth, you are banished from heaven and from the central reed plains as well. Go forth with all speed to the netherland. We have had enough of your wicked ways!"

Sun goddess Amaterasu emerging from the cave (she had previously retreated there, depriving the world of light, after her brother the storm god Susano had neglected his duties. She was enticed out by the other gods making much noise). © The Art Archive / Victoria and Albert Museum London / Eileen Tweedy.

So Susano-o-no-Mikoto left heaven forever and began his journey to the netherland.

Children of the Sun   (Rosenberg 1994: 473–76) (Mesoamerica, Inca) Part of the Inca attempt to claim all achievements of their inherited and borrowed civilization, this myth is a good example of how one culture can appropriate stories from others.

In times of old, our land was one of shrubs and small trees and tall mountains. The people were unmannered and untaught. They lived as wild animals live, without clothes made from woven cloth, without houses, and without cultivated food. They lived apart from other human beings in small family groups, finding lodging as nature provided it, within mountain caves and in hollow places beneath the great rocks. They covered their bodies with animal skins, leaves, and the bark of trees, or they wore no clothes at all. They gathered whatever food they could find to eat, such as grass, wild berries, and the roots of plants, and sometimes they ate human flesh.

Father Sun looked down from the heavens and pitied these humans who lived like wild creatures. He decided to send one of his sons, Manco Capac, and one of his daughters, Mama Ocllo Huaco, down to earth at Lake Titicaca to teach them how to improve their lives.

When his children were ready to leave, the Sun said to them, "I devote myself to the well-being of the universe. Each day, I travel across the sky so that I can look down upon the earth and see what I can do for the human beings who live there. My heat provides them with the comfort of warmth. My light provides them with the knowledge that comes from sight. It is through my efforts that fields and forests provide food for them, for I bring sunshine and rain, each in its proper season.

"Yet all this, good as it is, is not enough. The people live like wild animals. They know nothing of living in houses, wearing clothing, or raising food. They have no villages, they use no tools or utensils, and they have no laws.

"Therefore," Father Sun continued, "I am making you the rulers of all the races in the region of Lake Titicaca; I want you to rule those peoples as a father rules his children. Treat them as I have treated you, with tenderness and affection, with devotion and justice. Teach them as I have taught you, for the races of human beings are my children also. I am their provider and their protector, and it is time they stopped living like animals.

"Take this golden rod with you," the Sun concluded. "It is only two fingers thick and shorter than the arm of a man, yet it will tell you how good the soil is for cultivating crops. As you travel, whenever you stop to eat or to sleep, see if you can bury it in the land. When you come to the place where the rod sinks into the earth with one thrust, establish my sacred city, Cuzco, city of the sun. Soft soil as deep as this golden rod will be fertile soil."

So Manco Capac and Mama Ocllo Huaco went down to Lake Titicaca and set out on foot to examine the land. Wherever they stopped they tried to bury the golden rod, but they could not do it. The soil was too rocky.

Finally they descended into a valley. The land was wild and without people, but the plant growth was lush and green. They climbed to the crest of a hill (the hill where Ayar Cachi and Ayar Ucho had turned to stone) and pressed the golden rod into the soil. To their great pleasure, it sank into the earth and disappeared.

Manco Capac smiled at Mama Ocllo Huaco and said, "Our father, the Sun, intends us to rule this valley. Here we will build his sacred city, Cuzco. Let us now go separate ways, you to the south and I to the north. Let us gather together the peoples we find and bring them into this fertile valley. Here we will instruct them in the ways of human beings, and we will care for them as our father has commanded us."

Manco Capac and Mama Ocllo Huaco set out for the mountain plateaus to collect the peoples of the land. The men and women they found in the barren regions were impressed with their clothing and pierced ears, their regal bearing, and their message. "Let us teach you how to lead a better life," the children of the Sun announced. "Let us teach you how to build houses, make clothes, and raise cattle and crops. Right now you live like wild animals. Let us teach you how to live like human beings. Our father, the Sun, has taught us and has sent us here to teach you."

The peoples of the land placed their confidence in these children of the Sun and followed as they led the way toward a new and better way of living. When many people had gathered together, Manco Capac and Mama Occio Huaco divided the group into those who would be responsible for gathering food and those who would learn how to build houses. Their new life had begun.

Manco Capac taught the males which foods were nourishing so their diet would include both grains and vegetables, how to choose the best seeds, and how to plant and cultivate each kind of plant. In the process, he taught them how to make the tools and equipment necessary for farming and how to channel water from the streams in the valley for irrigation. He even taught them how to make shoes. Meanwhile, Mama Ocllo Huaco taught the women how to weave wool and cotton into cloth and how to sew that cloth into clothing.

So it came to pass that the Incas became an educated people. In honor of their great provider and protector, the Sun, the people built a temple on the crest of the hill where Manco Capac and Mama Ocllo Huaco had plunged the golden rod into the earth and from which they had set out to gather the Inca people together and teach them. Their prosperity drew other peoples to join them and learn their ways. Manco Capac finally taught the men how to make weapons—such as bows and arrows, clubs, and lances—so that they could defend themselves and extend their kingdom. The Incas were on their way to becoming a great people.

Modern: Gaia as Earth   (Leeming 1990: 145–46) (Contemporary Ecology) "In recent years the theory of British scientist James Lovelock has suggested that Earth—'a planet-sized entity...with properties which could not be predicted from the sum of its parts'—can best be seen as a living organism with the capability of organizing its own biosphere. This theory is now seriously discussed by scientists who study Earth's ecology. [James] Lovelock and others have given their newly discovered giant organism a name, which they have taken from an earlier mythological version of the theory: Mother Earth, or Gaia" (145).

The concept of Mother Earth or, as the Greeks called her long ago, Gaia, has been widely held throughout history and has been the basis of a belief which still coexists with the great religions. As a result of the accumulation of evidence about the natural environment and the growth of the science of ecology, there have recently been speculations that the biosphere may have been more than just the complete range of all living things within their natural habitat of soil, sea, and air. Ancient belief and modern knowledge have fused emotionally in the awe with which astronauts with their own eyes and we by indirect vision have seen the Earth revealed in all its shining beauty against the deep darkness of space. Yet this feeling, however strong, does not prove that Mother Earth lives. Like a religious belief, it is scientifically untestable and therefore incapable in its own context of further rationalization.

Journeys into space did more than present the Earth in a new perspective. They also sent back information about its atmosphere and its surface which provided a new insight into the interactions between the living and the inorganic parts of the planet. From this has arisen the hypothesis, the model, in which the Earth's living matter, air, oceans, and land surface form a complex system which can be seen as a single organism and which has the capacity to keep our planet a fit place for life.

We have since defined Gaia as a complex entity involving the Earth's biosphere, atmosphere, oceans, and soil; the totality constituting a feedback or cybernetic system which seeks an optimal physical and chemical environment for life on this planet. The maintenance of relatively constant conditions by active control may be conveniently described by the term "homoeostasis."

Gaia, Goddess of the Earth, relief from the tympanum of the Temple of Artemis, Corfu. 6th century. © Erich Lessing / Art Resource, NY.

Gaia has remained a hypothesis but, like other useful hypotheses, she has already proved her theoretical value, if not her existence, by giving rise to experimental questions and answers which were profitable exercises in themselves. If, for example, the atmosphere is, among other things, a device for conveying raw materials to and from the biosphere, it would be reasonable to assume the presence of carrier compounds for elements essential in all biological systems, for example, iodine and sulphur. It was rewarding to find evidence that both were conveyed from the oceans, where they are abundant, through the air to the land surface, where they are in short supply. The carrier compounds, methyl iodide and dimethyl sulphide respectively, are directly produced by marine life. Scientific curiosity being unquenchable, the presence of these interesting compounds in the atmosphere would no doubt have been discovered in the end and their importance discussed without the stimulus of the Gaia hypothesis. But they were actively sought as a result of the hypothesis and their presence was consistent with it.

If Gaia exists, the relationship between her and man, a dominant animal species in the complex living system, and the possibly shifting balance of power between them, are questions of obvious importance.... The Gaia hypothesis is for those who like to walk or simply stand and stare, to wonder about the Earth and the life it bears, and to speculate about the consequences of our own presence here. It is an alternative to that pessimistic view which sees nature as a primitive force to be subdued and conquered. It is also an alternative to that equally depressing picture of our planet as a demented spaceship, forever travelling, driverless and purposeless, around an inner circle of the sun.

Sedna (She Down There)   (Rosenberg 1994: 522–25, edited and condensed by WGD) One of the myths still changing as it is transmitted orally among the Inuit from Alaska to Siberia, this reflects the obsession with finding adequate food among people living in a mostly hostile environment. Sedna is the absolute focus of Inuit myth and ritual, the divine intermediary between the people and the animals needed for survival. Restrictive religious taboos and commands enable and regulate social cohesion.

Long ago, an Inuit man lived alone with his daughter, Sedna, in a skin-covered tent on the shore of their lonely land. Sedna grew to be a beautiful maiden whom many young men wished to marry. However, no matter who approached her father and asked for her hand, he was not appealing to Sedna, and she refused to marry him.

Meanwhile, in another land across the water, a proud seabird—a stormy petrel or a fulmar—looked upon the female birds in his community with disdain and decided, instead, to choose a human wife from among the Inuit people. He flew over one Inuit household after another until he found the woman of his choice. Then, he fashioned a striking sealskin parka to adorn his human form and he built a swift kayak for his long journey.

As he expected, the bird-man found Sedna by the shore of the sea, busily working at her tasks. Without beaching his kayak, he attracted Sedna's interest by calling to her from the water. Then, once her eyes rested upon him, he sang, "Come with me, my dear, to the land of my people, the land of the birds. There, you will live in a beautiful skin tent, and you will sleep on the softest bearskin mat. My people will bring you whatever you wish. With the feathers they bring you, you can make your clothes. With the oil they bring you, you can light your lamp, and with the meat they bring you, you can cook your food. For my part, I will make you a necklace of ivory as a token of my love. Marry me, and put an end to cold, put an end to darkness, and put an end to hunger!"

Sedna was immediately impressed by such a handsome man. She loved the stranger's beautifully dark and intelligent eyes. She admired his magnificent sealskin parka. And she longed for the luxury that he promised her in his song. Finally, a suitor had come whom she could not resist. She ran to the tent, collected her few belongings in a sealskin bag, and told her father that she was leaving to marry the man. She did not care that the stranger was a bird-man, and no argument of her father's could dissuade her from the marriage.

So it came to pass that Sedna became the wife of the well-dressed, promising stranger. The sea journey was difficult and tiring, and when the couple finally reached his land, Sedna found that the bird-man's song had been nothing but a ruse to win her. Instead of having a tent made from beautiful skins, she had to live in a tent fashioned from smelly fish-skins that made so poor a cover that every blast of wind and flake of snow found its way inside. Instead of sleeping on a mat of the softest bearskin, she spent sleepless nights on the hard hide of the walrus. And instead of having tasty meat to eat, she had to eat whatever raw fish the seabirds brought her.

Sedna did not care that her husband loved her. She spent her long days and longer nights remembering all the suitors whom she had rejected with her proud heart. She would sing longingly to her father, saying, "Oh, Father! If you only knew how miserable I am, you would put your kayak into the water, paddle to this dreadful land, and rescue me from this terrible people! My tent does not shelter me; my bed does not comfort me; and my food does not nourish me! Oh, how I want to go home to my own people!"

When the warm spring winds caused the ice to break up, Sedna's father paddled off in the direction that he had seen the stranger take his daughter, for he wanted to visit Sedna in her husband's homeland. He arrived to find that the bird-man was away fishing and that Sedna was home alone.

When Sedna's father saw how she was living, and when he heard Sedna's tales of her life among the arctic seabirds, his heart filled with rage. As soon as her husband returned, Sedna's father killed the deceitful bird-man who had enticed his daughter to come to this dreadful place. Then he took Sedna away with him in his kayak and paddled as quickly as he could toward their homeland.

When the other seabirds returned they found that their friend had been murdered and that his wife had disappeared. Crying mournfully over their friend's death, they set out to sea in order to find and punish Sedna. Nor did they did have to fly far over the sea before they spied the kayak. Immediately, they swooped down upon the water, stirring up a terrible windstorm as they violently flapped their wings. Their bodies darkened the sky, and the winds caused the waters of the sea to rise above the kayak in mountainous waves. The small boat was doomed to swamp and sink in such a sea!

Sedna's father knew that he was about to die unless he could think of a way to save himself. "This is no fault of mine!" he exclaimed to himself. "If Sedna had accepted a husband from one of our own people, this never would have happened! If I get rid of her, the seabirds may take pity on me and call off the storm-winds that are threatening my life!" Sedna's father then grabbed his daughter and threw her overboard into the icy waters of the sea. "Take her, seabirds, if you really want her!" he shouted. "And let me return safely home!"

Having no wish to die an early death, Sedna swam to the surface and grabbed onto the edge of the kayak with her freezing fingers. Despite the tumult of the waves, she desperately hung on for her life! Sedna's father, crazed by his own fears, took his sharp fishing-knife and cut off Sedna's fingers from her nails down to the first joint. As her fingertips fell into the waves, her nails became whalebone, and her flesh became whales. They quickly swam away, very much at home in the tumultuous sea.

Sedna still had no wish to die an early death. So she once again grabbed onto the edge of the kayak, this time with what was left of her freezing fingers. Sedna's father, now more determined, took his knife and cut off Sedna's fingers from her first joint to the middle joint. As these fell into the waves, these pieces of her fingers became ringed seals. Like the whales, they quickly swam away, very much at home in the tumultuous sea.

Sedna still had no wish to die an early death. So she grabbed onto the edge of the kayak with what was left of her freezing fingers. But again Sedna's father took his knife and, with two blows, first cut off the last of Sedna's fingers and then cut off her thumbs. As her bones and flesh fell into the waves, these pieces of her fingers became bearded ground-seals, while her thumbs became walruses. Like the whales and the ringed seals, the walruses quickly swam out to sea. However, the bearded seals swam in search of the nearest shore on which to make their home.

Watching the scene from above, the arctic seabirds flew away once Sedna's father had chopped off the last of her fingers and her thumbs. They knew that Sedna could no longer hang onto the kayak and, therefore, they were satisfied that she would drown. Their departure caused the winds to subside and calm waters to return.

Sedna's father then helped his daughter climb back into the kayak, and he paddled her back to their home. All the way home Sedna's heart pounded with rage against her father, and she thought and thought of how best to punish him for what he had done to her. As soon as they arrived, they were greeted by her huskies. "That's the way!" Sedna exclaimed to herself. That night, when her father was asleep, she called her dogs into their tent and encouraged them to feed upon her father's hands and feet.

Her father awakened in agony and hurled a curse upon himself, his daughter, and her dogs. To his surprise, the earth began to rumble with a low roar. And as it rumbled, it began to shake, at first so that one might hardly feel it, but then more and more violently. Suddenly, the earth gave way beneath their home, engulfing daughter, father, dogs, and tent. Down, down, down they fell into the land of Adiivun, the Underworld. There, Sedna became its ruler and the supreme power in the universe.

From that day to this, Sedna lives at the bottom of the sea, where she rules over the living and the dead. Her hair remains in two fat braids, just as she wore it in her earlier life, although she no longer has the fingers that are necessary in order to comb it. The animals that she created respond to her commands, giving themselves to those who are good, and hiding from everyone else.

Sedna insists that the Inuit people cook sea animals and land animals separately. To disobey this taboo angers her, and whenever Sedna becomes angry, her braided hair becomes tangled. She then withholds her animals from the Inuit hunters and creates the storms that swamp their kayaks and claim their lives.

Whenever this happens, the Inuit people must perform special, solemn ceremonies to win back Sedna's affection. Their shaman must make a spirit pilgrimage to her home beneath the sea, where he combs the tangles from her braided hair and pleads with her to forgive his people for breaking her taboos and to provide them with meat once again. On these occasions, Sedna is so happy to have the shaman's help that she generously rewards him and his people. Then, once again, the Inuit hunters find the animals that they desperately need in order to have food, clothing, and shelter in their harsh world.

The Race of Mud   (Willis 1993: 91) (China) "Nü Gua is said to have come to live on earth from heaven after the separation of the heavens and the earth and the creation of the hills, rivers, animals and plants. The following myth relates how she formed the human race from mud" (91).

After some time on earth Nü Gua grew lonely, feeling that something was still missing from the world. One day she saw her reflection in a pool and had an idea. She scooped up a handful of mud and fashioned it into a tiny copy of herself: the first human. When the goddess put the creature down, it came to life at once and started to shout and dance with joy. Pleased with her handiwork, Nü Gua took more mud and made a host of people. They wandered off into the countryside, but she could always hear their voices and never felt lonely again.

The goddess soon realized that to populate the whole world she must produce people more rapidly and efficiently. She dipped a vine in watery mud, then flicked it so that the mud flew off in all directions. Each drop of mud turned into another human being. Nü Gua soon populated the world and could rest from her labours. Later, when some people had grown old and died, she taught humans how to reproduce and raise children.

Changing Woman   (Leeming and Page 1994: 93–95) (Navajo, American Southwest) Changing Woman is the very important divinity who gives birth to the twin Navajo heroes, who help adjust living conditions on earth by vanquishing troublesome monsters.

When First Man and First Woman and the other emergent people came into this, the Glittering World, they were followed by monsters that had been born of their self-abuse in the previous world. And before too long, the monsters had devoured everyone but First Man and First Woman and four others. First Man hoped that the gods would help them, but First Woman doubted it, saying that they didn't yet know what pleased or displeased the gods. One morning, First Man noticed that a dark cloud covered the crest of the mountain known today as Gobernador's Knob. He decided to investigate, saying that he would protect himself by surrounding himself with songs. Just as he got to the peak, amid lightning, thunder, and driving rain, he heard an infant cry. Finding the spot in spite of the blinding storms, he discovered a small piece of turquoise in the form of a female, which he took down the mountain to First Woman, instructing her to care for it.

In an elaborate ceremony, a female baby was created from the turquoise figure, and she would become Changing Woman. When she came of age, reaching puberty, a ceremony was held in order that she would be able to bear children. She was dressed in white beads and ran four times in the direction of the rising sun. Talking God, one of the Holy People, sang twelve songs.

Sometime after the ceremony, which is called a Kinaaldá to this day, Changing Woman grew lonely and wandered off. She lay down on a flat rock near a waterfall with her feet facing east, and she felt the warmth of the sun come over her and fill her being. In time, she gave birth to twin boys, who would come to be known as Monster Slayer and Child Born of Water. As they grew up, they were challenged to ever greater feats by Talking God and the Wind, until they were fit to take on the greatest challenge facing the world: the monsters that still roamed the land.

In a series of great battles, they fought the monsters and slew them. Then they traveled to the four sacred mountains, from which they could see that there were no more monsters to be slain. There was now order and harmony in the world. With their father, the sun, they buried the corpses of the monsters under the blood of one of the monsters, Big Giant, which had spilled down the sides of Mount Taylor and can be seen today as what some people think of as lava.

Five days later, the sun came to Changing Woman and asked her to go with him to the west. There, he said, he would establish a home for her, so that they could be together at the end of his daily labors. But Changing Woman would have nothing to do with him. She knew, for example, that he also had a home—and a wife—in the east. He tried to persuade her: "What use is male without female? What use is female without male? What use are we two without each other?" Still Changing Woman resisted the sun's warm embrace, but she began to think that perhaps she was lonely after all.

After a long silence, she explained that she would want a beautiful house, as beautiful as the sun's eastern house, "floating on the shimmering water," away from war and disharmony, surrounded instead by gems and animals to keep her company during the long hours each day when the sun was away. Nonplussed, the sun asked her why she made such demands, and she said: "You are of the sky, and I am of the earth. You are constant in your brightness, but I must change with the seasons." And she said: "Remember, as different as we are, you and I, we are of one spirit. As dissimilar as we are, you and I, we are of equal worth. As unlike as you and I are, there must always be solidarity between the two of us. Unlike each other as you and I are, there can be no harmony in the universe as long as there is no harmony between us. If there is to be such harmony, then my requests must matter to you."

So it was agreed in those olden times, and Changing Woman went to live in the west beyond the farthest shore, joined each evening by the sun. But Changing Woman soon found her days long and lonely, and she yearned for mortal company. Her breasts swelled, her hips, her abdomen. The Holy People came and laid her down, head pointing west, and rubbed her body into perfection. And by rubbing skin from her breast, her back, and under each arm, Changing Woman then created the clans who would become the Dineh, the people—the Navajo.

For the Dineh, Changing Woman remains the ideal for which all women strive. And it is remembered even today that if the sun and Changing Woman, the creatrix of the people and the goddess of the earth and the seasons, do not get along, then no Navajo can walk in beauty.

Fire Theft

How People Got Fire   (Segal 2000: 106–7) (Karok Indians, northwest California)

There was no fire. Coyote went all over looking for fire. Coyote discovered fire in the far north. He returned and told people he had seen fire, he had found it. They talked over the means of getting the fire. They lined up with Frog next to the river. Grouse said, "I'll be on top of the mountain. I am pretty slow, but I can fly down the hill."

The Bear said he could run down the hill, so they put him on the next mountaintop.

Turtle said, "I can run down too. I'll draw in my feet and head and roll down."

Aixlechton (a bird on A'u'ich which is white below, brown above, and calls like a seagull) said, "I can travel over two mountains, two ridges."

Fox said, "I'll take a hand in it, too."

Measuring Worm said, "I can go over about ten ridges and mountains and not have to run downhill."

Coyote went up north where the fire was. The girls there were Yellow Jackets. Coyote said to them, "You all sit around and I'll make you pretty." Coyote said, "Come on, girls. We'll all go into the house."

Coyote took black oak bark and put it in (the) fire to burn. To the girls, he said, "You all close your eyes. You will not be pretty if you open your eyes." While they had their eyes shut he pulled the bark out of the fire with his heel. "Keep your eyes closed. I've got to go outside for a minute. Don't open your eyes while I am gone."

Then he ran and ran and ran with the fire. He became exhausted and passed it to Fox.

After a time the girls opened their eyes and realized Coyote was gone. They set out in pursuit and finally spied Fox with the fire.

Fox ran until he came to Measuring Worm and passed the fire on to him. Measuring Worm wriggled around, as he reached from mountain to mountain. He went a long way. Then Measuring Worm passed it to Bear. Bear ran down the mountain, but was slow in climbing up the next mountain.

Bear passed it to Grouse. Grouse went a long way with it. Grouse passed it to the bird Aixlechton. He passed it to Turtle, and Turtle rolled down the mountain to Frog, who had his mouth wide open to receive the fire.

The Yellow Jackets grabbed the Frog, but Frog jumped into the river with the fire in his mouth. The Yellow Jackets gave up. It was no use. They went back. Frog came up and spat out the fire to willow trees. Now you can get fire from willows. Willow roots are used for fire drills.

Prometheus   (Jordan 1993: 163–64) (Greek, but subsequently adopted into Roman culture) The mythology surrounding Prometheus is one of confrontation with Zeus, who regards him as an equal in wit and therefore a potential source of challenge.

In [Hesiod's] *Theogony* Prometheus is one of the sons of the Titan Iapetos and his sister Klymene (other traditions identify his mother as Asia). Prometheus's brothers include Epimethius, Atlas and Menoetius [...]. In one episode Zeus becomes jealous of Prometheus and binds him with chains to a rock in the Caucasus, driving a lance through the victim's stomach and employing an eagle, generally assumed to be one of the monstrous offspring of the demonic nymph Echidna, to torture him each day by tearing at his liver. The suffering is perpetuated because, being an immortal, Prometheus recovers each night so that by morning his liver is fully restored. His suffering is ended by the heroic god Herakles (Hercules), who slays the eagle and releases Prometheus from his chains while journeying to collect the Golden Apples of the Hesperides.

In a further confrontation, on an occasion when the gods are assembled at Mecone, Prometheus cuts up an ox and divides it into two unequal shares. One contains the flesh and innards deceptively wrapped in the hide on which is placed the stomach (making the choicest meat appear to be the offal), the other contains only the bones disguised attractively with fat. Prometheus offers Zeus the choice of portions and the god selects what appears to be the best (the suggestion in the *Theogony* is that Zeus knows he is being deceived). Bitter at Prometheus's powers of trickery which he has also taught to mortal man, Zeus withholds the boon of fire from the human race, but Prometheus, not to be outdone, steals the fire in a fennel stalk from the crippled blacksmith god, Hephaestos, and gives it to mankind. Out of spite for this impertinence, Zeus burdens the world with the first mortal woman, Pandora, and her troubles.

Prometheus is generally depicted as a benefactor and ally of humanity and he is also credited, though not in the *Theogony*, with having created mankind out of lumps of clay.

Descent into the Underworld

Inanna (Ishtar)   (Leeming 1973: 223–24) (Babylonian and Sumerian) A chilling story that contains the basic elements of the primal myth of the descent: the search for a loved one and the struggle with and conquering of death in the underworld.

Inanna, queen of heaven, the goddess of light and love and life, has set her heart upon visiting the nether world, perhaps in order to free her lover Tammuz. She gathers together all the appropriate divine decrees, adorns herself with her queenly robes and jewels, and is ready to enter the "land of no return."

Queen of the nether world is her elder sister and bitter enemy Ereshkigal, the goddess of darkness and gloom and death. Fearing lest her sister put her to death in the nether world, Inanna instructs her messenger, Ninshubur, who is always at her beck and call, that if after three days she shall have failed to return, he is to go to heaven and set up a hue and cry for her in the assembly hall of the gods. Moreover, he is to go to Nippur, the very city where our tablets have been excavated, and there weep and plead before the god Enlil to save Inanna from Ereshkigal's clutches.

If Enlil should refuse, he is to go to Ur, Ur of the Chaldees, whence according to Biblical tradition Abraham migrated to Palestine, and there repeat his plea before Nanna, the great Sumerian moon-god. If Nanna, too, refuses, he is to go to Eridu, the city in which Sumerian civilization is said to have originated, and weep and plead before Enki, the "god of wisdom." And the latter, "who knows the food of life, who knows the water of life," will restore Inanna to life.

Having taken these precautions, Inanna descends to the nether world and approaches Ereshkigal's temple of lapis lazuli. At the gate she is met by the chief gatekeeper, who demands to know who she is and why she came. Inanna concocts a false excuse for her visit, and the gatekeeper, upon instructions from his mistress Ereshkigal, leads her through the seven gates of the nether world. As she passes through each of the gates part of her robes and jewels are removed in spite of her protest. Finally after entering the last gate she is brought stark naked and on bended knees before Ereshkigal and the seven Anunnaki, the dreaded judges of the nether world. These latter fasten upon Inanna their "look of death," whereupon she is turned into a corpse and hung from a stake.

So pass three days and three nights. On the fourth day, Ninshubur, seeing that his mistress has not returned, proceeds to make the rounds of the gods in accordance with his instructions. As Inanna had foreseen, both Enlil of Nippur and Nanna of Ur refuse all help. Enki, however, devises a plan to restore her to life. He fashions the *kurgarru* and *kalaturru*, two sexless creatures, and entrusts to them the "food of life" and the "water of life," with instructions to proceed to the nether world and to sprinkle this food and this water sixty times upon Inanna's suspended corpse. This they do and Inanna revives. As she leaves the nether world, however, to reascend to the earth, she is accompanied by the shades of the dead and by the bogies and harpies who have their home there. Surrounded by this ghostly, ghastly crowd, she wanders through Sumer from city to city.

Terracotta relief of Inanna-Ishtar (winged goddess of heaven, earth, and underworld) / Lilith (wife of Adam) wearing crown of lunar horns and rainbow necklace with lions and owls, from Mesopotamia, c.2000 B.C., Larsa period. © The Art Archive / Christies / Elieen Tweedy.

The Underworld Journey of Re   (Jordan 1993: 268–69) (Egypt) From the *Book of Gates,* inscribed in the tombs of Ramesses VI and Seti I; and the *Book of Caverns,* inscribed in the tomb of Ramesses VI. The *Book of Caverns* offers variations on the preceding mythic account in which Re passes through a series of 12 caverns on his nocturnal voyage. The *Book of Gates* recounts a similar story in the course of which Re passes through 12 gates.

According to the *Book of Am-Duat* Re sets out from the western horizon to begin his nocturnal journey through the underworld. He is to travel through the Twelve Hours by sailing the river of the underworld in his solar barque [boat]. He takes with him a crew of deities and—as he enters the First Hour he takes human form, surmounted with the head of a ram. In the Second Hour, he provides fertile land for the gods of agriculture. In the Third Hour he revitalizes the underworld god Osiris. In the Fourth Re passes through the gates guarded by serpents. The Fifth Hour encompasses thoughts of resurrection. In the Sixth Hour, Re meets with the god of wisdom, Thoth, in the guise of a baboon who holds a sacred ibis. He also confronts his own corpse in the form of the scarab beetle, Khepri, engulfed by a serpent. The Seventh Hour finds Re guarded by three obscure deities, a serpent god identified as the "Flesh of Osiris," a feline god with a knife and a third who binds opponents of Re with a rope. In the Eighth Hour the demonic underworld god, Apophis, depicted as a huge serpent, is subjugated and wounded though never destroyed.

In the Ninth Hour the enemies of Re are destroyed by magical weapons. In the Tenth the symbols of Re's emergence for the start of the new day appear. The scarab beetle holds an egg from which Re will come at sunrise and the sun discs also appear in the scene. Twelve guardian deities act as a vanguard to check the safety of the eastern horizon. In the Eleventh Hour, the adversaries of Re in the underworld are consigned to a fiery pit. Finally comes the Twelfth Hour during which, within the body of a huge serpent whose bowel Re has entered, he transforms into his daytime form and becomes the scarab beetle which climbs from the snake's mouth. The god of the air, Su, closes the gates of the underworld and Re hovers above his head. Re sails in his solar barque up the legs of the creator goddess Nut and so begins his daytime journey.

Emma O (Jordan 1993: 262–63) (Japanese Buddhist) Emma O, the lord of the dead, is derived from the Hindu Vedic god of death, Yama.

After death the soul sets out upon a long journey to the Yellow Springs, the home of Emma O, in the underworld kingdom of Yomi. To provide for the journey the dead are accompanied by food and money. During Bommatsuri, the Festival of the Dead (13–16 July), lanterns are also lit to guide them on their way. When the soul reaches the dried-up bed of the river of the dead, the Sanzu no Kawa, the old woman who controls the crossing, Sodzu Baba, must be paid to allow it permission to pass.

The soul eventually arrives in purgatory, Gakido, the so-called "Demon Road," where it is judged by Emma O and pays for sins committed during life according to the Law of Buddha. Purgatory is the lowest point in the existence of the soul. The benign and merciful guardian goddess, Guan Yui (Kuan Yin), modeled on the *sakti* of the Buddhist *boddhisattva* Avalokitesvara, may intervene to exonerate and raise it to a peaceful and immortal afterlife. If the person has lived a good mortal life and made pilgrimage to the thirty-three shrines of Guan Yin scattered around Japan, this intercession is more likely. Even if they have sinned she may still act on their behalf, ameliorating their penance. For those who have been truly wicked there is only the prospect of Emma O, who tosses them into a vat of molten metal. Guan Yin once threatened to turn the underworld into a kind of paradise, but Emma O insisted that it remain a sober place, so she returned to earth.

Jizo, the benevolent male counterpart of Guan Yin, also plays a role in the protection of souls. He is modeled on the Buddhist *boddhisattva* Ksitigarbha (woman of the earth) and is the guardian of the graveyards. His responsibility is to keep *oni* or evil spirits at bay. These are demonic creatures possessing three eyes, horns and talons. Jizo hides souls in his clothing to prevent the *oni* from seizing them. He also ministers to the spirits of the dead in purgatory, saving them from the worst excesses of Emma O.

Sometimes souls may wander, seeking rest. These spirits are perceived as fiery glowing spheres called Shito Dama.

> **Kitamba and the Death of Muhongo**   (Jordan 1993: 263–64) (Kimbundu, Angola, southwest Africa) "The myth appears to have several messages. Firstly it reinforces the global understanding of mankind that ordinary mortals, even those who assume mythical dimensions, cannot return from the underworld once they have passed through its portals. It also offers a typically confused view of many shamanistic societies about the powers of tribal priests. Certain select individuals may travel between earthly, upper and lower realms as messengers, but even they are not immune from death. This resignation is tinged, however, with the equally universal optimism that out of death in the natural world comes regenesis of life" (262).

King Kitamba's wife, Muhongo, has died. The distraught king directs a celebrated herbalist and shaman known as a *kimbanda* to intercede for her in the underworld. First the *kimbanda* collects medicinal plants in the forest and then lays himself on his own hearth. He instructs his sons to cover him with earth and his wife to sprinkle him each day with water. Thus interred, he discovers a subterranean pathway leading to the underworld. Following it he comes across the hut of the dead queen and greets her, pleading that she shall come back with him to the upper world where her husband mourns her loss. Muhongo replies, however, that, like all deceased, she is a now a servant of the ruler of the dead, Kalunga-Ngombe, and can never return to the land of the living.

The shaman's wife continues dutifully to water the mound of earth under which he lies and eventually she sees her husband's nose sprout through the soil like a courgette [zucchini squash]. She can see that he begins to breathe again, so she harvests him, like a big sweet potato.

COMMON THEMES IN SEVERAL CULTURES; COMPARATIVISM

Until the last decade or so, I have found repeatedly that students have a pretty solid idea about utopian thought—perhaps it is part of the youth orientation of our culture or of the progressive-evolutionary development of society that the West in particular has long anticipated. The Future was more often anticipated than the End was discussed, except perhaps within ecological or astronomical circles.

Within the last decade, which has seen an amazing proliferation of conservative, if not fundamentalist, religious teachings, things have changed, particularly because of evangelical Christian fascination with revenge upon the ungodly, in a period when the righteous will supposedly get to bash in their heads during the "Rapture." That idea, although only emphasized quite recently within Christian thought, has a long history, dating back to the Apocalypse to John (or Book of Revelation) in the New Testament. That book itself has had a checkered history of interpretation, having been rejected from the biblical canon by major branches of the faith, at other times studied as a sort of allegorical code to world history, and sometimes merely considered to be innocent religious poetics providing lovely symbols of glory or "pie in the sky."

Much of that imagery derived from the Jewish temple and synagogue liturgy and the astrological year, dependent in some of the base metaphors and figures upon books such as Ezekiel and Daniel in the Tanakh or Old Testament. Several contemporary religious movies have featured grand schemes of the world run amuck that are taken to prefigure a final period of world-darkening before a climactic End (or apocalypse—which seemed terribly threatening when the atom and hydrogen bombs were threatening much of world population).

Works in the Hellenistic world of late-biblical Judaism and early Christianity claimed to have "revelations" of future history, particularly with respect to End-time events. *Revelation* is developed from *reveal*; the re- prefix in its Latin roots meaning what we understand in English in the prefix "un-." Hence to re-veal is to un-*veil*, to uncover a prophecy of the future supposedly written in the past (some of them were attributed to Adam!). *Uncover* in Greek is *apokalyptein,* to take away or open (apok-) something that is hidden or veiled, which names the literary type we have been talking about: the Apoc-

Four Horsemen of the Apocalypse, 1511. Courtesy of the Library of Congress.

alypse to John is literally the same as the Revelation to John (often inaccurately called "Revelations").

Cultures other than these we have been referring to have also prefigured times of the End (or Ends!) in terms of long stretches of time, typically arranged in tapewormlike segments, each with its dramatic symbol. A dramatic example of apocalyptic myth comes from Traditional Hopi prophecy, as told to Frank Waters (1963: 408–9; see the impassioned application of this prophecy to ecological issues 35 years later, Mails 1997). It deals with the Emergence to the Fifth World:

> The end of all Hopi ceremonialism will come when a *kachina* removes his mask during a dance in the plaza before uninitiated children. For a while there will be no more ceremonies, no more faith. Then Oraibi will be rejuvenated with its faith and ceremonies, marking the start of a new cycle of Hopi life.
>
> World War III will be started by those peoples who first received the light [the divine wisdom or intelligence] in the other old countries [India, China, Egypt, Palestine, Africa].
>
> The United States will be destroyed, land and people, by atomic bombs and radioactivity. Only the Hopis and their homeland will be preserved as an oasis to which refugees will flee. Bomb shelters are a fallacy. It is only materialistic people who seek to make shelters. Those who are at peace in their hearts already are in the great shelter of life. There is no shelter for evil. Those who take no part in the making of world division by ideology are ready to resume life in another world, be they of the Black, White, Red, or Yellow race. They are all one, brothers.
>
> The war [of the end time] will be "a spiritual conflict with material matters. Material matters will be destroyed by spiritual beings who will remain to create one world and one nation under one power, that of the Creator."
>
> That time is not far off. It will come when the Saquasohuh [Blue Star] Kachina dances in the plaza. He represents a blue star, far off and yet invisible, which will make its appearance soon. The time is also foretold by a song sung during the Wuwuchim ceremony. It was sung in 1914 just before World War I, and again in 1940 before World War II, describing the disunity, corruption, and hatred contaminating Hopi rituals, which were followed by the same evils spreading over the world. This same song was sung in 1961 during the Wuwuchim ceremony.
>
> The Emergence to the future Fifth World has begun. It is being made by the humble people of the little nations, tribes, and racial minorities. "You can read this in the earth itself. Plant forms from previous worlds are beginning to spring up as seeds. This could start a new study of botany if people were wise enough to read them. The same kinds of seeds are being planted in the sky as stars. The same kinds of seeds are being planted in our hearts. All these are the same, depending how you look at them. That is what makes the Emergence to the next, Fifth World."

These comprise the nine most important prophecies of the Hopis, connected with the creation of the nine worlds: the three previous worlds on which we have lived, the present Fourth World, the future three worlds we have yet to experience, and the world of Taiowa, the Creator, and his nephew, Sótuknang.

One of the best-known apocalyptic stories is in the Norse myth of Ragnarök. "The gods themselves are doomed in this myth of the end of the world (from the ancient *Voluspa*, the soothsaying of the *volva*, or seeress), movingly retold by the thirteenth-century Icelandic writer Snorri Sturluson in his *Prose Edda*. Many recognizable [apocalyptic] events are present here: the earthquakes, the darkening of the sun, the rising of monsters, Armageddon, the destroying fire followed by the renewal of life" (Leeming 1990: 85):

Then Gangleri said: "What is there to relate about Ragnarök? I have never heard tell of this before."

Teutonic mythology—Ragnarök. The World-doom of the Gods, in Nordic mythology, is called Ragnarök, the story of which is told in the *Prose Edda*. In this scene, the wolf is Fenrir, the snake the Midgard Serpent. After a painting by Johannes Gehrts. © Charles Walker / Topfoto / The Image Works.

High One said: "There are many and great tidings to tell about it. First will come the winter called Fimbulvetr [Terrible Winter]. Snow will drive from all quarters, there will be hard frosts and biting winds; the sun will be no use. There will be three such winters on end with no summer between. Before that, however, three other winters will pass accompanied by great wars throughout the whole world. Brothers will kill each other for the sake of gain, and no one will spare father or son in manslaughter or in incest. As it says in the *Sibyl's Vision:*

Brothers will fight
and kill each other,
siblings do incest;
men will know misery,
an axe-age, a sword-age,
shields will be cloven,
a wind-age, a wolf-age,
before the world's ruin.

"Then will occur what will seem a great piece of news, the wolf will swallow the sun and that will seem a great disaster to men. Then another wolf will seize the moon and that one too will do great harm. The stars will disappear from heaven. Then this will come to pass, the whole surface of the earth and the mountains will tremble so [violently] that trees will be uprooted from the ground, mountains will crash down, and all fetters and bonds will be snapped and severed. The wolf Fenrir will get loose then. The sea will lash against the land because the Midgard Serpent is writhing in giant fury trying to come ashore. At that time, too, the ship known as Naglfar will become free. It is made of dead men's nails, so it is worth warning you that, if anyone dies with his nails uncut, he will greatly increase the material for that ship which both gods and men devoutly hope will take a long time building. In this tidal wave, however, Naglfar will be launched. The name of the giant steering Naglfar is Hrym. The wolf Fenrir will advance with wide open mouth, his upper jaw against the sky, his lower on the earth (he would gape more widely still if there were room) and his eyes and nostrils will blaze with fire. The Midgard Serpent will blow so much poison that the whole sky and sea will be spattered with it; he is most terrible and will be on the other side of the wolf.

"In this din the sky will be rent asunder and the sons of Muspell ride forth from it. Surt will ride first and with him fire blazing both before and behind. He has a very good sword and it shines more brightly than the sun. When they ride over Bifröst, however—as has been said before—that bridge will break. The sons of Muspell will push forward to the plain called Vígríd and the wolf Fenrir and the Midgard Serpent will go there too. Loki and Hrym with all the frost giants will also be there by then, and all the family of Hel will accompany Loki. The sons of Muspell, however, will form a host in themselves and that a very bright one. The plain Vígríd is a hundred and twenty leagues in every direction.

"When these things are happening, Heimdall will stand up and blow a great blast on the horn Gjöll and awaken all the gods and they will hold an assembly. Then Ódin will ride to Mímir's spring and ask Mimir's advice for himself and his company. The ash Yggdrasil will tremble and nothing in heaven or earth will be free from fear. The Aesir and all the Einherjar will arm themselves and press forward on the plain. Ódin will ride first in a helmet of gold and a beautiful coat of mail and with his spear Gungnir, and he will make for the wolf Fenrir. Thór will advance at his side but will be unable to help him, because he will have his hands full fighting the Midgard Serpent. Frey will fight against Surt and it will be a hard conflict before Frey falls; the loss of the good sword that he gave to Skfrnir will bring about his death. Then the hound Garm, which was bound in front of Gnipahellir [cliff-cave leading to Hel], will also get free; he is the worst sort of monster. He will battle with Týr and each will kill the other. Thór will slay the Midgard Serpent but stagger back only nine paces before he falls down dead, on account of the poison blown on him by the serpent. The wolf will swallow Ódin and that will be his death. Immediately afterwards, however, Vídar will stride forward and place one foot on the lower jaw of the wolf. On this foot he will be wearing the shoe which has been in the making since the beginning of time; it consists of the strips of leather men pare off at the toes and heels of their shoes, and for this reason people who want to help the Aesir must throw away these strips. Vídar will take the wolf's upper jaw in one hand and tear his throat asunder and that will be the wolf's death. Loki will battle with Heimdall and each will kill the other. Thereupon Surt will fling fire over the earth and burn up the whole world. . . .

Then Gangleri asked: "What will happen afterwards, when heaven and earth and the whole world has been burned and all the gods are dead and all the Einherjar and the whole race of man? Didn't you say before that everyone will go on living for ever in some world or other?"

Then Third answered: "There will be many good dwelling-places then and many bad. The best place to be in at that time will be Gimlé in heaven, for those that like it there is plenty of good drink in the hall called Brimir that is on Ókolnir [Never Cold]. There is also an excellent hall on Nidafjöll [Dark Mountains] called Sin-dri; it is made of red gold. Good and righteous men will live in these halls. On Nástrandir [Corpse-strands] there is a large and horrible hall whose doors face north; it is made of the backs of serpents woven together like wattle-work, with all their heads turning in to the house and spewing poison so that rivers of it run through the hall. Perjurers and murderers wade these rivers...

Then Gangleri asked: "Will any of the gods be living then? Will there be any earth or heaven then?"

High One said: "At that time earth will rise out of the sea and be green and fair, and fields of corn will grow that were never sown. Vidar and Vali will be living, so neither the sea nor Surt's Fire will have done them injury, and they will inhabit Idavöll where Ásgard used to be. And the sons of Thór, Módi and Magni will come there and possess Mjöllnir. After that Baldr and Höd will come from Hel. They will all sit down together and converse, calling to mind their hidden lore and talking about things that happened in the past, about the Midgard Serpent and the wolf Fenrir. Then they will find there in the grass the golden chessmen the Aesir used to own...

"While the world is being burned by Surt, in a place called Hoddmimir's Wood, will be concealed two human beings called Líf and Lífthrasir. Their food will be the morning dews, and from these men will come so great a stock that the whole world will be peopled...

"And you will think this strange, but the sun will have borne a daughter no less lovely than herself, and she will follow the paths of her mother...

"And now, if you have anything more to ask, I can't think how you can manage it, for I've never heard anyone tell more of the story of the world. Make what use of it you can."

The next thing was that Gangleri heard a tremendous noise on all sides and turned about; and when he had looked all round him [he found] that he was standing in the open air on a level plain. He saw neither hall nor stronghold. Then he went on his way and coming home to his kingdom related the tidings he had seen and heard, and after him these stories have been handed down from one man to another. (Leeming 1990: 85–89, citing the ed. and trans. of *The Prose Edda* by Jean Young [Berkeley 1973: 86–93].)

Lest we conceive of apocalyptic Ends as remaining strictly thematic to antiquity, Leeming reminds us that modern science provides us with its own pictures of the end of the world. "This 'myth' might best be read in conjunction with the Hindu myths of the destruction of the world at the end of each eon" (Leeming 1990: 88, citing Jeremy Rifkin, *Entropy: A New World View.* New York: 1980: 44–45):

> Whenever scientists begin speculating about the second law, the question ultimately arises as to how broadly it can be applied. For example, does the Entropy Law apply to the macroworld of stars and galaxies that make up the universe? In fact, the Entropy Law is the basis of most cosmological theories. Scientist Benjamin Thompson became the first to draw the cosmological implications of the second law back in 1854. According to Thompson, the Entropy Law tells us that
>
>> within a finite period of time past, the earth must have been, and within a finite period of time to come the earth must again be, unfit for the habitation of man as at present constituted, unless operations have been, or are to be performed, which are impossible under the laws to which the known operations going on at present in the material world are subject.
>
> Two years later Helmholtz formulated what has become the standard cosmological theory based on the Entropy Law. His theory of "heat death" stated that the universe is gradually running down and eventually will reach the point of maximum entropy or heat death where all available energy will have been expended and no more activity will occur. The heat death of the universe corresponds to a state of eternal rest.
>
> Today the most widely accepted theory about the origin and development of the universe is the big bang theory. First conceptualized by Canon Georges Lemaitre, the big bang theory postulates that the universe began with the explosion of a tremendously dense energy source. As this dense energy expanded outward, it began to slow down, forming galaxies, stars, and planets. As the energy continues to expand and become more diffused, it loses more and more of its order and will eventually reach a point of maximum entropy, or the final equilibrium state of heat death. The big bang theory coincides with the first and second laws. It states that the universe started with complete order and has been moving toward a more and more disordered state ever since. If this the-

ory appears familiar, it should. Both the ancient Greek and the medieval Christian view of history share much in common with the cosmologists' notion of the history of the universe.

One last example, from Puranic Hindu India concerns the myth of Kalkin, who is

the final incarnation or *avatar* of the god Vishnu, the only one who is yet to appear at the end of the present age of mankind, the age of the goddess Kali. He will herald in the new Krta Age. Kalkin is thus envisaged as the avenging sword of righteousness who will cleanse the world of the evil symbolized by Kali. Some authorities consider that the idea of a messianic coming in Hinduism first took shape at the time of the Scythian and Parthian invasions of India in the third and fourth centuries C.E. There are strong parallels to be drawn with the prophetic Christian myth to be found in the Book of Revelation 19.11. Kalkin is also the counterpart of the Buddhist Salvationist *manusibuddha* (future human Buddha) Maitreya.

The kings of the Age of Kali are corrupt and power-hungry to the extent that ordinary people will become greatly impoverished and seek refuge in the remote mountain valleys, where they will eke out an existence foraging for honey, roots and wild vegetables. The population will wear ragged clothes, it will become too large for the scarcity of the land to support and it will face great physical hardship from the elements. Since the longest that anyone will live is twenty-three years, the entire race is faced with destruction.

The Vedas and other sacred texts will become scattered and, when all seems lost, a messiah will come riding upon a white horse, to punish evil and reward good. He will be a part of the creator god Brahma. This champion of a new order, the tenth incarnation of the god Vishnu, will be named Kalkin, 'the Fulfiller' and he will be born in the house of the chief brahmin of the village of Sambala. He will destroy all invaders of India and everything that is evil to herald in the new and flawless Age of Krta." (Jordan 1993: 121–22)

Common themes appear across various cultures, although not necessarily illustrated by the same mythological or natural figures. A section of the Pantheon of the Gods in Doty (2002: 228–29) summarizes a wide range. Animals, for instance, appear as part of the divine appearances in several cultures: "Egypt's cow goddess Hathor is associated with fertility, and India's elephant god Ganesha with wisdom. In some mythologies, including Maori, animals are the ancestral people, while many African and North American myths refer to a time when all creatures, including humans, lived together in harmony and shared the same language" (228).

There are many explanations about the origins of the world, of the earth, of the stars—in fact of many specific aspects of human life and experience. Nature and agriculture, hunting, something like the origin of the olive tree grove can all figure in mythic accounts. The Greeks kept lists of "First Finders" to whom various cultural artifacts and behaviors were attributed. Local events may be related to wider myths about the founding of clans and tribes, even peoples; and local variants of myths shared across a large pantheon of gods may be said to be more important than the canonical shaping of such materials by a Homer or Hesiod.

Many rituals are known to be associated with myths: Theodor Gaster's *Thespis: Ritual, Myth, and Drama in the Ancient Near East* (1961) creatively restages many of the great Ancient Near Eastern rituals using available mythological texts. Many of the selections of myths gathered in this volume have come from works in the loosely defined field of comparative mythology, and I conclude this chapter with reflections on what sort of "comparison" has been assumed.

In a climate in which comparative literature, semantics, education, biology, physiology, psychology, zoology, endocrinology, archaeology, genomics, and legal studies are common, it may be a bit surprising to learn that the area of comparative mythology or comparative religion has been suspect for several generations now. This quick historical sketch will set in context the sorts of comparative texts presented in the first three segments of this chapter.

The issue arose in the latter part of the nineteenth century, when extensive accounts of life on parts of the planet other than Europe began to accrue. Explorers and early anthropologists' accounts were usually published quickly and often devoured by curious audiences in magazines and newspapers. James Frazer's *The Golden Bough*, eventually encompassing 13 large volumes, was initially two volumes published in 1890. It amassed accounts of myth and magic, folklore, and religion, and delighted in showing parallels between "primitive" myths and rituals and those of Christianity. The work was discussed everywhere, and it had an enormous influence on early twentieth-century writers, anthropologists (usually with great reservations), and students of "primitive" cultures (see Vickery 1973: chap. 1 for the intellectual context in which the work appeared; Manganaro 1992: chap. 1 for analysis of the ways Frazer played to the concept of "vanishing peoples").

Frazer still wrote prose accessible to the general educated public, as did Darwin, Freud, and Marx; their successors wrote for specialist scientists. In fact, it was more in literary criticism and the disciplines of the humanities than in scientific fields that the *Golden Bough* worked its magic—not surprising, because it is itself, in a way, a great mythic cycle, "less a compendium of facts than a gigantic *romance of quest* couched in the form of objective speech" (Vickery 1973: 128, my emphasis); "the myth underlying *The Golden Bough*—the myth beneath the myths, as it were—is that of Theseus and the Minotaur" (135).

Precisely by the inclusiveness of the accounts in his volumes (usefully condensed into one by T. H. Gaster, 1959), Frazer contributed to a developing cultural pluralism, in which some of the automatic assumptions of Western European superiority began to shatter. A similar work oriented to folk customs by William Graham Sumner, *Folkways: A Study of the Sociological Importance of Usages, Manners, Customs, Mores, and Morals,* published in 1906, was also influential in demonstrating and to some extent commending the "difference" found in non-European cultures.

A second type of comparativism was developed in the school of religious studies that tried to improve upon the methodology of cross-cultural analysis, namely what was called the phenomenology of religion or the history of religions. Perhaps the most obvious example is found in the work of a Romanian scholar who eventually held chairs in both Paris and Chicago, Mircea Eliade (for a comprehensive reader of his many-sided works, see Beane and Doty 1975). Eliade's influence has been enormous and spread, much like Frazer's earlier influence, well beyond any one field. His work found deep significances in "primitive" materials from several continents. Like Frazer, he was what is known as an "armchair anthropologist"—both of them compiled their extensive collections of myths and rituals from the accounts of business people, anthropologists, and missionaries in foreign lands.

Much of Eliade's work connected themes and symbols from antiquity with modern culture. He thought that novels were replacing myths, for instance, suggesting that they and movies "concentrate time," make it special apart from the secular everyday. Symbolism fascinated him, whether from antiquity or from modern ethnographic reports, and like Frazer, he gathered examples from across the planet, seeking in nearly every instance to find some universal philosophical or theological aspects they held in common.

Eliade practically made shamanism a part of the twentieth-century religious vocabulary, but he also introduced the function of sacred diagrams (yantras and mandalas), ritual performances seeking to restore the original purity of life disclosed "back then," to bring it into the present ritual moment on the analogy with the "real presence" of the Christ that Christian theology finds in the Mass. His fascination with ethnographic materials led him to be one of the first to focus on Australian materials, although so far as I know, he never traveled there.

By contrast, mid-twentieth-century ethnology turned sharply against armchair anthropology, demanding instead what has since become an established requirement in the anthropological disciplines: in-depth, hands-on participation in the societies one will later write about. Comparative works were ruled as subject to generalizations and universalizations of cultural elements that could not really be shown to be universal at all. The ideal became microstudies in single isolated sites—to the extreme that Edmund Leach wanted his students to omit anything observed that had not been documented by videotapes!

Generally interest shifted from myths in general to specific types of myths. There were attempts to study Freud's Oedipus complex in various social setting—almost all of which denied its presence in the societies studied. Or there were compilations of origin (creation, emergence, first-beginning) myths that simply laid them on the table side by side, with no attempt to point to comparable features or themes or universal meanings.

Most recent volumes of "world mythology" continue this approach, although there is most frequently a desire today to include more of the world's cultures than was true in earlier compilations and more emphasis upon contemporary cultures than those of antiquity. Scholars such as Wendy Doniger (who occupies the Mircea Eliade Distinguished Service Professor of the History of Religions chair at the University of Chicago) are often quite critical of Eliade's context-free approach to mythological traditions: He seldom accounts for the perspective of the collectors or how they might differ from those of the informants, nor does he pay much attention to the social functioning of such materials, looking instead at religious assertions that he often seems to interpret with a strong bias toward Christian theology.

Luther Martin identifies the problem of ignoring such material contexts as "discounting of any historical and cultural significance"; the "'recurrent' themes have tended to be derived from religious traditions of the Western scholar, the autonomous character attributed 'the sacred,' for example" (2000: 52). A volume edited by Laurie Patton and Wendy Doniger attempts both to critique the older comparativist connotations of terms such as the sacred and profane, binary opposition, the "Center of the World," and the static, ahistorical systematization of narrative they imply, while stressing how analysts' definitions and emphases have affected "the course of Western intellectual history—whether it be in the study of Gnosticism, the study of ritual, or the study of literature" (1996: 22).

In a more recent volume, Doniger herself urges that careful cross-cultural comparisons—of, say, only a few cultures at a time—can usefully set parallel yet differing mythical accounts side by side in order to explore precisely their variations and difference, rather than their universal qualities. In such comparisons we will speak less in the old terms of powerful sources and diffusions from ancient master stories, and more in terms of "analogues, influences, and borrowings" (1999: 4)—indeed, "*all* cultures [...] are recipients" (5). Certainly the cross-cultural comparativist will be alert to the fact that "often [...] different cultures will draw radically different, even opposite conclusions from the same plot" (303, with ref. to Doniger 1998: chap. 4); elsewhere she suggests that "the comparison of myths from other cultures opens up our political vision" (27).

For further information about this topic, see especially Patton and Ray (2000) and the highly influential if rather technical essay by Smith (1982). A volume whose title, *Parallel Myths* (Bierlein 1994), might lead us to expect engagement with some of the issues discussed here never even defines how "parallel myths" are parallel and, in fact, rings alarm bells at the author's attempt to show that "the 'primitive' and the 'modern' are not all that different as we might think. In reading these myths, the gaps between cultures narrow [how?—WGD] to reveal what is constant and universal in human experience" (xiv)—precisely the overlooking of sociohistorical differences and the importance of specific contexts that most academic comparativism recognized years ago. The only myths explicitly identified as "parallel stories" are the Blackfoot (Sihasapa) "Story of Two Brothers," the Egyptian story with the same title, that of the Greek Bellerophon, and the episode of Joseph and Potiphar's Wife in Genesis 39. They are parallel in that "All four have the same basic plot" (178), and the last three are thought to exhibit interborrowing, but the first can be regarded as a parallel only if one ignores specific boundaries of cultural time and space.

WORKS CITED

Beane, Wendell C., and William G. Doty, eds. 1975. *Myths, Rites, Symbols: A Mircea Eliade Reader.* 2 vols. New York: Harper and Row.

Bierlein, J. F. 1994. *Parallel Myths.* New York: Ballantine.

Birrell, Anne. 1993. *Chinese Mythology: An Introduction.* Baltimore: The Johns Hopkins UP.

———. 2000. *Chinese Myths.* The Legendary Past. Austin: British Museum P in cooperation with U of Texas P.

Campbell, Joseph. 1968. *The Hero with a Thousand Faces.* 2nd ed. Bollingen ser., 17. Princeton, NJ: Princeton UP.

Doniger, Wendy. 1998. *The Implied Spider: Politics and Theology in Myth.* New York: Columbia UP.

———. 1999. *Splitting the Difference: Gender and Myth in Ancient Greece and India.* Chicago: U of Chicago P.

Doty, William G., gen. ed. 2002. *The TIMES World Mythology.* London: Times Books-HarperCollins. (USA: *World Mythology.* New York: Barnes and Noble.)

Erdoes, Richard, and Alfonso Ortiz, eds. 1998. *American Indian Trickster Tales.* New York: Viking.

Gaster, Theodor H., ed. 1959. *The New Golden Bough: A New Abridgement of the Classic Work by Sir James George Frazer.* New York: Criterion.

Gaster, Theodor H. 1961 [1950]. *Thespis: Ritual, Myth, and Drama in the Ancient Near East.* Rev. ed. Garden City, NY: Doubleday.

Halifax, Joan. 1982. *Shaman: The Wounded Healer.* The Ill. Lib. of Sacred Imagination. New York: Crossroad.

Hynes, William J., and William G. Doty, eds. 1993. *Mythical Trickster Figures: Contours, Contexts, and Criticisms.* Tuscaloosa: U of Alabama P.

Jordan, Michael. 1993. *Myths of the World: A Thematic Encyclopedia.* London: Kyle Cathie.

Leeming, David Adams. 1973. *Mythology: The Voyage of the Hero.* Philadelphia: Lippincott; 3rd ed. 1998, Oxford UP.

———. 1990. *The World of Myth: An Anthology.* New York: Oxford UP.

———. 1998. *Mythology: The Voyage of the Hero.* 3rd ed. New York: Oxford UP.

Leeming, David Adams, and Jake Page. 1994. *Goddess: Myths of the Female Divine.* New York: Oxford UP.

———. 1996. *God: Myths of the Male Divine.* New York: Oxford UP.

Mails, Thomas E. 1997. *The Hopi Survival Kit.* New York: Stewart, Tabori and Chang.

Manganaro, Marc. 1992. *Myth, Rhetoric, and the Voice of Authority: A Critique of Frazer, Eliot, Frye, and Campbell.* New Haven: Yale UP.

Martin, Luther. 2000. "Comparison." In *Guide to the Study of Religion,* ed. Willi Braun and Russell T. McCutcheon, 45–56. New York: Cassell.

Patton, Kimberley C., and Benjamin C. Ray, eds. 2000. *A Magic Still Dwells: Comparative Religion in the Postmodern Age.* Berkeley: U of California P.

Patton, Laurie, and Wendy Doniger, eds. 1996. *Myth and Method.* Charlottesville: UP of Virginia.

Reesman, Jeanne Campbell, ed. 2001. *Trickster Lives: Culture and Myth in American Fiction.* Athens: U of Georgia P.

Rosenberg, Donna. 1994. *World Mythology: An Anthology of the Great Myths and Epics.* 2nd ed. Lincolnwood, IL: NTC.

Segal, Robert A., ed. 2000. *Hero Myths: A Reader.* Malden, MA: Blackwell.

Smith, Jonathan Z. 1982. "In Comparison a Magic Dwells." In *Imagining Religion: From Babylon to Jonestown,* 19–35. Chicago: U of Chicago P. Repr. in Patton and Ray 2000: 23–44.

Stevens, Anthony. 1998. *Ariadne's Clue: A Guide to the Symbols of Humankind.* Princeton, NJ: Princeton UP.

Sumner, William Graham. 1940 [1906]. *Folkways: A Study of the Sociological Importance of Usages, Manners, Customs, Mores, and Morals.* Boston: Ginn.

Vickery, John B. 1973. *The Literary Impact of "The Golden Bough."* Princeton, NJ: Princeton UP.

Waters, Frank. 1963. *Book of the Hopi.* Drawings and source materials recorded by Oswald White Bear Fredericks. New York: Ballantine.

Weigle, Marta. 1989. *Creation and Procreation: Feminist Reflections on Mythologies of Cosmogony and Parturition.* Philadelphia: U of Pennsylvania P.

Willis, Roy, gen. ed. 1993. *World Mythology.* New York: Holt.

Four
Scholarship and Approaches

The definitional situation with respect to myth, as discussed in chapter 2, is complex. As we have seen, there are more definitions that one can shake a stick at, so that the approaches that drive scholarly analysis are regulative in important ways. The very concept of what constitutes myth discloses that it has been conceptualized differently at different times. Hence it is not surprising that the academic approaches to the study of mythography vary enormously as well. Both Paul Veyne's *Did the Greeks Believe in Their Myths?* (1988) and Marcel Detienne's *The Creation of Mythology* (1986) emphasize the importance of recognizing that the very notion of "myth" in classical Greek culture differs extensively from what Western analysts usually presume from the eighteenth century forward.

J. F. Bierlein's "Views of Myth and Meaning" (1994: chap. 12) provides a quick survey of statements on how myth ought to be regarded, by nineteenth- and twentieth-century writers including Freud, Jung, George Santayana, Alan Watts, Thomas Mann, Bruno Bettleheim, and Joseph Campbell. Few of these extracts give more than a hint of the developed positions of the figures mentioned (for instance, Carlos Fuentes: "Myth is a past with a future, exercising itself in the present"), but the selections surely demonstrate how many opposing mythographic positions can be affirmed. Most introductions to classical mythology or to myths in general have at least a short résumé of the history of development of perspectives on myth.

A quick lay of the land can be obtained from some surveys of mythography such as my own *Mythography: The Study of Myths and Rituals* (2000; beyond the text, the annotated "Selected Introductory Bibliography" should be useful) or the indispensable anthology of mythographic texts, *The Rise of Modern Mythology 1680–1860* (Feldman and Richardson 1972), or the detailed *Modern Construction of Myth* (Von Hendy 2002) and Kees Bolle's survey, "Myths and Other Religious Texts" (1983).

HISTORY OF THE CONCEPT OF MYTH

Discussion of the topic of "the concept of myth" is fairly recent, even though what it describes has been around as far back as we can reach in the history of human civilization. Surviving written materials, which were commercial records, appear about 3000 B.C.E., and shortly thereafter, mythic materials appear. But that does not really date the origins of myths, because for the most part, writing initially represented what had been passed around for generations by word of mouth, family or civic traditions, in schooling and religions, and in the arts, especially epic, drama, and poetry.

The nature of myth at the earliest points was quite in flux, as it is yet today among the wandering contemporary bards who perform the way their predecessors did, moving from court to court or camp to camp, receiving temporary board and room as payment for entertainment on festive occasions or merely evening gatherings around campfires. Writing is usually described as the freezing of traditions passed around orally, and of course it is the basis for canonical accounts, which can be laid side by side for comparison, and one or another declared authentic.

Nonetheless, written myths also change as they are rewritten in different historical periods or for different purposes. Stephen Wilk sketches some of the possible amendments in written accounts:

> [M]yths can change through time by the addition of elements prompted by any number of causes. They can reflect bits of natural science or engineering cleverness (as with the explanation of the Golden Fleece), or they can be explanations for place names (as with Helle and the Hellespont), or they can relate bits of genealogy, or they can be marvelous devices and ideas imported from other sources (the flying golden ram, or perhaps the Round Table itself). Rationalizations can make their way into tales (as with the pagan Celtic Graal, which became the Christian Grail, the cup that many said was used at the Last Supper). Story elements may be added to suit the medium used, as with Superman or Wilgefortis, and may then be retained when the story is transferred to another medium. (2000: 14)

Hence to suggest that myth means only one thing ignores the multiplicity of ways in which any particular myth may be regarded. The same mythical material can be realized as a folktale at one level, as revered myth at another—perhaps even both simultaneously. Wilk notes that "it is easy for a story to lose its concrete localizations over time or to become associated with a strong hero from another story. At any point in its life history, a myth can go in a number of directions, acquiring new associations or losing old ones" (14).

A number of mythic stories were familiar to many people, and the performers orchestrated their own versions to please audiences they were addressing, just as a good teacher will catch the attention of a class by references to contemporary films. Some internal poetic constraints were carried along in these epic entertainments, so that we refer to oral formulaic poetic performances: certain clusters of descriptive adjectives were associated with particular heroes. But such mythic narratives certainly were not standardized, even though audiences were quick to point out variations among singers. That is true today even among the Navajos of the American Southwest, where perfection in singing the religious mythic narratives is demanded, yet each chanter has a particular version.

The common body of knowledge within a culture is such that only when it begins to fade away does self-conscious "collection" in a "mythology" become necessary. Earliest versions are fragmentary, and the literary collectors draw from a range of sources. Now it is important to identify how each mythical figure is related to each other, and there is a sort of obsession with genealogy and patterns of influence. Contemporaries would simply recognize characters and traits and plots they heard or read repeatedly. We can imagine a future generation in which Superman has become a faint memory having to explain who Lois Lane and Clark Kent are, and how they are related; or that Dubya refers to President George W. Bush, The Terminator to Arnold Schwarzenegger.

The use of the concept of myth increased when the philosopher Plato, in *The Republic,* idealized the training of future leaders as one that would include careful training in the philosophical thought of the day and exclude much of the popular lore about the world passed along by nursemaids. Among the uses of the term *mythos/myth,* he excluded stories he did not want transmitted, even while making up what we certainly would call myths to convey some pretty sophisticated philosophical ideas. The myth of the cave in *Republic* book 7 is the most famous example, but also in the *Symposium* (189c–190e) Plato demonstrated how he can make up a myth—about the feeling of being one with a lover—and make it sound like a tradition retold by his fictitious "Aristophanes." (Luc Brisson's *Plato the Myth Maker* [1998] is the most extensive study of Plato's uses of myths; see also Morgan 2000.)

Among the uses of the term *mythos/ myth,* Plato excludes stories he does not want transmitted, even while making up what we certainly would call myths to convey some sophisti-cated philosophical ideas. Courtesy of Thommes.

Aristotle also used the word *mythos,* but in a rather different sense, namely for what structured literary expressions. That is what we call *plot,* and he ex-plored how literary and dramatic plots function in his *Poetics.* Shortly there-after the definition of myth gets complicated, initially because Aristotle's use of the word was, to some degree, conflated with Plato's—and possibly others'. But centuries later, when Latin theorists and philosophers talked about plot in the sense of structure, they used the word that leads to English fable, namely *fabula.*

That happened at a point when Plato's *negative* use of the term had led to a trivializing of the concept so that it included old wives' tales and all sorts of fantastic stories. Hence instead of standardizing a Latinized form of the Greek *mythos,* Latin philosophers used the same word for both meanings—*fabula*— and that word carried over into the European languages based on Latin. (It is a bit of a problem for us because we have to remember that what English calls *fable* has developed a different usage, namely to designate talking-animal stories and the like; think of the famous *Aesop's Fables*.)

The situation is also complicated (for us, not for the early Greeks) by the fact that within the development of the sort of sciences Aristotle was influential in shaping, *mythos* and a term also meaning simply "word," *logos,* came into opposition as *concepts.* Recently it has been proposed and widely accepted that the traditional distinction of myth versus logos/reason in European thought must be reconsidered. Bruce Lincoln has argued that our usual picture is just reversed, that *mythos* was actually the word of asserting power spoken by a leader, whereas *logos* referred to materials that had no innate authority, but had to be argued for (1999).

A conference at the University of Bristol in 1996 entitled "Mythos into Logos?" (papers are in Buxton 1999) featured a rigorous reconceptualizing of perspective, suggesting in general that the two terms were probably *very seldom opposed* in the manner that later thought has assumed, especially because of the influence of rationalism developed in the period of the Enlightenment—which began to idealize Ancient Greece and look negatively at other civilizations, particularly the Near East, that have different ways of conceptualizing the natural world.

It is also true that within Greek and Roman thought, several rationalistic interpreters of myth (Thales, Palaphaitos) followed Euhemeros of Messene (330–260 B.C.E.), who in a novelistic travel book (a popular Greek genre) claimed to have seen on an island in the Indian Sea a very ancient temple of Zeus. Supposedly a golden column there displayed magnificent deeds of Ouranos, Kronos, and Zeus, the creator deities of Ancient Greece. The three were not depicted as magnificent creatures, however, but as ordinary human heroes, mortals! (Within this culture, to be sure, the two classes, deities and heroes, were never sharply distinguished.)

Euhemeros developed a way of looking at mythic figures that considered them to have been merely powerful leaders who later had become deified at some point. Euhemeristic mythography was developed by Roman writers and then later, especially by Christian theologians who treated myths as debased or trivial accounts, rather than stories important to high culture.

Early Christian religious references were primarily negative, referring to what *others* believed (in Timothy 1.4, even the teachings of Hellenistic Judaism from which Christianity derived are referred to as "myths and endless genealogies"—see also I Timothy 4.7 and Titus 1.14). In the Gospel of John, "Mythos, logos, and history overlap in the prologue [...]; there, Jesus, the Christ, is portrayed as the Logos, who came from eternity into historical times" (Long 1997; this Logos is not so much the rational thought of the Greek sciences as a quasi-divine spiritual being of Hellenistic mystical religions and Stoic philosophy).

The Christian founding stories came to be considered "revelation," opposed to "history" as "what really happened," the factual. Today, however, using nonreligious but primarily literary criteria, many of the happenings claimed in Christian teaching to be ultimately "historical" (the Exodus, the Resurrection of the Christ) are considered to be essentially myth or theology, from a strictly formal point of view. Such a perspective explores the creative imagining central to any religious movement and is seldom concerned with establishing historical or factual veracity. It is more interested in why a people would tell such a story—the psychological motivation.

During the Christian Middle Ages, allegorical or tropological interpretations dominated within Christian preaching and teaching (famously: the ass upon which the wounded man is laid in the parable of the good Samaritan represents the Holy Church). Scripture that would not yield a pious interpretation by means of allegory was treated to at least three other types of secondary interpretation, moving from the most literal to the most moralistic (and often leaving the elements of the original passage far behind; Eco 1985 provides a good survey).

Meanwhile, in strong opposition to the dominant Christian religion, non-Christian ("pagan") Europeans, some of great antiquity themselves, continued to influence much of the population, especially in the country (*pagani* originally meant those who lived outside the Roman cities). Many of these (such as the arbitrarily reconstructed "Celtic" peoples) were extremely rich in mythological traditions.

The Renaissance (ca. 1500–1700) brought a recovery of Greek and Latin literature from antiquity, and now what we call "myth" began to have a more positive reception. The language of ancient Greece was in particular idealized, and artists and architects portrayed motifs found in remaining ruins—sometimes in fantastic applications that bear almost no resemblance to the originals.

The term and a now-positive concept of myth began to resurface (first used in English, in the eighteenth century). Thinkers during the Enlightenment (1700s) sought *to understand* religion and mythology, not just to dismiss it as trivial or low class. The growth of objectivism and rationalism now polarized the spheres represented by the shorthand terms *myth* and *reason* (logos). A developmental model proposed that societies evolve from a "primitive" social level in which myth is the natural mode of expression toward truly scientific thinking and reasoning where only facts and data count.

Romantics (late 1770s–early 1800s) rediscovered many more traditions from the past, especially old Indo-European myths about nature, such as the windswept alpine crag or the mysterious deep forest. Here the wild spirit of creativity was to be found outside the pallid life of the growing urban areas. Emotionalism rather than cool rationalism was prominent in the arts and literature; the mythical figure of Prometheus reappears repeatedly (Powell 2004: 116–17).

Barry Powell notes, "Whereas thinkers of the Enlightenment attacked myth as a product of primitive mental and emotional states, the Romantics

The mythical figure of Prometheus, shown here, reappears repeatedly during the Romantic period. Lithograph on paper, 1938 (at Smithsonian) by Rockwell Kent. Courtesy of the Library of Congress.

returned to myth as a vehicle for regaining lost truths" (2004: 646). "The folk" (*das Volk* in German) were discovered to have sheltered many customs and superstitions, myths, and tales that might be recovered in a renewal of contemporary culture. Later, in the Modern period, such materials would be regarded as part of the interior psychological dimension of both culture and individual, a romantic inheritance that Von Hendy (2002) discloses as still very much alive in several schools of myth interpretation.

Early in the Modern period (1800–1900s) myth was understood primarily as the texts that were scripts for rituals (by Frazer and the Cambridge Ritualists, in particular), leading to claims to be able to reconstruct New Year's Festivals across ancient Mesopotamia. These supposedly featured a yearly battle for the kingship in which the reigning leader had to vanquish all contenders or be replaced by the winner among them.

The concept of myth as *delusion* appeared in the publications and lectures of Karl Marx: An apparently innocent myth (or other social expression) represented merely a deception, a distracting surface cloaking a hard-hitting economic reality. This tradition, although not just pointing to economic hidings, was continued later by the myth analyses of the French critic Roland Barthes (1972)—he particularly pointed to ideological impulses behind publicity images, advertising, and popular entertainments such as wrestling matches.

Another negative attitude toward myth and ritual was developed by Sigmund Freud, who considered them merely props for the weak; a person who had undergone a thorough psychoanalysis ought to see through their superficial covering over traumatic incidents from the past (mostly sexual) that could now be integrated. Or not: Freud suggested that many of a culture's highest artworks and most noble contributions were the products of "sublimation" by which the artist directs all attention to the artwork in order to subdue interior psychic turmoil.

More positively inclined, Carl G. Jung pointed toward huge and lasting cultural images ("archetypes," but a term used some differently than by Plato) that he thought provided an immaterial substrate to the somewhat uniform human psyche that is realized either positively or negatively in any specific society, individual, or mythic expression. Also positive in interpretation, historian of religions Mircea Eliade argued that the mythic and religious materials of primitive societies represent a sort of ontology that still explains—to those religious persons who heed them—the nature of the universe and the divine.

Sociologist Émile Durkheim, on the other hand, stressed the manner in which societies set out models of the divine that actually just reflect what is most important to them at the time; these models subsequently form the basis of social cohesion and cooperation. Anthropologist Bronislaw Malinowski recognized that many such myths function as charters for social organization and activity. Others in the recent past have pointed to the role of mythic images in social construction of symbols by which a culture projects understandings upon the world (Ernst Cassirer, Paul Ricoeur). One such symbol would be that represented by the heroes of a culture—Joseph Campbell and others note how similar heroic stories are in many societies (see *In Quest of the Hero* [1990]). Campbell's very influential *Hero with a Thousand Faces* (1968) treats the hero monomyth as a paradigm of the development of the individual's journey (primarily the *male's*) out of the home into adulthood.

An exhaustive scientific interpretation of hundreds of myths reduces them to algebraic structures: Claude Lévi-Strauss took the myths of the Americas as his database to indicate how the varying mythic units (mythemes) combine in almost algebraic regularity, ultimately leading to ways of tolerating the fundamental human opposition between being and not-being. Structuralism is more interested in relationships between mythemes than in what we normally consider "content": Meanings can be sketched no matter what the content involves. The position of a myth in a corpus results from its role in structuring the ways a society resolves certain dilemmas—and for Lévi-Strauss such resolutions include myth interpretations, which become part of the sum total of all versions of a particular myth.

At least partly in reaction to the scientific tendencies in structuralism, postmodernist (late twentieth century onward) myth criticism has emphasized the manner in which myths are the basis for symbolic embodiments of values in the social universe. This is seen, literally, in the raft of books published on various representations of the human body and more abstractly in the principle of "social construction," in which mythic and ideological models are seen both to reflect society and to operate as ideals.

The phrase "just a myth!" would certainly not be heard in such circles, which recognize the ways in which mythological orientations (such as the heroic body) can lead to psychophysiological diseases (bulimia for women, manorexia [male anorexia] for men). Postmodernist citation of the past (in architecture, initially, then in literature and the other arts) proceeds cautiously, therefore, hoping to avoid baleful influences from the neuroses of earlier societies on the one hand and turning to various previously excluded attitudes typical of New Age grab bags of beliefs and practices.

Although all sorts of subjects are now encompassed within myth criticism, two passing examples will have to suffice: Jon Wagner and Jan Lundeen explore *Deep Space and Sacred Time:* Star Trek *in the American Mythos,* finding the television series to portray "a secular American mythology" that "constructs a humanist mythos that fulfills many of the same functions that myth has served in more traditional cultures" (1998: 3). One of the most widely experienced mass media entertainments of all time, the series' devotees have organized into the equivalent of religious groups who "explore life's ambiguities in a way that preserves our appreciation of their complexity while at the same time allowing for a sense of enhanced understanding, and perhaps even personal or collective empowerment" (4).

When the *New York Times* Sunday magazine devoted an entire issue to the subject of American baseball, I was by no means the only one (as letters to the editor revealed) who was outraged. Yet I should have remembered the national impact of the film *Field of Dreams* (1989; "If you build it, they will come"). Deeanne Westbrook contributes a very rich study of myth criticism under the title *Ground Rules: Baseball and Myth.* In the spatial metaphor of "gap," that distance between an archetypal mythic theme and its realizations, Westbrook elevates the popular sport to philosophy: "The gap of myth is a great void of nonmeaning, nonsense, or contradiction in which the mythic purpose operates within the medium of language, attempting to fill that emptiness with meaning, to render experience intelligible, to create narrative bridges across the abyss" (1996: 17). Baseball as mythic provides a way of making sense of human lives and action; it marks out sacred spaces and conforms to strict procedural rules. Westbrook's focus is on baseball in contemporary fiction, but she does not shirk adding a philosophical dimension to her literary analyses.

Philosophers with a Continental bent have indeed begun to reconsider the importance of myth, as witnessed by Lawrence J. Hatab's *Myth and Philosophy: A Contest of Truths* (1990) and especially a conference volume, *Thinking Through Myths: Philosophical Perspectives* (Schilbrack 2002; I contribute a chapter entitled "Myth and Postmodernist Philosophy"). Here philosophical perspectives on myth touch upon a wide array of current preoccupations: the environment, interpretation theory (semiotics and hermeneutics), feminism, moral philosophy, politics and ideology, postmodernism, and the language of science.

COMPARATIVE MYTHOGRAPHY AND FOLKLORE STUDIES

In the next sections of this chapter I will note how various academic disciplines have approached and do still approach myth in cultures; in the remaining part of this section I indicate the relationship of myth studies to folklore studies, one of the first academic areas that developed technical treatment of myths.

Many of the attitudes toward myth within early American folkloristics were negative. In the first issue of the *Journal of American Folklore,* published

Baseball considered as mythic provides a way of making sense of human lives and action; it marks out sacred spaces and conforms to strict procedural rules. Courtesy of the Library of Congress.

in 1888, William Wells Newell's programmatic essay on "Folk-Lore and Mythology" restated the traditional evolutionary-developmental perspective that associated mythology of "primitive" peoples and other evaluations of the material (as summarized by Dundes 1975: 4):

> Primitive peoples had *mythology;* civilized peoples had folklore, which was thought to be survivals from primitive times. The distinction also suggested that mythology was living while folklore was dying. That Newell was quite serious in making the distinction is apparent in his remark that had it not been out of regard for brevity, the *Journal of American Folklore* might have might have been titled the *Journal of American Folklore and Mythology.* Among most twentieth-century American folklorists, the distinction is [but now no longer—WGD] made. Mythology is usually considered to be a subdivision of folklore.

Part of the situation derived from the devolutionary premise in folklore theory that Dundes notes that "by 1890, Newell had come to realize that the distinction was a false one and he saw that the term folklore had to be more inclusive" (5). Dundes explains:

> The generally negative attitude towards change [i.e., in folklore, as we have seen, earlier considered to devolve or degrade in time—WGD] has been clearly reflected in folklore methodology. Just as ethnographers carefully sifted through unavoidable details obviously only recently added through acculturative contact in an attempt to discover the pure unadulterated original native culture, so practitioners of the Finnish historic-geographic method [influential on folkloristics worldwide—WGD] sought to work backwards through the unfortunate changes (or in [Stith] Thompson's terms, the mistakes and errors) in order to find the pure unadulterated original ur-form. The difficulties of searching for the ur-form, too often presumed to be hopelessly hidden by the destructive, deteriorative effects of oral transmission were considerable, but not always insurmountable. (19; he goes on to cite biblical form criticism as a *good* example, and in Dundes 1999, he expressly treats "the Bible as folklore")

Certainly contemporary folklorists seldom search for "earliest occurrences," which might be considered to have canonical priority. Barre Toelken emphasizes:

> [A]ll folklore participates in a distinctive, dynamic process. Constant change, variation within a tradition, whether intentional or inadvertent, is viewed here simply as a central fact of existence for folklore, and rather than presenting it in opposed terms of conscious artistic manipulation vs. forgetfulness, I accept it as a defining feature that grows out of context, performance, attitude, cultural tastes, and the like. (1996: 7)

Precisely what characterizes living folk materials is that they are subject to many changes as they are transmitted, so that *variation* is a sign of health: "Variation in the particular appearance of one item is probably the most reliable hallmark of life folklore available to the student. It is not based on the belief that folklore is more 'pure' than anything else, but on the observation that folklore is produced and maintained in a distinctive way" (39).

"Folklore," yes, but also written materials that express multiple tag-lines: Georges and Jones document some seven alternative explanations to the Zuni tale "The Deserted Children" (1995: 258, box 8–6). In the New Testament, the parable of the unjust steward (Lk 16.1–8a) is followed in 16.8b-12 with five bumbling attempts to say what that story "meant." Evidently even the later redactors could not agree and so left the varying explanatory verses in a heap.

The second main point to be made here involves oral and literary *types* or *genres* of materials. Most contemporary folklore approaches recognize that the earlier strict distinctions between saga, epic, legend, folktale (often called fairy tale, yet few include any fairies!), fable, and myth are actually untenable, because they are almost indecipherable to the "folk" being studied. So Garry Gossen notes with respect to the Chamula people of Mexico that "if our consideration of Chamula oral tradition were restricted to what we call myth, folk tales, legend, folk music, or pun, we could hope for no more than a distorted view of the collective representations of the community" (1972: 165). Those "would account for no more than a fraction of the vast amount of information contained in the many classes of Chamula verbal behavior."

Here, as elsewhere within ethnology and folkloristics, native categories have firmly resisted limited classifications familiar from European and American folklore, and some of their categories *add to* what classifications the whites have utilized. Gossen notes that the assumption that only certain genres are appropriate for the most important cultural information is belied by the recognition that Chamula categories corresponding to our *gossip* may carry important "information about cosmology and social categories" (165). Work in Middle America by Dennis Tedlock has disclosed similar situations, such as the Mayan oral conventions that correspond to our paper book jackets (1983: 163).

There is also the important factor of audience reception. Eliott Oring suggests that myth, legend, and folktale are terms that "do not refer to the *forms* of narrative so much as to the *attitudes* of the community toward them" (1986: 124). Oring is pressing beyond separative definitions to look at "the place of folk narrative in some larger context of belief and behavior." He goes on to suggest that "the folklorist must attempt to understand why people tell stories in the first place, why listeners appreciate them, and why they favor some stories over others" (135).

Oring calls for a holistic study of narrative that would include the performative factors: "The study of performance [...] would attend to the full range of ideas and behaviors that bear upon a communicative interaction. Narration is conceptualized as an *event* taking place in time and space. It is more than a text and its constituent elements" (138)—that is to say, words, plots, themes, and narrative structures.

The study that Oring proposes would not just look at the "sweetness and light" elements that most popular folk collections emphasize:

Folk narratives are reflections of the societies and individuals which create and transmit them; consequently they reflect a wide range of human ideas and emotions. Often one must get used to the fact that folk narratives do not just document the triumphs of good over evil and injustice, the sacrifices and martyrdoms in the pursuit of a righteous cause, or acts of humility and charity for which supernatural rewards are bestowed. Certainly such tales exist, but we must remember that folk narratives represent themes of violence, hatred, cruelty, racism, prejudice, sexuality, obscenity, and scatology as well. (133)

Recognizing such features even in "noble myths" casts some doubt on the widely established association of myths and the sacred, an issue to which we turn shortly. Such recognition helps remove mythological materials from the gilt-edged Western classic books context and returns them to the frames of the ordinary social settings within which they surely arose.

A point made by Dan Ben-Amos is well taken: Having separative definitions of myth does not mean it has to refer to materials kept *outside* other aspects of folklore, such as "jokes and myths, gestures and legends, costumes and music" (1972: 3). In fact the "cultural attitude toward" the materials is more important functionally than specific generic classification because the same unit of folk material may *function* as "myth for one group and [as] *Märchen* [wonder tales] for another" (4). Myth, after all, is but "one genre out of several hundred genres of folklore" (Dundes 1999: 2), and it would be silly to suggest that generic boundaries would always operate as restrictively as some theorists have tried to set them out in the past.

Steven Swann Jones emphasizes that "like legends, epics, myths, and other forms of folk literature, the folktale genre is a product of oral tradition, evolving over years, passing from performer to performer, spanning cultures and continents, and outliving generations" (1998: 291). "Like" legends, epics, and myths!—some of the early folklorists' strict literary differentiations are clearly less useful to more recent analysts.

One of the deans of the folkloristics field, Alan Dundes, would not find my argument convincing and indeed would probably refer to it as an example of the "madness in method" with which he titles a rejection of mythographic approaches to myth that do not take its *sacred character* seriously enough (1996, an essay that reaffirms the separative definition, widely regarded in folklore, of William Bascom 1965). I return to that issue later.

Sometimes myth in Durkheim's sense is regarded as a mirror of culture. At other times it becomes little but data-fodder for computerized analytics, as in structuralism. Observing that most folklorists and anthropologists consider myth not as literature or philosophy, but as a mirror of culture, Claire Farrer reflects on the "enduring" nature of myth: "At still other times, myth has been pointed to as the philosophy of the unlettered, completely ignoring that the lettered also have and believe in their own myths. What is enduring is myth itself. It does not vanish with increased complexity of social life. Worldwide trade and politics [in the contemporary world—WGD] do not cause it to wither and die from lack of use" (1997: 580).

Certainly myth appears at all levels of society, although folklorist Barre Toelken reminds us of the recurrent tendency to suggest that it is important only at "primitive" levels of social development:

> Perhaps the most subtle battle in modern folklore is the constant attempt of scholars to reform the widespread journalistic use of the words *folklore* and *myth*. In the newspapers, and in the common understanding of many people, the terms have come to mean "misinformation" or "misconception" or "outmoded (and, by implication, naively accepted where believed) ideas." The misunderstanding and misapplication of these terms seems to stem from a modern continuation of [the] notion that only backward or illiterate people have folklore; where it exists among us, by implication, it represents backward or naïve thinking. [...T]his use of *folklore* [and by extension, *myth*—WGD] to imply intellectual deficit is simply not borne out by the facts: something we call folklore [myth] is found in great plenty on all levels of society, and scholars are at some pains to account for its persistence and development. (1996: 3)

Anyone who denies this has to account somehow for what is usually called urban folklore, frequently distributed by photocopied pages or by e-mail or on the Internet—not exactly sites associated with the illiterate! And as we will see in chapter 5, mythologies remain vital across the entire spectrum of the arts and literature. Already in the 1970s, Edmund Leach noticed the amount of redundancy in mythic expressions, demonstrating "how myth is fluid, rather than being fixed for all time" (cited by Farrer 1997: 579).

Farrer sees this as evidence of the "permeability" of myth, its openness to accommodation and reinterpretation, to incorporation of the new as well as celebration of the old. It has been widely documented in contemporary times how frequently traditional Native American mythological traditions have been altered as the people find mythic ways to incorporate items acquired only after contact with Anglos and successfully to stake land claims on the basis of geographical information in their mythological accounts.

DEFINITIONAL: THE SACRED

As already noted, Alan Dundes decries contemporary mythographers' usage, because for his definition *the sacred* is always central. Accordingly, "most of these academic discussions of 'myth' have little or nothing to do with myth in the strict and technical sense of the term" (1996: 147)—"strict and technical" in the separative way earlier folklore studies defined the differentiations between genres. I suspect Professor Dundes is particularly sensitive to the fact that "the study of myth by folklorists tends to be virtually ignored by these would-be mythologists"—a complaint that is more than accurate when we see how seldom cross- or interdisciplinary scholarship is supported by the institutions in which most academics work (having coedited several volumes on the subject, I am not speaking out of ignorance).

The "purist" definitional scope Dundes demands is evident in his *Sacred Narratives* (1984: 1, first sentence: "A myth is a sacred narrative") no less than in the "Madness in Method" essay just referred to: "For the folklorist, a myth is a sacred narrative explaining how the world and mankind came to be in their present form" (1996: 147). Hence the Oedipus myth as normally discussed "is *not* a sacred narrative offering an explanation of how the world and mankind came to be in their present form. It is the standard folktale, namely, Aarne-Thompson tale-type 931, Oedipus" (148–49; the reference is to a standard collection of myths listed by means of folkloristic types; see also Thompson 1946).

Carrying out his strict folklorist-purist agenda, Dundes then suggests (149) that in a widely referred to contemporary volume, Accardi et al., *Recent Studies* (1991), "more than half the entries have nothing whatever to do with myth in the folkloristic sense. Most of these tend to refer to either themes or patterns, but definitely not myths" (149). The same author has repeatedly suggested that only Freudian, never Jungian, interpretations of myth are legitimate (152). (I write this out of some astonishment because I have found Dundes's interpretations so compelling over the years. Yet I have repeatedly factored them into a more-forgiving, multidisciplinary context.)

I suspect that the nub of the problem has to do with traditional modernist definitions (please recall the discussions in chapter 2) in which rationalist outlines of what delimited one item from another were absolute, and never flexible. But as I have just suggested, today most postmodernist definitions acknowledge that slippage between one or another genre or definition is simply to be expected. Hence Wendy Doniger suggests that "the sacred" cannot be limited to supernatural beings, although she as well wants to include the "religious" nature of myth.

My own preference as part of my complex definition (2000: chap. 2–3) is for a phrase something like "intervention of suprahuman entities" (74). I like what Toelken does when he encounters the traditional "sacred" of the usual definitions: the mythic mode comprises materials reaching "toward the ineffable, the Beyond" and possessing "the aura of universal power" (1996: 396). Perhaps even better is Philip Wheelwright's suggestion that myth and ritual "imply in their turn a belief in a penumbral reality, something extending beyond yet interpenetrating with the affairs of mortal men" (1966: 60).

This is hardly what our society refers to as "sacred" or "religious," but I think Matti Megged is absolutely correct in suggesting that myth "is not based anymore on sacred traditions or collective rituals" (1985: 2), and that "modern man is a product of a nonmythological world, modes of thinking, ways of life" (3). Clearly myth has been based on the sacred in many sociohistorical settings and may well yet be so for more traditional, less technologically-oriented peoples today. But for anyone fully immersed in the common, contemporary Western consciousness and praxis, it derives from arbitrary external influences like the mass media (driven as they are by corporate profit factors, *not* any sort of collectively considered or accepted religious values).

IN THE ANALYTICAL HUMANITIES AND SOCIAL SCIENCES

Myth criticism has no single disciplinary "home," but occurs across a wide spectrum of the humanities and social sciences. It has surfaced at various times in philosophy, religious studies, literary studies, psychology (depth and psychoanalytical, primarily), anthropology, political science and economics (especially with respect to ideology), history, classics, biblical studies, folkloristics, and American and cultural studies—and many of these disciplines are at least represented in other primary domains. It is not unusual to find a historian such as one of my own colleagues who specializes in studying attitudes toward myth in a particular period of European history.

At times myth criticism is truly cross- or interdisciplinary in a very fruitful manner—I think of the beautifully illustrated book, *A City of Images: Iconography and Society in Ancient Greece* (Bérard et al. 1989). The seven authors worked in two French academic institutions to provide information about the life of the artisans of the Kerameikos, the ceramics production center in ancient Athens. They focus upon imagery in the pottery, reading it as presenting signs of the culture. Consider how young men are portrayed, for example, and you can extrapolate rules and taboos, clothing styles (indicating rank, profession, differences between age groups), traditional associations with others, activities engaged in typically (athletics, schooling, military training), sexual patterns, and participation in civic and religious ceremonials. Sometimes mythological materials are clarified from recognizing the way the artisans represented heroes and deities. We can to a certain extent sit alongside an ancient Greek person, as we learn how a world of representations comes to be established and then copied faithfully (Woodford 2003 is also very instructive in this respect). At such a point, the culture is millennia away from conventions of realistic representation in the arts such as photography (mid-nineteenth century).

Conventions include shrinking a complex set of indicators, such as those of the prized warrior, to an icon, in this case his weapons: "This is not a still life [...] but a picture reduced to its essentials" (Bérard et al. 1989: 51). Representations of rituals disclose that meat is eaten only at sacrifices, and that the sacrifice was thought to reproduce, around the smoking and bloody altar, the very order of the universe (53).

The initiatory hunt, the logical opposite to war with others, is associated with an erotically tinged fascination with adolescent male beauty. Women are represented as much more active than literature would suggest: The vases meant for household use showing women at the communal fountain and in other situations would not have been acceptable had these been onerous occupations (89–96).

The scenes of rituals demonstrate both the importance of the *performance* and its *images*. We are reminded that the central most important element of the mystery at the center of a philosophico-religious cult was a "sermon without words" that could neither be spoken about nor illustrated (117). We gather a sense of the place of the wine cult famously associated with Dionysos. The point was not getting drunk, but obtaining experiences that might blur distinctions between humans and deities (138). And most of all, we realize that only a study completed collaboratively from as many analytical perspectives as this one fully provides a dense, rich evocation of mythological scenes that are all too often reduced to "the symbol of god X is Y" in the familiar myth handbooks.

Interpretive possibilities stemming from several disciplines that are not necessarily often in communication with others are also important. I have to admit to a longing to see more studies such as that summarized in *A City of Images*. How fascinating it would be to have some early American rock paintings examined by professions such as sociology, art history, psychology, anthropology, history, and literature, each bringing to bear its own most sophisticated contributions, and then seeing how what others bring to the table calls into question, amplifies, or adds to one's own contribution.

Certainly within the last century our understanding of the meanings of myths has been multiplied by several of the modern analytical disciplines. I make no pretense to complete discussion here but will highlight some of the understandings of myth that seem to me to have been the most fruitful for persons working in myth studies in the several disciplines I listed earlier. We might as well begin with that "new science" of psychoanalysis that was given its greatest creditability through the work of Sigmund Freud. I start here because perhaps his most influential publication, *Die Traumdeutung/The Interpretation of Dreams,* was published in 1899, but dated to appear as one of the first books of the new century, in 1900.

Beginnings are always important, and Freud certainly relied upon the *anamnesis,* a recollection of one's earliest beginnings in the memories of infancy and childhood. But he had the sense not to focus exclusively on the point of inception, but also upon the psychological issue, whatever it was, that worked itself out in everyday life—in jokes, artworks, or literature. "The issue" was normatively rooted in infant sexuality (this in itself was quite a shocking thought to the Victorian culture in which Freud's work appeared); deviances from expected refined persons' behavior (called neuroses) were simply the most recent appearance of the childhood traumas.

Most notable was the Oedipus complex. Freud chose to stress one of the several strands of ancient myth about the Greek Oidipous—and ignored *Oidipous epi Kolonoi/Oedipus at Colonus,* precisely the version that told of the nonviolent death of Oidipous, even though he was estranged from his sons.

Freud's approach to mythology was that of a highly cultured Viennese whose education included intensive instruction in the Greek and Latin literature of antiquity. His working desk was edged with a number of miniature antique statues of goddesses and gods. No wonder, then, that his worldview was considerably influenced by classical mythological thought.

He often found mythological names and figures to personify what he considered to be the basic drives of the human psyche: Eros, the impulse toward connectivity, especially sexual; Thanatos, the impulse toward destruction, death; and Ananke, the recognition of a sort of Fate (from the Latin, *fatum,* what is pronounced) that overwhelms whatever individually desired concentration upon doing "the right thing."

Much dependent upon Aristotle, Freud understood Greek tragedy as a portrayal of what is inescapable about the human condition: humans are always tempted to overreach their limited capabilities and aspire to godhood, total control of the world around them. Freud's great insight was that dreams and other expressions of the unconscious soul (psyche) within all of us provide ways for our kind to tap into the "beyond-me" aspects of experience, indeed, into eons of mythological expression, the knowing down deep that we are more than our purely individual self (his follower Carl Jung will refer to this dimension as the archetypal).

Freud also recognized that dreamwork is much like the work of all culture: it seeks to cloak fairly base human impulses in symbols that are pure and

Sigmund Freud's worldview was considerably influenced by classical mythological thought. Most notable was Freud's Oedipus Complex. Courtesy of the Library of Congress.

clean, hence the shock of realizing that tall up-reaching edifices might be a displacement for the penis, the artfully crafted box or purse a displacement for the vagina. Hence Freud's interpretive theory—vastly influential upon literary and artistic criticism in the middle of the twentieth century—functions as a hermeneutics (interpretation theory and practice) of "deceit." One must be wary about surface appearances, because they may cloak totally the fundamental underlying human impulses (not always pleasant to confront) that provided the motivation for the material.

Dream mechanisms have a great deal to do with veiling and disguising, so that *The Interpretation of Dreams* provided a scout handbook to people in many disciplines who were interested in understanding the basic motivations of artistic production. Freud introduced a sense of regularization of seeing through the most noble community contributions to their fundamental bases in individual and collective human needs. He did not suggest we should shun the community worker or artist's productions, but he did believe the life of the individual would be more satisfying, were she or he to confront the "real" psychological issues surfacing (Jung spoke similarly about the importance of recognizing the "shadow" dimension).

Freud felt that Western civilization is near the peak of scientific expectations for the human race. The psychologically mature person will be able to understand that the "fate" of antiquity and the ultimately dependent reliance upon an external divine figure are but shaky canes that can be easily discarded so that the individual can walk entirely without supports. The "primal father" is just something that can be left behind, when we realize that we are our own "father" in some unique way. And that way for him involved Logos with a capital L: like many early Modernists, Freud thought that Logos/Rationality/Science would replace the dependencies of the premodern upon external divine principles and figures, and "mankind will surmount this neurotic phase, just as so many children grow out of their similar neurosis" (1961: 53).

Postmodernist thought relies much less upon the positive evolutionary thought echoed in Freud's works, indeed questions its very viability apart from specifically identified historical context. Freud's emphasis upon the repression of religious ritual and the "ritualistic" aspects of human behavior generally, however, have come to roost across much of late-twentieth-century culture. "Ritualistic" has come to mean something like inauthentic, pathetic, useless, although it ought to be obvious that any society has formal, repeated behaviors that indicate little except standard social conditioning or individual choice (dare I mention TV surfing?).

Followers of Freud with respect to mythological issues included Otto Rank (1959) and Géza Roheim, who tacked Freudian perspectives onto Lord Raglan's (1937) mapping of the Western heroic model. These studies suggested that Freudian principles *could* be applied to mythological materials, as did E. R. Dodds's *The Greeks and the Irrational* (1951), one of several cultural studies that applied Freud's concepts of cultural shame and guilt to traditionally elevated cultural mythological expressions. Alan Dundes has developed Freudian explications of many sorts of socially produced literary materials, although countervoices have found his and similar works overreaching and hard to duplicate.

"Beyond Freud" means, of course, not only neo-Freudian interpretations but especially Jungian ones. Carl Gustav Jung split from what he felt to be restrictive orthodox Freudian interpretations of cultural materials when he abandoned the purely sexual/erotic Freudian emphases. For Jung, "erotic" need not mean "sexual," but could mean "connective." Expanding Freud's range of "the mythological," Jung brought into play ancient Gnostic materials as well as Eastern religious thought Freud had never considered. His respect for ancient mythological materials was vastly greater than Freud's, so that instead of primal psychological malfunctions, Jung saw within the same materials primal building blocks of the human psyche, indeed "archetypes" of meaning expressed and graphed many centuries ago.

According to Jung, such materials were important within civilized expressions primarily as they reflected advanced representations of common experiences familiar to all cultures. Jung turned to the study of iconography and mythic expressions out of frustrations working with purely personal materials. Part of his psychotherapy included having the patient read widely in mythological sources—indeed, even today the Jungian psychoanalyst is extensively trained in mythological narratives and archetypal symbolism.

For Jung, dreams were less symptoms than they were harbingers, bearing symbolic meanings that could point the way to potential growth in the psy-

Carl Jung's respect for ancient mythological materials was vastly greater than Freud's—Jung saw within the same materials primal building blocks of the human psyche, indeed "archetypes" of meaning expressed and graphed many centuries ago. Courtesy of the Library of Congress.

che. Dreams, mythological images, and figures to which the patient is attracted can point to vocational paths otherwise left unexplored. In this sense a vast "objective psyche" of the culture (the collective unconscious, in earlier Jungian diction) can be posited: Jung thought of it as a sort of rhizome whose roots are infinitely ancient, but whose sprouts still surface in the most contemporary life. Dream images may also alert one to unconscious aspects of the way one is living—and by extension, mythological images may have a similar cultural function.

Although it is always difficult to be aware of the culturally important images that rule a generation, such identification can be an important source of cultural criticism and renewal. A day when "reality TV," superhero kung fu heroes, or shapely "angel" crime fighters predominate the entertainment media may be a day very unsure of its own future, even its own "reality." But identifying a cultural mythos or worldview may be difficult precisely when we are within it.

Daniel Noel's *Approaching Earth: A Search for the Mythic Significance of the Space Age* (1986) quite successfully identifies the reconsideration of our own planet made necessary by having looked back at it from outer space. Many of our short-term concerns pale before the sort of expanse of time and space that we now have to take into consideration. Most importantly, perhaps, we are directed to some of the mythically inspired interests of recent decades in Goddess religions, earth art, and aerial archaeology—where we can find what Noel calls "geometaphors" that may redirect our habits of wasting our natural resources and failing to plan adequately for the quality of life on the planet.

Jungian-influenced works have produced some classics in mythical and iconographic analysis, such as Erich Neumann's *The Great Mother: An Analysis of the Archetype* (1963), a rich treasure trove of ideas as well as images spanning the many representations of the feminine in the arts. Several contributors with Jung produced *Man and His Symbols* (Jung and von Franz 1964), a volume whose illustrations today seem curiously out of date, but whose content still provides a useful orientation to the Jungian positions on mythological materials. Marie Louise von Franz, Jung's coeditor for *Man and His Symbols,* has produced several Jungian-oriented volumes, treating creation myths and fairy tales (1972a, 1972b, 1997). *Mirrors of the Self: Archetypal Images that Shape Your Life* (Downing 1991) provides a convenient introduction to a wide range of archetypal motifs and figures.

James Hillman has brought post-Jungian analysis of mythological themes and materials into the postmodernist framework. For years he edited *Spring: A Journal of Archetype and Culture* and contributed frequently to it (in Doty

2000: 15–17, I provide a chart identifying where Hillman has published on some 16 mythical figures/themes). Hillman conceives of myths not as merely referents lying "behind" contemporary thought, but as having ongoing creative powers in their own rights. In several of his essays ("City, Sport, and Violence" [1994] or "A Psyche the Size of the Earth" [1995]) he demonstrates how rewarding it can be to track mythical energies running loose in urban streets today, and how much attention we are *not* giving to channeling them in healthy ways.

Hillman conceives of mythical metaphors not as causal explanations of anything so much as "perspectives toward events which shift the experience of events" (1996: 93); they are possible interpretations growing out of the power of an image to provoke the imagination. They counter our culture's excessive rationality and "hit home" like a bolt out of the blue (or don't): "The relevance of a myth to life strikes like a revelation or a self-evident proposition, which cannot be demonstrated by logic or induced from factual evidence. The best evidence is anecdote, the telling example that lights up an obscure idea in a clear intuitive flash" (100).

We must ask what is myth-ing us, how the image(s) speak in ways that discursive talk does not, what else is animating our cosmos besides our natural and technological sciences. Hillman is thoroughly conversant with traditional philosophy, but especially with Renaissance thought that tried to see beyond the traditional. Hearing him speak gives one a sense of what it can be like to have a *real* conversation, one in which the past is not a foreign time, but one in which the future as well as the present is being imaged and reexperienced anew. (*A Blue Fire: Selected Writings by James Hillman,* edited by Thomas Moore, provides an excellent introduction to Hillman's world of thought in his own terms.)

Other post-Jungian writers and speakers include Jean Shinoda Bolen, Clarissa Pinkola Estés, Allen Chinen, and James Hollis. They hardly speak with one voice, but their popularity demonstrates how some sort of application of Jungian thought to mythological stories and images has found a ready audience today.

Myth studies taking place mostly within literature departments and now increasingly within cultural studies (and in America, within departments in American Studies) have provided many insights into the construction of mythological narratives and the ways languages work as systems of meaning-symbols. The last named flourished in the 1960s and 1970s, especially in the semiotics of Roland Barthes. His articles written between 1954 and 1956 for a French periodical were published in *Mythologies* and addressed many instances of ideological formation in everyday life, from the upper-class values revealed in the ways Sunday newspaper supplements presented foods in elaborate fashion, to wrestling matches, to the image of the French Legionnaire abroad.

Although Barthes also worked in literary analysis, these articles address commercial interests and political applications as they seek to sway consumers or voters. More or less in the Marxian tradition, he attempts to demystify the items he studies and hence interrogates the way the symbols are created and manipulated. Myth functions to reduce the actual historic place of objects it touches or to move meaning from one sphere to another: a detergent is given a mythicized framework when it is advertised as cleaning "deeply" or "naturally." Soaps don't really reach down and lift out, but recite the new connection a few times, and one forgets the added meaning in the semiotic overlay.

The dietary advice that a substance in red wines has health benefits is recent; but there's a long tradition in France about how it is vital to the national identity—a connection Barthes believes to have been promoted by commercial interests, rather than any actual historical referent. His demythologizing claims to see between the myth and the historical referent. One might say that Barthes is suggesting political allegories replace the real. His attention to the levels of signs is helpful in understanding how transference of meanings across different domains can take place—a first order sign in one system can become a secondary-order sign with a different signified meaning, as in an automobile advertisement where an attractive young woman drapes herself seductively over a rather phallic sports car.

Barthes's attention to the ideological aspects of created mythic discourse is amplified by John Girling's *Myths and Politics in Western Societies* (1993), where the author shows how ideological materials appeal both to logical concepts and to the emotions. And David Kertzer notes the role of repetition in political rituals: "Ritual action is repetitive and therefore, often redundant, but these very factors serve as important means of channeling emotion, guiding cognition, and organizing social groups (1988: 9).

Lance Bennett has shown how political myths have subliminal appeals that are seldom blatantly obvious to anyone yet are very functional:

Myths condition the public to the powerful symbols used by politicians. Myths underwrite the status quo in times of stability and they chart the course of change in times of stress. In the day-to-day business of politics myths set the terms for most public policy debate. When mythical themes and myth-related language are stripped away from policy discourse, very little of substance remains. Most political controversy centers around disagreement over which myth to apply to a particular problem. (1980: 168)

WORKS CITED

Accardi, Bernard, David J. Charlson, Frank A. Doden, Richard F. Hardin, Sung Royal Kim, Sonya J. Lancaster, and Michael H. Shaw. 1991. *Recent Studies in Myth and Literature, 1970–1990: An Annotated Bibliography.* Bibliog. and Indexes in World Lit., 29. New York: Greenwood.

Barthes, Roland. 1972. *Mythologies.* Trans. Annette Lavers. New York: Hill and Wang.

Bascom, William. 1965. "The Forms of Folklore: Prose Narratives." *Journal of American Folklore* 78: 3–20. Repr. in Dundes 1984: 5–29.

Ben-Amos, Dan. 1972. "Toward a Definition of Folklore in Context." In Paredes and Bauman 3–15.

Bennett, W. Lance. 1980. "Myth, Ritual, and Political Control." *Journal of Communication* 30 (4): 166–79.

Bérard, Claude, Christiane Bron, Jean-Louis Durand, Françoise Frontisi-Ducroux, François Lissarrague, Alain Schnapp, and Jean-Pierre Vernant. 1989. *A City of Images: Iconography and Society in Ancient Greece.* Trans. Deborah Lyons. Princeton, NJ: Princeton UP.

Bierlein, J. F. 1994. *Parallel Myths.* New York: Ballantine.

Bolle, Kees. 1983. "Myths and Other Religious Texts." In *Contemporary Approaches to the Study of Religion,* ed. Frank Whaling, 297–363. Berlin: Mouton.

Brisson, Luc. 1998 [1994]. *Plato the Myth Maker.* Trans., ed. Gerard Naddaf. Chicago: The U of Chicago P.

Buxton, Richard, ed. 1999. *From Myth to Reason? Studies in the Development of Greek Thought.* New York: Oxford UP.

Campbell, Joseph. 1968. *The Hero with a Thousand Faces.* 2nd ed. Bollingen ser., 17. Princeton, NJ: Princeton UP.

Detienne, Marcel. 1986 [1981]. *The Creation of Mythology.* Trans. Margaret Cook. Chicago: U of Chicago P.

Dodds, E. R. 1951. *The Greeks and the Irrational.* Berkeley: U of California P.

Doty, William G. 2000. *Mythography: The Study of Myths and Rituals.* Revised 2nd ed. Tuscaloosa: U of Alabama P.

Downing, Christine, ed. 1991. *Mirrors of the Self: Archetypal Images that Shape Your Life.* A New Consciousness Reader. Los Angeles: Tarcher.

Dundes, Alan. 1963. *The Study of Folklore.* Englewood Cliffs, NJ: Prentice Hall.

———. 1975. *Analytic Essays in Folklore.* Studies in Folklore 2. New York: Mouton.

———. ed. 1984. *Sacred Narrative: Readings in the Theory of Myth.* Berkeley: U of California P.

———. 1996. "Madness in Method, Plus a Plea for Projective Inversion in Myth." In *Myth and Method,* ed. Laurie Patton and Wendy Doniger, 147–59. Charlottesville: UP of Virginia.

———. 1999. *Holy Writ as Oral Lit: The Bible as Folklore.* Lanham, Md.: Rowman and Littlefield.

Eco, Umberto. 1985. "At the Roots of the Modern Concept of Symbol." *Social Research* 52 (2): 383–402.

Farrer, Claire R. 1997. "Myth." In *Folklore: An Encyclopedia of Beliefs, Customs, Tales, Music, and Art,* ed. Thomas A. Green, 575–81. Vol. 2. Santa Barbara, CA: ABC-CLIO.

Feldman, Burton, and Robert D. Richardson. 1972. *The Rise of Modern Mythology 1680–1860.* Bloomington: Indiana UP.

Freud, Sigmund. 1961. *The Future of an Illusion.* Trans. and ed. James Strachey. New York: Norton. [In Standard Edition, v. 21.]

Georges, Robert A., and Michael Owen Jones. 1995. *Folkloristics: An Introduction.* Bloomington: Indiana UP.

Girling, John. 1993. *Myths and Politics in Western Societies: Evaluating the Crisis of Modernity in the United States, Germany, and Great Britain.* New Brunswick, NJ: Transaction.

Gossen, Gary H. 1972. "Chamula Genres of Verbal Behavior." In Paredes and Bauman 145–67.

Hatab, Lawrence J. 1990. *Myth and Philosophy: A Contest of Truths.* La Salle, IL: Open Court.

Hillman, James. 1989. *A Blue Fire: Selected Writings by James Hillman.* Intro. and ed. Thomas Moore. New York: Harper and Row.

———. 1994. "City, Sport, and Violence." In *Psyche and Sports: Baseball, Hockey, Martial Arts, Running, Tennis,* ed. Murray Stein and John Hollwitz, 1–16. Wilmette, IL: Chiron.

———. 1995. "A Psyche the Size of the Earth: A Psychological Forward." In *Ecopsychology: Restoring the Earth, Healing the Mind,* ed. Theodore Roszak, Mary E. Gomes, and Allen D. Kanner, xvii–xviii. San Francisco: Sierra Club Books.

———. 1996. *The Soul's Code: In Search of Character and Calling.* New York: Random House.

In Quest of the Hero. 1990. Reprinted essays by Otto Rank, Lord Raglan, and Alan Dundes. Intro. Robert A. Segal. Mythos: The Princeton/Bollingen Ser. in World Mythology. Princeton, NJ: Princeton UP.

Jones, Steven Swann. 1998. "Teaching the Folktale Tradition." In *Teaching Oral Traditions,* ed. John Miles Foley, 291–97. MLA of Amer. Options for Teaching. New York: MLA.

Jung, Carl G., and Marie-Louise von Franz, eds. 1964. *Man and His Symbols.* Garden City, NY: Doubleday.

Kertzer, David I. 1988. *Ritual, Politics, and Power.* New Haven, CT: Yale UP.

Lincoln, Bruce. 1999. *Theorizing Myth: Narrative, Ideology, and Scholarship.* Chicago: U of Chicago P.

Long, Charles. 1997. "Mythology." *Microsoft Encarta 97 Encyclopedia* CD-ROM.

Megged, Matti. 1985. "Editor's Introduction." Myth in Contemporary Life. *Social Research* 52 (2): 211–15.

Morgan, Kathryn A. 2000. *Myth and Philosophy from the Pre-Socratics to Plato.* New York: Cambridge UP.

Neumann, Erich. 1963. *The Great Mother: An Analysis of the Archetype.* 2nd ed. Trans. Ralph Mannheim. Bollingen ser., 47. Princeton, NJ: Princeton UP.

Noel, Daniel C. 1986. *Approaching Earth: A Search for the Mythic Significance of the Space Age.* Amity, N.Y.: Amity House.

Oring, Eliott, ed. 1986. *Folk Groups and Folklore Genres: An Introduction.* Logan: Utah State P.

Paredes, Américo, and Richard Bauman, eds. 1972. *Toward New Perspective in Folklore.* Publ. of the Amer. Folkl. Soc., Bibliogr. and Spec. Ser. 23. Austin: The U of Texas P.

Powell, Barry B. 2004. *Classical Myth.* 4th ed. Upper Saddle River, NJ: Pearson/Prentice Hall.

Raglan, F.R.R.S. 1937. *The Hero: A Study in Tradition, Myth, and Drama.* New York: Oxford UP.

Rank, Otto. 1959. *The Myth of the Birth of the Hero and Other Writings by Otto Rank.* Ed. Philip Freund. Trans. F. Robbins and S. E. Jelliffe. New York: Random House.

Schilbrack, Kevin, ed. 2002. *Thinking through Myths: Philosophical Perspectives.* New York: Routledge-Taylor & Francis.

Tedlock, Dennis. 1983. *The Spoken Word and the Work of Interpretation.* Philadelphia: The U of Pennsylvania P.

Thompson, Stith. 1946. *The Folktale.* New York: Holt, Rinehart and Winston.

Toelken, Barre. 1996. *The Dynamics of Folklore.* Logan: Utah State UP.

Veyne, Paul. 1988 [1983]. *Did the Greeks Believe in Their Myths?: An Essay on the Constitutive Imagination.* Trans. Paula Wissing. Chicago: U of Chicago P.

von Franz, Marie-Louise. 1972a. *Patterns of Creativity Mirrored in Creation Myths.* Zürich: Spring Publications.

———. 1972b. *Problems of the Feminine in Fairy Tales.* New York: Spring Publications.

———. 1997. *Archetypal Patterns in Fairy Tales.* Stud. in Jung. Psych. by Jung. Analysts, 76. Toronto: Inner City.

Von Hendy, Andrew. 2002. *The Modern Construction of Myth.* Bloomington: Indiana UP.

Wagner, Jon, and Jan Lundeen. 1998. *Deep Space and Sacred Time:* Star Trek *in the American Mythos.* Westport, CT: Praeger-Greenwood.

Westbrook, Deeanne. 1996. *Ground Rules: Baseball and Myth.* Urbana: U of Illinois P.

Wheelwright, Phillip. 1966. "Notes on Mythopoeia." In *Myth and Literature: Contemporary Theory and Practice,* ed. John B. Vickery, 59–66. Lincoln: U of Nebraska P.

Wilk, Stephen R. 2000. *Medusa: Solving the Mystery of the Gorgon.* New York: Oxford UP.

Woodford, Susan. 2003. *Images of Myth in Classical Antiquity.* New York: Cambridge UP.

Five

Contexts and Transmissions

To ask how myths arose in human civilization is about like asking for the time when the imagination was born. Or when dreams began. Of course, one can chart when certain types of myths are first recognizable, but mythmaking itself must have begun when the first communities shared their dreams or imaginings, when its members first understood themselves as being related to one another through this or that primary story, and not just the necessities of hunting and gathering.

WHENCE COME MYTHS?

Myths are not all chartering narratives, but most narratives that serve as founding charters for societies have the sort of aura that myths readily assume when recited or read. Such materials are rarely treated lightly: they are approached with the focused attention that indicates that the hearer or reader recognizes in them significance not found in comic strips or romance novels. Their authority probably stems from being told and retold within a particular community; one tells a community's most important myths because such stories reflect its own identity.

Likewise in personal development, one finds myths important that refer to larger than personal issues. Not much help on dealing with a pesky younger brother, perhaps, but for the major life crises—birth, marriage, death—highly revered mythic explanations are all important. Death is a bit less fearsome if one has a sense of another plane of existence beyond it. Marriage only gains in personal significance when one realizes that all partnerships have resonances with mythical patterns in all known cultures.

Because at least the "major myths" have such importance, such far-reaching associations, they are usually passed along within the contexts of religions, politics, civics, philosophy, or literature. And they are often associated with particular ceremonies or rituals: that is obvious in the case of religious stories, but applies as well to the political—just think of the congressional campaigns for election! Or think of how the Disney Corporation's adaptations of tales and myths ritually *shape* the traditional materials they relate (Lawrence and Jewett 2002: chap. 2, is an excellent exposé of the whole Disney enterprise; Lyon 2000 applies sociological perspectives to the Disneyfication of America).

Disney's *The Lion King,* for instance, is framed (as are *Aladdin, Pocahontas,* and *Tarzan*)

> by the romance genre, where sexual fulfillment and partnership are linked with some acceptance of permanent responsibility for the welfare of a community. In effect, these stories revert to the pattern of the classical monomyth [of the hero—WGD]. But like most traditional stories of departure-testing-return, they have nothing to do with the symbolic affirmation of democratic ideals. And they are told with Old Walt's starkly simplistic understanding of good and evil, which can be overcome only by those who exhibit the sweet innocence of stereotypically feminine love. (Lawrence and Jewett 2002: 194)

These authors are not entirely in agreement with the judgment that *The Lion King* falls fully within what has been termed "Disney-fascism," but they do point out some of the tendencies that also appear in *Tarzan:* "Not a single African appears on the screen of this film about Africa" (196). And in *Lion King,* "the symbolism of the fable is inescapable: the most powerful, provided they show a little compassion, shall rule the rest; and the ruled shall be happiest when they festively celebrate their oppressors. [...] The film thereby provides a model for human interaction that sanctifies domination and violence" (196).

Looking at how readers can search for more positive mythic scenarios, Susan Mackey-Kallis argues that "effective mythic stories 'open up' rather than 'close down' interpretive possibilities while often inviting other, possibly competing versions of the myth to exist in the same culture or age" (2001: 234). She finds that *Lion King* "provides an example of a mythic story that turns the circle of life specifically, and creation mythology generally, into a justification for hierarchy. Although Mustafa's and Simba's dominion over the beasts of the jungle and birds of the air offers a benevolent monarchy, it is a monarchy nevertheless" (234). This Disney production "provides an example

Susan Mackey-Kallis finds that Disney's *The Lion King* "provides an example of a mythic story that turns the circle of life specifically, and creation mythology generally, into a justification for hierarchy." Courtesy of Photofest.

of a cultural interpretation of an archetypal myth that may close down, rather than open up, interpretive possibilities for audiences and for the culture at large" (235).

Mackey-Kallis provides a careful critical analysis of the film (92–101), concluding with a section "Problematizing Class, Race, Sexual Orientation, and Gender in *The Lion King*" (101–3): the animals "walk and talk the language of hierarchy and privilege, implying that if it works for the animals, then why not for their human counterpart as well?" (101). Furthermore, "*The Lion King* not only celebrates monarchy; it also champions patriarchy as well," and "Sexual orientation and race are also presented in a stereotypical and often demeaning fashion. [...] Racial stereotyping also occurs in the characters of Rafiki, the shaman/wiseman, and the lead hyena, whose voice is provided by Whoopi Goldberg. Although Rafiki is a powerful figure and a positive force in the life of the pride, he is portrayed with a black African accent and takes the form of a monkey, which may reinforce a particularly demeaning stereotype about African Americans" (102).

Mackey-Kallis concludes her critique: "Thus, although *The Lion King* offers a powerful and moving portrait of 'the circle of life,' the grail quest, the sacred marriage quest, and most significantly, the father quest, it does so in a fashion that raises many troubling questions about privilege and hierarchy, gender roles, racial identity, and sexual orientation" (103). Other films Mackey-Kallis critiques include *E. T.*, the original *Star Wars* trilogy, *Field of Dreams*, *The Piano*, and *Thelma and Louise*, stressing the hero-quest elements in each. Her analysis usefully indicates the need to recognize long-respected mythological elements in contemporary films and as usefully reminds us of the interpreter's responsibility to indicate whether those elements are appropriate to the development of wholesome community values.

Uncommonly influential stories about hero figures such as King Arthur apparently satisfy deeply rooted needs for guiding images of heroism and leadership. Arthur's legend began in the fifth or sixth century and acquired features in various periods, especially the twelfth and fifteenth centuries. It continues to be retold in versions that emphasize one or another story line, even in the popular musical *Camelot* and the 1960 cinematic version starring Richard Burton and Julie Andrews. Terry Gilliam's movie *The Fisher King*, 1991, brought the Arthurian materials to Manhattan's down-and-out streets, complete with the Holy Grail motif that was first introduced to the body of myths in the twelfth century by Chrétien de Troyes in the literary genre he created, the Arthurian romance. Chrétien also introduced the theme of Camelot itself.

Alfred, Lord Tennyson, in the groups of poems comprising *Idylls of the King*, 1859–1885, brought Camelot and the Round Table's knightly members together with the Grail Quest in a manner that suggested how the search for the famous chalice, although worthy in its own right, eventually contributed to the fall of the glory of Camelot insofar as it distracted the knights to the extent where they even killed one another. The fall of Arthur to a blow by his illegitimate son (by his half-sister Morgause) led either to his death or to his semimiraculous escape to the island of Avalon. Focusing on that location, the American novelist Marion Zimmer Bradley developed, in *The Mists of Avalon* (1982), yet additional side plots, involving in this case relationships between the women of the legend who had never been featured previously.

But then across European history (and in most of its languages; see Zink 1996) Arthuriana expanded to fit local interests. Arthur remains for all an image of stalwart leadership (of course, one has to cut some slack for the sexual dalliances developed throughout the legends), a figure who not only set Britain free from the attacking Saxons, Picts, and Scots, but also led to the takeover of Ireland and Iceland. Born of royal blood, he was reared as a commoner, a squire who turned out to have the extraordinary power of extracting a sword from an anvil set in a boulder—proving himself worthy of becoming king.

King Arthur and his knights setting sail to find the
Holy Grail. Stories about hero figures such as King
Arthur apparently satisfy deeply rooted needs for
guiding images of heroism and leadership. © The Art
Archive / Biblioteca Nazionale Turin / Dagli Orti.

The way legendary materials may vary is seen in the fact that in some accounts it is the anvil that he alone is able to extract from the stone, and in others it is the famous magical sword *Excalibur* that was at the core of his
astonishing powers. And the mother of Arthur's illegitimate son Mordred
may be treated as a more distant relative than his sister: it really does not matter because it is Mordred whom Arthur killed for taking over his throne while
he was away Grail questing, but who earlier had wounded Arthur.

Nor does the lack of a tomb or other evidence of Arthur's actual death matter. What ultimately matters was caught perfectly by the fifteenth-century *Le Morte d'Arthur/The Death of Arthur* by the English knight and writer Sir Thomas Mallory: "Yet some men say in many parts of England that King Arthur is not dead, but had gone by the will of Our Lord Jesu into another place; and men say that he shall come again, and he shall win the holy cross. I will not say that it shall be so, but rather I will say, here in this world he changed his life. But many men say that there is written upon his tomb this verse: HIC IACET ARTHURUS, REX QUONDAM REXQUE FUTURUS." The Latin reads in English: "Here lies Arthur, the once and future king," and the reference is to the ancient prophecy that the still-alive Arthur will return to save England in some time of dire straits.

Hope for salvation from The Great Beyond, what could be more attractive? Something of the Christian hope for a future manifestation of the Christ surely influences this shading of the Arthurian materials. They have provided a framework for an astonishingly widespread literary and artistic outpouring since the seventh century. Even Mark Twain rode the bandwagon with his seriocomic play, filmed several times, *A Connecticut Yankee in King Arthur's Court;* Richard Wagner's operas develop the figures of Parsifal and of the love between Tristan and Isolde. And of course, there are the two films, *Monty Python and the Holy Grail* (1975), directed by Terry Gilliam, and *Excalibur* (1981), directed by John Boorman. In Gilliam's *The Fisher King,* street people envision themselves as knights in pursuit of the Holy Grail—mocked by one of the characters as "Jesus's juice glass"—and the ill Fisher King is brought back to health by Robin Williams's jester-fool Parry (a modern Parsifal).

Some stunning images from the Arthurian tradition can be found on the Microsoft Encarta CD Encyclopedia, including the 1875 image, *The Passing of Arthur,* an elaborately staged studio-drama photo by the great English photographer Julia Margaret Cameron. I realized just how important the editors of the encyclopedia thought Arthurian materials are in our culture when I noted *15* media clips available—surely more than for most figures of merely legendary stature (Wilk 2000: 9–10 lists the steps in the development of the Arthurian traditions; Mathis 2002 treats Arthurian influences in Twain, Barthelme, Steinbeck, Chandler, and Gardner).

Looking in another direction—that of speculative (or "science") fiction—I think there are some similarities in the way so many of such novels recycle classical motifs familiar in traditional mythologies. Robert Silverberg's revisions of the Gilgamesh epic, for instance, are rightly given lurid paperback covers that remind one of women's romance or historical novels. But just about every mythological figure one can recall has had several incarnations within the genre of speculative fiction. Although some of these remain fairly well within the framework of the earlier story, the great narrative freedom in the genre to take plot lines in new directions—not bound by usual limitations of time and space—is eagerly exploited.

Often figures from vastly different eras are presented in the same time framework—I just named an example of this, Twain's *Connecticut Yankee*. Here a contemporary male is transported to a medieval setting, leading not only to hilarious misunderstandings but also to the "dark" side of Twain, which was quite negative about the "benefits" of modern technology. There is always a sense of curious attraction to seeing a contemporanization, whether it be a classical figure like Adonis, appearing in a *Star Trek* episode, or the most recent filming of a movie that has been remade repeatedly.

And looking in yet another direction, the realm of fantasy and the "little people" (leprechauns, elves, faeries) are featured in a series of books by Jody Lynn Nye and Robert Lynn Asprin. Nye's titles bear the term *mythology* in them, whereas Aspirin's bear the term *myth* or the acronym *M.Y.T.H.* Nye's *Applied Mythology* (2000) is an omnibus of *Mythology 101* (1999), *Mythology Abroad* (1991), and *Higher Mythology* (1993). The two have collaborated on collections of fantasy short stories. The Elf Master as a college professor seems even more foolish to me than the real variety, but clearly there is an enormous readership for this sort of writing.

Collaboration of another sort can be found in the creation of new volumes of Isaac Asimov's Foundation Trilogy by three leading speculative fiction novelists of the day, Gregory Benford, Greg Bear, and David Brin. And of course, one has to wonder if a *fourth* Indiana Jones movie will be released. Or whether *The Matrix* trilogy will expand through additional episodes, although that project is unique in that the directors had mapped out the contours of the three films before shooting the first.

RETELLING TRANSMISSIONS

As mentioned previously, transmission of myths can sometimes be located in ritual contexts, but actually, every retelling is a transmission that adds or subtracts something from an earlier version. It is shaped for the particular hearers or readers, so much so that it is almost impossible to speak of exact repetition: even if the words of a second telling are precisely the same, the performance (another form of ritualization) will vary as the teller takes into account the interests and situations of the listeners.

Over a long period of time, some myths fascinate creative artists, who use their imagery or elements of their plots in any number of new presentations:

works such as Pierre Brunel, ed., *Companion to Literary Myths, Heroes, and Archetypes*, 1996, or Jean Chevalier and Alain Gheerbrant, *A Dictionary of Symbols*, 1994, are two of the best compilations of artistic revisions. Jane Davidson Reid, *The Oxford Guide to Classical Mythology in the Arts, 1300–1990*, 1993, treats more than 30,000 works of art (including music, dance, drama, literature, sculpture, and painting) with brief descriptions, rather than the discursive texts of Brunel's contributors or Chevalier and Gheerbrant.

Myths are as close to hand in the contemporary world as televised episodes of *Northern Exposure* that adapt classic mythological stories, or the movie *Clash of the Titans*, featuring the adventures of Perseus—or as *Hercules* and *Xena* appear on television, relating to new generations classic mythological stories while inventing new ones. *Star Trek* has taken its adventurers in outer space through frightening experiences weekly, experiences that usually were extrapolated from traditional mythic stories. One episode, "Who Mourns for Adonais?" has the adventurers encounter a Zeus-like hunk who demands their worship; "Darmok" retells important parts of the Gilgamesh myth. More recently, the delightful film *O Brother, Where Art Thou?* (2000) somewhat ramblingly retells themes from Homer's *Odyssey*, set to American bluegrass music.

In the *Star Trek* episode "Who Mourns for Adonais?" the crew encounters a Zeus-like hunk who demands their worship. Courtesy of Photofest.

The film *O Brother, Where Art Thou?* (2000) retells themes from Homer's Odyssey, set to American bluegrass music. Here, Everett Ulysses McGill (George Clooney) and Pete (John Turturro) meet the sirens. Courtesy of Photofest.

An extraordinary book analyzing the alliance between film and America by Paula Marantz Cohen, *Silent Film and the Triumph of the American Myth,* returns to the thematic of "American myth" or "myth of America" that surfaces several times in this book. Cohen suggests that it was well in place by the 1820s (2001: 6). She agrees with the classical judgment by R.W.B. Lewis that America seemed a second chance for the human race, after the first chance had been so disastrously fumbled in the darkening Old World. It was a new Eden, with no traditional fetters holding back progress.

Already silent cinema "consolidated and rendered believable the American myth that had circulated in truncated, scattered, and inchoate form in the nineteenth century. It gave birth to a new kind of consciousness, centered on the dynamic image, that would have far-reaching effects on our future as a nation and on the shape of the world" (19). And this film became so much a part of the story because of its intimacy with the viewer—for whom it could seem the film had been expressly and personally crafted. It was especially effective because it grew out of elements associated with lower-class, specifically American forms of popular entertainment, markedly in contrast to the "artful" elitism of Europe (9).

And it was part of the movement in American culture toward surface aspects, the body, the exterior rather than the interior (French existentialism's moodiness never really caught on in the States, for instance). Film contributed to the developing sense of self that could be nurtured, even in individuals with no education or social standing: "Whereas the literary representation of an internalized self had linked it to the past (since what was buried was invariably what had been constructed or implanted before), the visual dynamism of film placed a new emphasis on the self as immediate and forward-looking, formed in the 'here and now,' a value in motion" (134).

In *Once and Future Myths*, Phil Cousineau gathered from the *New York Times* references to stories, images, icons, and presences that he considers to constitute the American Myth of Progress, certainly a major thematic since the country's founding. Other contemporary references Cousineau identifies include

> myths of love and romance in the movies; the myth of killer sharks; the mythic aspirations of George Lucas' *Star Wars* trilogy; the twisted myth of Frankenstein as mad gene-splicing scientist; the mythmaking machine of political campaigns; the crippling effects of family myths; the legendary outsider status of Marlon Brando and the Olympian influence of Wall Street insiders; the fabled genius of Leonardo da Vinci and the legendary curse on the Boston Red Sox; and a much ballyhooed story of the pre-Christian nomadic discoveries of dinosaur bones in Asia centuries before Christ who inspired the headline, "Monster Myths Born of Fossils?" and [...] "Evolution: Myth or Fact?" (2001: 10–11)

Cousineau identifies even more contemporary references to the American Myth of Progress in conversations with Rollo May: "the Myth of Paradise, the Golden Age, the Lone Pioneer, Rugged Individualism, the Age of Melancholy, the American Dream" (14). In *Myths America Lives By,* Robert Hughes traces the historical importance of the myths of the Chosen Nation, of Nature's Nation, the Christian Nation, the Millennial Nation, and the Innocent Nation, along with submyths of these, such as Manifest Destiny and Capitalism. Some I would add include Youth, Success, Power, Health, Religion, Athletics, the Perfectible Body, Mentoring, Parenting, the City, the Farm, and the Automobile.

We are not accustomed to seeing some of these ideals as "mythological" because we have been so conditioned to think of myth as "old" and expressing only issues found in classic mythological accounts and traditions. Perhaps in analogy to the now-customary term *factoid* for materials consciously devised to support an American presidential action, we might use the term *mythoid*— suggesting that although the materials do not satisfy traditional definitional requirements, they continue to exert strong influences on our daily actions and thoughts.

Cousineau argues that "despite the brash claims of scientific materialists and religious moralists, myth still suffuses and enlivens everyday life" (11). A highly seasoned traveler, Cousineau tracks mythological aspects of life and assumption in a number of places around the world: from the impressive glamour of Paris to the flat American Midwest (the mythologization and then demythologization of Detroit), from Easter Island to Silicon Valley. His assumption is that "myth is Janus-faced: one face turned to the ancient world of brilliantly colorful gods and goddesses, heroes and monsters; the other face turned inward, personal, soulful" (7). Mythical patterns and stories and rituals are Cousineau's sources for exploring how such materials constitute the inner self, the psyche, in our culture.

Somewhat similar opinions are found in *Literature and Film as Modern Mythology*, by William Ferrell. He suggests that today novels and film play the role of ancient rituals, ceremony, and myth, especially as they inculcate certain patterns for living (2000: 18). "Myth, in the form of novels and films, forms a natural opposition to the mechanization and secularization of contemporary society. More important, they allow us to view reality in a form we can understand. In addition to opening our own minds, novels and film open lines of communication through dialogue and discussion because they connect to our spiritual side by their restructuring of the mythological base" (19).

Ferrell's book treats a number of movies in some detail: *The Shawshank Redemption, One Flew over the Cuckoo's Nest, Shane, The Color Purple, The English Patient, The Last Picture Show, Field of Dreams,* and others receive chapter-length discussions. The book is designed for class use, with Midterm Perspective and Research Project appendices as well as a Reading and Film List including many films.

An earlier *Classics and Cinema* volume has been thoroughly revised and edited by Martin M. Winkler as *Classical Myth and Culture in the Cinema.* The volume reflects attention to movies within classics courses beginning in the late 1960s. Several chapters relate recent films to classical prototypes (*Chinatown; The Searchers; The Cook, the Thief, His Wife and Her Lover;* and *Star Wars*). Other chapters treat the ways classical civilization and mythology are represented in "serious" films meant to portray that culture. Erling B. Holtsmark's "The *Katabasis* Theme in Modern Cinema" (2001) is a quite stunning analysis of the classical mythological pattern of a hero's "descent" into a strange or threatening world to accomplish some task or rescue someone. The figure is often accompanied by a Hermes or Charon character, and there are echoes of Joseph Campbell's monomyth of the classical hero here.

The pattern is analyzed in a number of movies such as the western (*The Wild Bunch,* and *Shane*), the thriller (*Absolute Power*), science fiction (*Johnny*

Mnemonic), contemporary drama *(Beyond Rangoon* and *Pure Country*), and especially Vietnam War films *(Platoon, Full Metal Jacket,* and *Apocalypse Now*). (A very full review by Ilja Kuschke 2001 also lists earlier books on classics and cinema.)

The Poet Laureate of the United States and Consultant to the Library of Congress, 1993–95, Rita Dove, published *Mother Love,* a collection of poems exploring the love between Demeter and Persephone (1995). The romance of Amor (Eros) and Psyche is explored by the British writer C. S. Lewis in *Till We Have Faces,* and there is an insightful Jungian commentary on the myth by Erich Neumann (1956).

A number of volumes have explored the role of myth in poetry—although most of them have focused upon Modernist poets. One of the most solid studies, *Ancient Myth in Modern Poetry,* by Lillian Feder (1971), analyzes several aspects of mythology incorporated in the works of W. B. Yeats, Ezra Pound, T. S. Eliot, and W. H. Auden. Two other small volumes, by William Righter and K. K. Ruthven, treat mythological literary criticism and reflect the Modernist issues raised by the group of poets just mentioned: Is myth something timeless? Are there mythological ways of making poetry? What is the future for myth in literature? I discuss other approaches to mythlitcrit in chapter 8 of *Mythography,* including the seasonal analogies with literary tropes developed by Canadian Northrop Frye.

A wonderfully rich compendium, Nina Kossman's *Gods and Mortals: Modern Poems on Classical Myths* (2001), has us all in her debt for this almost-300-page anthology that is wonderfully inclusive of a very wide range of poetries. The segment on Odysseus, for instance, includes poems by Margaret Atwood, W. S. Merwin, Jorge Luis Borges, Gabriel Zaid, Louise Glück, and Wallace Stevens. Her editor's eyes are set on Greek myths reflected in contemporary international poetry in the light of contemporary sensibilities, and within that scope, "the basis for the selection was that a poem be a provocative or unusual treatment of a particular myth" (2001: xvii).

Chapters showing the ongoing influence of stories of the Greek goddesses and gods and heroes are complemented by thematic chapters on "The Way to the Underground," "Lovers," "Transformations," "Trespassers," and places such as Crete and Thebes. Kossman is not interested in mere retellings—which have become about as boring as endlessly repeated Jungian analyses of archetypes. Rather, we have a focus here upon materials that "provide an unexpected twist to a familiar story" (xix).

This editor has a sensitivity to nuance, recognizing that "myth in poetry" is not a matter of routine application of formulas. With respect to H.D., she writes: "The venerable tradition of donning a Greek mask is often used by poets in order to speak of things they would have found difficult to approach otherwise. H.D. is one such poet. She holds the mask so close that at times it is hard to distinguish her own features behind it; the poet becomes the mask" (xix)—this strikes me as a poetic analysis in itself!

Gregory Orr's *Orpheus and Eurydice: A Lyric Sequence* (2001) orchestrated in 32 marvelously fresh poems a new take on the figures in its title. Seldom has a poet found a contemporary way to speak what is touched in the ancient accounts of Orpheus, but Orr's voice is quiet and restrained, yet passionate in the period of the lonely wandering of Orpheus. The love between the two has seldom been voiced so beautifully. (Kossman 2001 collects 35 modern and contemporary poems on Orpheus and Eurydice.)

Theatrical plays have featured various classical figures, such as that of Aphrodite in G. B. Shaw's *Pygmalion* (the basis for the musical *My Fair Lady*) or the ironic naming of a poor neighborhood The Elysian Fields, in Tennessee Williams's *A Street Car Named Desire.* In 2000, theatre patrons viewed an eight-million-dollar production of *Tantalus,* an adaptation by Peter Hall of John Barton's epic ten-play cycle tracing the Trojan War from its beginnings to its aftermath. It was presented in a 13-hour marathon with breaks for lunch and dinner. A drama adapted by Rina Yerushalmi from Aeschylos's trilogy, *The Oresteia,* premiered in 2003—in Hebrew—at the La Guardia, New York, Dance Theatre in 2003. A comprehensive study by Angela Belli, *Ancient Greek Myths and Modern Drama: A Study in Continuity,* 1969, is helpful in exploring this topic.

Classical Mythology in English Literature, edited by Geoffrey Miles, provides introductory materials on classical myths resurfacing in literature (primarily poetry) from England, the United States, Australia, New Zealand, and English-speaking parts of Africa, the Caribbean, and the Pacific. Three depth trenches from Miles's "Classical Traditions in English Literature" course at Victoria University of Wellington, New Zealand, treat Orpheus, Venus and Adonis, and Pygmalion materials as they have resurfaced from antiquity to the late 1990s, in a rich anthology of actual texts. Introductions and notes are wise and helpful.

In order to demonstrate the ongoing presence of mythical materials across several of the arts, I have simply picked a number of artists whose works are explicitly in touch with a mythical figure, choosing only four mythological figures as they have been represented in the last several decades. I have made selective use of Jane Davidson Reid's massive, two-volume *Oxford Guide to Classical Mythology in the Arts, 1300–1990.* I look at Achilles, Adonis, Hermes, and Medea, choosing primarily very-well-known artists listed by Reid and other sources.

Education of Achilles in the art of hunting by centaur Chiron, from *Iliad* by Homer, 1782. © The Art Archive / Musée du Louvre Paris / Dagli Orti (A).

ACHILLES

- H.D. [Hilda Doolittle], poem: "The Education of Achilles" (Part 3, *Helen in Egypt,* 1952–56)
- Yvor Winter, poem: "Chiron," 1932
- Giorgo de Chirico, paintings: many on Achilles
- Karl Shapiro, poem: "Scyros," 1945
- Marguerite Yourcenar, poem: "Achilles, ou, Le mensonge," 1936
- Thom Gunn, poem: "My Sad Captains," 1961
- Louise Glück, poem: "The Triumph of Achilles," 1955

Reproduction of a mural in the Library of Congress Jefferson Building showing Adonis lying on a rock after being killed by a wild boar. Courtesy of the Library of Congress.

- W. H. Auden, poem: "The Shield of Achilles," 1955
- Robert Lowell, poem: "Achilles to the Dying Lykaon," 1973
- Oskar Kokoschka, lithograph: "The Fall of Achilles," 1969
- Robert Duncan, poem: "Achilles's Song," 1969
- Randall Jarrell, poem: "When Achilles Fought and Fell," 1965
- Maurice Béjart, dance: *Notre Faust* (as Achilles figure), 1975
- Daryl Hine, poem: "Patroclus Putting on the Armor of Achilles," 1965
- Constantine P. Cavafy, poem: "The House of Achilles," 1975

Adonis

- Carol Orlock, novel: *The Goddess Letters,* 1987
- Earl Staley, painting cycle: "Venus and Adonis," 1982
- Hugo Weisgall, opera: *The Gardens of Adonis,* 1980
- H.D., poem, "Adonis," 1916
- Alan Hovaness, music: "The Garden of Adonis," 1971
- John William Waterhouse, painting: "The Awakening of Adonis," ca. 1900
- Kenneth Rexroth, poems: "Adonis in Winter," 1944; "Adonis in Summer," 1966
- Daryl Hine, poem: "The Wound," 1957

Hermes (Mercury) killing Argus in order to rescue the nymph Io, ink drawing, 19th century. © The Art Archive / Donizetti Museum Bergamo / Dagli Orti (A).

- Ted Hughes, poem: "Venus and Adonis," 1997
- T. S. Eliot, poem: *The Waste Land,* 1922; part IV
- Constantine Trypanis, poem: "The Elegies of a Glass Adonis," 1972

HERMES

- Tony Harrison, drama: *The Trajectory of Oxyrhynchus,* 1988
- W. H. Auden, poem: "Under Which Lyre," 1946
- Seamus Heaney, poem: "The Stone Verdict," 1987
- Robert Graves, poem: "The Accomplice," 1975
- Leonard Baskin, sculpture: "Hermes," 1973
- Sten Nadolny, novel: *The God of Impertinence,* 1997
- Ronald Bottral, poem: "Hermes," 1984
- Zbigniew Herbert, poem: "Hermes, Dog, and Star," 1977

Medea uses magic to send the guardian
dragons to sleep, enabling her lover Jason
to steal the Golden Fleece. © Mary Evans
Picture Library.

Medea

- Martha Graham, ballet: *Cave of the Heart,* 1946
- Margaret Zimmerman, ballet: *Jason and Medea,* 1982
- Teresa Procaccini, music: *Medea,* 1981
- Kathleen Raine, poem: "Medea," 1980
- Leonard Baskin, drawings and sculptures: "Medea," 1976, 1981, 1982
- Ray Edward Luke, opera: *Medea,* 1979
- John Gardner, novel: *Jason and Medea,* 1973 (he also cowrote a modern version of *Gilgamesh*)
- Pier Paolo Pasolini and Andrei Serban, drama: *Medea,* 1972
- Gavin Bryars and Robert Wilson, opera: *Medea,* 1984
- Theodore Antoniou, opera: *Medea,* 1976

Hollywood and associated film centers are—you better believe—greatly aware of the potential of mythological materials and figures to drive plots. One recent volume, *The Writer's Journey: Mythic Structure for Writers,* by Christopher Vogler (1998), builds upon the mythic pattern of the (mostly male) hero popularized in Joseph Campbell's *The Hero with a Thousand Faces.* Vogler has made a sort of cottage industry out of the situation, both in terms of advising screenwriters and directors for the quick but dirty evaluation process of the hundreds of manuscripts that come before them, and of producing scripts/movies that touch deeply into the core of interest in matters mythological possessed by the viewing public.

Vogler's volume appeared in 1993; it was so well received that a second edition appeared in 1998. Although there is no index to mythic figures, it is not difficult to identify the archetypal figures associated with each genre and then see which movies Vogler analyzes. He suggests, for instance, that Dorothy, in *The Wizard of Oz,* has a whole series of Mentors, such as Glinda, the good witch, who helps her adjust to the new realities of the Land of Oz. The Wounded Hero is studied in movies such as *The Fisher King* or *Lethal Weapon.*

Stuart Voytilla developed *Myth and the Movies: Discovering the Mythic Structure of 50 Unforgettable Films,* with commendatory preface by Vogler, in 1999. "Designed as a companion to Christopher's invaluable work" (3), this volume organizes its studies according to cinematic genres: action adventure, western, horror, thriller, war, drama, romance, romantic comedy, comedy, and science fiction and fantasy. Expanding upon Vogler's "character arc," which represents "phases of growth that a character experiences during the course of the study" (Voytilla 1999: 7, developed on p. 157), Voytilla adds visual icons of the characteristic elements of the hero's journey. Screenwriter Voytilla meticulously charts 51 classic and recent films, even providing the precise timing of when each element of the arc occurs.

Examples include *The Godfather, Citizen Kane, Unforgiven, Dances with Wolves, The Silence of the Lambs, Jaws, Raiders of the Lost Ark, Platoon, Beauty and the Beast, Star Wars,* and many others. Two paragraphs illustrate how he highlights the hero monomyth elements in *Boyz n the Hood,* directed by John Singleton in 1991. The JOURNEY of the Styles family

begins in 1984. South Central L. A. An ORDINARY WORLD of gangs and drugs. Gunshots, police sirens, helicopters fill the night. This violent ORDINARY WORLD extends beyond the bullet-riddled and blood-stained alleys, into Tre's elementary school, where it is reflected in the children's drawings and Tre's interactions with other kids. When Tre is sent home after fighting with another boy (a CALL TO ADVENTURE), his mother, a single parent, realizes that Tre is approaching the THRESH-OLD of manhood. He needs the guidance that his father can provide to overcome his violent ways and prepare for that SPECIAL WORLD.

His father, Furious Styles, welcomes his "prince." And Tre is eager to revisit with his old friends, especially Doughboy and Ricky, half-brothers living across the street. But Tre must also accept his MEN-TOR'S strict rules that will prepare him for his SPECIAL WORLD of manhood. Tre may grimace at the chores (a REFUSAL to change) and prefer to play with his friends, but he accepts this new path of learning responsibility. And his MENTOR assures Tre that he has the advantage of a father who can teach him. His friends don't. Furious warns Tre that he will see the difference at JOURNEY'S end. (1999: 179–80)

A similar approach is to be found in screenwriter Victoria Lynn Schmidt's *45 Master Characters: Mythic Models for Creating Original Characters* (2001). She uses a vaguely Jungian approach to the archetypes, rather than Camp-bell's more restrictive model, and expands that model richly with her second chapter, "Creating Female Heroes and Villains." Here we meet a wide variety of permutations of Aphrodite, Artemis, Athena, Demeter, Hera, Hestia, Isis, and Persephone.

Jean Shinoda Bolen's 1984 *Goddesses in Everywoman: A New Psychology of Women* is somewhat comparable in its scope and organization, although it stresses psychological matters and relates to many other realms besides cinema. Her 1989 *Gods in Everyman: A New Psychology of Men's Lives and Loves* comple-ments Schmidt's chapter on "Creating Male Heroes and Villains." Something of Bolen's approach can be noted in two quotations: "Mythological stories [she refers almost exclusively to those of classical Greece] are like archaeological sites that reveal cultural history to us. Some are like small shards that we piece together and infer from; others are well preserved and detailed, like frescoes once buried in the ashes of Pompeii but now uncovered" (1989: 19).

When we know who the gods are, they can tell us more about who we are. In some of them, we can see reflections of ourselves, as they mirror the grandeur, meaning, and limitations of the archetypes we live out. Other gods tug at our memory, and we recall that we once did know them. In another, we might see the face of the god we rejected, the ar-chetype we feared made us unacceptable. (281)

Each chapter of Schmidt's *45 Master Characters* concludes with lists of tele-vision characters, film characters, and literary and historical figures who exemplify various aspects of the way each archetype has been realized. An example from "Aphrodite in Action": the seductive muse/femme fatale female TV heroes in *Sex and the City, Gilligan's Island, Twin Peaks,* and *All My Children;* the same figure in films: *Basic Instinct, The Postman Always Rings Twice, Cabaret;* and as literary-historical figures, Cleopatra, Delilah, Salome, Marilyn Monroe, Emma Bovary, and Scarlett O'Hara *(Gone with the Wind).*

"Athena in Action" is represented in characters in *Star Trek: Voyager, The X-Files, Murphy Brown,* and *Charmed; G. I. Jane, Working Girl, All About Eve,* and *Moonstruck;* and Kate, in Shakespeare's *The Taming of the Shrew,* Lady Macbeth in *Macbeth,* and Clarice Starling in *The Silence of the Lambs.* With respect to male models, Apollo ("The Businessman and the Traitor") is discerned in *Columbo, Gilligan's Island, Family Ties, Independence Day, Ghostbusters, Pretty Woman,* and *Annie Hall;* Dr. Alan Grant in *Jurassic Park,* Sherlock Holmes, Hercule Poirot in mystery novels by Agatha Christie, and Macon Leary in *The Accidental Tourist* by Anne Tyler.

Writers quickly learn that being familiar with sketches of mythological plots is just the first step in creating fascinating contemporary incarnations of their patterns: I have chuckled several times as students have headed out from seminars to devise contemporary realizations of the classical mythological figures, thinking it would be "a piece of cake." They often returned disgruntled, having tried many approaches that "just don't make it." I certainly do not suggest that persons who use the books just discussed will find an easy road to drama or movie writing—or any other sort of artistic expression, for that matter. But tracking the *sorts* of realizations of these "archetypal" or mythical patterns can be useful for becoming sensitized to the wide range of their appearances in all the arts.

This approach helps us understand something of the Protean nature of myth: apparently it can appear in an almost unimaginable number of incarnations, not only in traditional "classical" materials, but also in the soaps, commercials, children's rhymes, and even advertisements. Hence it is important not just to consider elevated and traditionally respected ancient Norse or Egyptian or Greek mythical figures as "mythic," but also to recognize large mythically formulated and transmitted themes, often ideologically reinforced, from a country's quite recent past.

The Myth of America has already appeared in this book, especially with respect to the myth of the Frontier or the American West, an adaptation of earlier myths about new beginnings in a new land that were primarily launched in the expansion of consciousness in the European Renaissance. The healing power of the new land is part of their appeal: the sickly teen-aged Theodore Roosevelt went west to develop himself, physically as well as psychologically.

Other mythic figures such as Daniel Boone, Kit Carson, Custer, and Buffalo Bill represented The American Task of civilizing raw nature and educating an untutored population.

Rollo May points out some dark parts of the American mythos (1991: chap. 6): the loneliness of frontier life (not just American—think of the Beatles' song "All the lonely people—Where do they all come from?"), probably a corollary to contemporary rootlessness. And that, of course, stems from the nation's dismissing the well-established and long-hoary traditions (religious, educational, political, and even with respect to food) and the American habit of constantly moving into new parts of the land. The Myth of the New was nurtured in the early frontier expansion experiences and matured in the more recent adoration of new technological innovations that can lead to a childish and unwarranted anticipation of a New Age.

This is not the *communal* sacred past, but the potential for *changing* into something not yet experienced: a myth of the shape shifter Proteus (May

Mythic figures such as Daniel Boone, Kit Carson, and Buffalo Bill represented the American task of civilizing raw nature and educating an untutored population. Pictured here is Daniel Boone protecting his family. Courtesy of the Library of Congress.

Kit Carson. Courtesy of the Library of Congress.

1991: 104) in its latest guise. It is an *individualistic* pattern, shorn of a meaningful past, and not yet into the fully new age that our culture constantly anticipates because *its* past has been just such an era. But from the 1970s onward it has been clear that this verges on being a culture of narcissistic self-adoration. In such a culture, the self-focused individual (often lacking any social maturity that is aware of the important dimensions of communal living together amicably and creatively) ends up feeling alone, isolated, and going she or he knows not where—because no one around her or him has any clue as to how collective values have to be acquired by study of past ideas and ideals long debated and reaffirmed.

Another aspect of identifying mythic traces in contemporary culture can be derived from looking carefully at our male and female heroes and our leaders as well as media celebrities. This includes Madonna and John Wayne, of course, but even the power of a figure like Elvis Presley continues across a culture that "ought to have" moved beyond his death in 1977. Yet Erika Doss has shown

The scout Buffalo Bill. Courtesy of the Library of Congress.

that there is a substantial cult around Elvis, a sort of pop religion that includes construction of elaborate home altars featuring representations treated as objects of veneration (2002: 69). There is a yearly Elvis Week at his Memphis home, complete with the astonishingly ritualized Candlelight Vigil, with offerings left at the tomb, and many other features easily identified in our culture as "religious." Followers speak of "deeply spiritual relationship[s] with Elvis" and consider him "a mediator, an intercessor, between [themselves] and other fans and God" (63). One worshipper says "He is like a bridge between us and God" (63); she finds her "personal relationship with Elvis—as well as the works of art she makes and the rituals she performs that express that relationship—[...] the most meaningful cultural and social practice in her life" (64).

Elvis Presley performing onstage, 1956. Erika Doss has shown that there is a substantial cult around Elvis, a sort of pop religion that includes construction of elaborate home altars featuring representations treated as objects of veneration. Courtesy of the Library of Congress.

The status of Presley as a mythic/religious figure is quite impressive:

in the years since his death, a veritable Elvis religion has emerged, replete with prophets (Elvis impersonators), sacred texts (Elvis records), disciples (Elvis fans), relics (the scarves, Cadillacs, and diamond rings that Elvis lavished on fans and friends), pilgrimages (to Tupelo, where Elvis was born, and Graceland), shrines (his grave site), churches (such as the Twenty-Four-Hour Church of Elvis in Portland, Oregon), and all the appearances of a resurrection (with reported Elvis sightings at, among other places, a Burger King in Kalamazoo, Michigan). Ritual activities that occur during Elvis Week are cited as further evidence of Elvis's cult status. (65)

As I was writing this, I was given a slickly printed brochure for EW.03, that is, Elvis Week, August 9–17, 2003. Every single day featured several commemorations for the thirty-fifth anniversary of Presley's 1968 television special, *Elvis,* and the thirtieth anniversary of his 1973 special, *Elvis: Aloha from Hawaii, via Satellite.* Graceland Events included brunch and gospel music. City-wide Events included pilgrimages to Tupelo, Mississippi, the birthplace, and an Annual Elvis World Lunch, as well as many concerts and meetings of adoring fan clubs.

Although it may seem a bit far-fetched to look at the pop culture figure of Elvis as "religious"—although from within the academic profession of religious studies, few would question the accuracy of such an analysis—another pop culture icon, Madonna, has likewise been regarded critically by Georges-Claude Guilbert, who teaches American literature, gender studies, and popular culture, in *Madonna as Postmodern Myth.* Guilbert is not interested in seeing how Madonna reincarnates or reflects an earlier mythical figure—although he does note her fascination with figures such as Eva Perón, Marlene Dietrich, Liza Minelli, and even Rita Hayworth. He is interested in the manner in which Madonna Louise Veronica Ciccone has *staged and managed* her series of identities and appearances.

In this sense, of course, she self-consciously "mythicizes" her persona in a very postmodern manner: "In the era of postmodernist art, myths are self-created, even more rapidly than modern myth, and they come equipped with ironic distance. Madonna devised various means to construct her own myth; she borrowed from different ethnic groups, for example, or pushed sex, the universal weapon" (Guilbert 2002: 35–36).

"Madonna did create herself and propelled herself to the top. Madonna's everywhere. [. . . S]he is undeniably part of our culture. Wherever you look, you will find Madonna or a Madonna echo" (37). Guilbert notes further: "In the American, British, Australian, and French press [. . .], it is generally taken for granted that Madonna is the most famous female in the world" (2). Her picture book *Sex* (1992) was one of the most spectacularly successful public events ever; a million copies were printed and sold in their poorly assembled metal boxes, the whole shrink-wrapped in plastic (Guilbert 2002: 54).

Ahead of the Elvis game, Madonna effectively organized her own cult, especially among gay people (62), and "More than any other star in history, Madonna approaches that total omnipresence which characterizes the divine

Madonna in concert at the Meadowlands. According to
Georges-Claude Guilbert, "Madonna devised various
means to construct her own myth." © Nancy Richmond
/ The Image Works.

in the majority of widespread religions. [...] Like a sort of Big Sister, she in-
vades our screens, our hi-fi equipment, our magazines, and our books. She is
a racially postmodern phenomenon which feeds upon itself, self-reproducing.
More than ten thousand Internet sites speak of her, more than a hundred are
entirely devoted to her. [...] Today, America knows more about Madonna
than about any passage of the Bible" (89).

Guilbert sees Madonna as both reflecting and modeling portions of the
American Dream: not so much the "anybody can make good" aspect, but
rather "anybody can become a superstar" (Guilbert 2002: 149, but my

phrases). Her recent album, *American Life,* released by Warner Bros. April 22, 2003, is most appropriately titled. Discussing that album with NBC's Matt Lauer on MSN, April 28, 2003 (Dateline NBC: "Madonna: An American Life"), Madonna actually stated "I am the epitome of the American dream. I came from nothing. You know I did something incredible with my life. And I realized a lot of dreams." Lauer comments: "She certainly has. *American Life* is her sixteenth album. She's had twelve number one hits and is worth a reported $300 million."

To stretch the study of myth in the customary sense to Madonna's life and career may seem a wide stretch from familiar approaches to "myth," but it also leads us to understand that contemporary mythic expression will doubtlessly be quite different in our postmodernist age. This is precisely a time when postmodernist writers "do not hesitate to borrow elements from genres traditionally seen as minor. [...] "Postmodernism seeks to blur if not totally dissolve the traditional oppositions and boundaries between the aesthetic and the commercial, between art and the market, and between high and low culture" (Guilbert 2002: 23). Hence we ought to expect that mythic materials today need to be approached afresh with methods that are only being worked out in cultural studies and popular culture studies. Michael Wetzl, professor of German Studies at the University of Bonn, offers an advanced study of the ways Madonna managed her representations in the media.

Neil Harris sets an interesting model in surveying the origins of the modern figure of Superman (Wilk 2000: 10–13 reaches a bit further back in the stream of influences on the figure). Initially two high school friends wrote and illustrated a short story, "Reign of the Superman," in 1932. After initial magazine publication, the two young men decided to start a comic strip with the theme of a hero with telescopic vision and enormous mental abilities. The writer, Jerry Siegel, had a vision one summer night of "a dual-identity human avenger, simultaneously a mild-mannered newspaper reporter and a cape-powered, tights-wearing, extraterrestrial being to be known simply as Superman" (Harris 1985: 243).

Four years later the pair met Harry Donenfeld, the founder of one of the first comic books (not just collections of strips previously published in newspapers). *Action Comics* then paid $150 and some additional fees for all rights to the short story, and in June 1938 issue number one appeared, bearing on its cover the now-familiar action figure. Success was astonishingly rapid, and within a year Superman had his own comic book—selling over a million copies an issue—and then of course, movies, television, movie cartoons. By 1941 the newspaper comic strips alone sold almost 25 million; "By 1943 the

A German refugee child, a devotee of Superman (1942). Courtesy of the Library of Congress.

sales of comic books had reached 18 million copies a month, more than the combined sales of *Life, Reader's Digest,* and the *Saturday Evening Post*" (244).

Writer Siegel was forthright in admitting the influence of mythical figures such as Samson and Herakles. A *New Republic* writer (Brown 1940, cited in Harris 245) considered Superman "handsome as Apollo, strong as Hercules, chivalrous as Launcelot, swift as Hermes...A Hero God...a protective deity," fulfilling desires for some strong religious experiences. The publishers didn't fail to exploit the classical references: "Like Moses, like Odysseus, like every abandoned baby of heroic myth, he was cast afloat by his parents only to survive and become a savior himself" (246).

Harris cites other observers troubled by the apparent connection of Superman and his many imitators with "the growing totalitarianism of their day and the gospel of action through violence" (247; on the latter, see especially Jewett and Lawrence 2003). In *Love and Death: A Study in Censorship*, critic Gerson Legman considers the formula merely a form of law by lynching:

" 'Superman' takes the crime for granted, and then spends thirty pages violently avenging it" (cited in Harris 1985: 247). From such a perspective, Superman could be seen as analogous with what the Ku Klux Klan advocated.

When I turned to the now-mythical figure of Harry Potter, I wondered if critics would find as much to take to task, and indeed I did find materials about his "moral development." However, it was mostly positive. The *Wisdom of Harry Potter* by Edmund Kern proposes that Harry's wisdom is that of Stoic philosophy, perhaps somewhat influenced by the neo-Stoic classic *The Book of Constancy* by Justus Lipsius (sixteenth century). The Potter books "might just comprise the most visible contribution to Stoicism's re-emergence as a viable, practical philosophy offering comfort and guidance in these uncertain times" (cited by Cohen 2003).

And Lana A. Whited and M. Katherine Grimes look at Harry's stories through the perspectives of Lawrence Kohlberg's influential moral-development model. Whew! Whereas Draco Malfoy, a schoolmate of Harry's who is motivated by the fact that "my daddy's an important person, so I can get away with this," ranks a mere Level 1/pure self-interest grade, by the *Chamber of Secrets,* Harry is at Level 5/prior rights and social contract, if not Level 6/universal ethical principles (complicated because 6 is not exemplified by Kohlberg, although others name in this context Gandhi, Mother Teresa, and Martin Luther King, Jr.)

It may be a bit odd to find Harry grouped with such figures, but by now the seriousness of the analogies has been well established in academic conferences and publications such as Whited (2002), Anatol (2003), Heilman (2003), and Kern (2003). Heilman's collection includes a number of morally important issues: technocultural issues and becoming human; content in children's literature; gender and identity studies; and civic and leadership policies. Certainly conservative Christians have resisted the Rowling series, in publications attacking its witchcraft as anti-Christian; they have attempted to ban the books from school libraries and classrooms. The director of the American Library Association's Office of Intellectual Freedom noted that the Potter books have been the No. 1 target of censors since 1999.

Clearly the development of the hero, the heroic quest, and the father/parental quest are central to such a figure as Harry. Rowling seems well aware of many classic accounts, and her novels are admired very much in the British tradition of boarding school coming-of-age accounts. They are admired as well by literally millions of people around the world, let it be said: her publisher Scholastic's Web site noted on July 21, 2003, that over 170 million Potter books had been sold; the books had been translated into 55 languages and distributed in over 200 countries. *Harry Potter and the Order of the Phoenix,*

The development of the hero, the heroic quest, and the father/parental quest are central to such a figure as Harry Potter. Courtesy of Photofest.

released in that summer, has combined first and second print runs of 8.5 million copies, "a figure unprecedented for any book."

Rowling has won impressive awards and was named an Officer of the British Empire. In 2000, she was ranked at the top of Great Britain's wealthiest women. *Forbes* magazine estimates that she earned $36 million in 2000 alone (Whited 2002: 2). This is pretty astonishing for a "children's literature" author and indicates the world is not unable to recognize larger-than-life mythic figures being created—in this case by just one author and the literary tradition out of which she writes.

An Internet search for "Harry Potter" in April 2004 brought 5,380,000 listings—it would take months to read them all. Harry has his own on-line Lexicon, *The Harry Potter Lexicon,* and the hpana.com Automatic News Aggregator, which is updated every 30 minutes to announce new discussions of Pottersville from sources around the world. In a season marked by *Terminator 3* and the second and third *Matrix* trilogy releases, featuring as they do the massing of enormous forces of technological powers of destruction, it is somehow reassuring that an interest in magic and witchcraft practiced responsibly and humanely can be so popular.

FUNCTIONS OF MYTHS

Although the formal school of anthropological analysis known as socio-functionalism peaked mid-twentieth century, some form of its "practical" attitude toward myth in society has had strong influences ever since. And that seems natural because the primary question to myths is: What does it DO? (The approach is discussed at greater length in my *Mythography* 2000: 128–37; Joseph Campbell's four functions—mystical/metaphysical, cosmological, sociological, psychological—are also discussed, 1968: 140–47.)

Émile Durkheim (1858–1917) is usually considered the founder of the view that myths express the highest aspirations of the social order, that they are attributed to "deities," and that they provide the social energies to keep members of the society bound willingly to one another in community. In surveying political, social, religious, ritual, and psychological approaches to *Star Trek*, Chris Gregory suggests that the television series is held together by precisely such a projected mythological system:

> It has evolved into an interconnected "web" of stories in a way that parallels the development of traditional sagas, odysseys, or mythic story cycles. Its characters tend to be representative figures of various aspects of the human condition, and they are invariably presented with "heroic" challenges that emphasize their symbolic roles. Like many traditional mythological systems, it has created its own "world," in which "fantastical" events such as physical transformations or "time shifts" may frequently occur. *Star Trek* stories, like mythical tales, are presented within the form of a highly conventionalized dramatic structure, into which is characteristically built an overriding moral imperative. (2000: 9)

What is striking is that Gregory so neatly addresses a fictional society oriented not around a mythos of the past—as were Western movies—but a mythos of the future! He notes that "the biggest Hollywood blockbusters of the last 20 years have almost all been SciFi movies, from *Star Wars* (1977) to *E.T.* (1982) to *Jurassic Park* (1992) and *Independence Day* (1996); he mentions likewise the television series *The X-Files, Dark Skies, Sliders,* and *Babylon 5.*

Also addressing the ways myths function in culture, Barbara Whitmer, focusing upon representations of social violence in contemporary societies, notes how a myth can be "a pattern of beliefs that articulates, often symbolically, the prevalent attitudes in a culture"; it "is a collection of beliefs; a cultural mindset; the framework that expresses a pattern of beliefs, attitudes, behaviors, discourses, and practices in a society." Hence

The violence mythos includes the war hero myth, the victimizer/victim dynamic of exploitation, the mind/body dualism, the cowboy myth, the myth of competitive individualism, the theory of innate violence, the myth of male aggression, the military-industrial complex, technological determinism (especially destructive technology), the subordination of women, the myth of the superiority of rationality over emotion and creativity, and the myth of the elite human species. (1997: 1)

I find it striking that these two analyses of mythological function in the contemporary world could be applied readily to the mythologies of many earlier cultures. And I like the way John Girling explains just how it is that such master myths can carry so many functions: he looks at the way myths function at an *affective* level, not just at a rational level: "Myths are emotionally charged beliefs, expressing the way people experience formative periods in their history [as in his study, "the crises of modernity"—WGD] whether economic (the ascendancy of capitalism), or political (the conjunction of nationalism and power), or cultural (changing conceptions of society)" (1993: x).

Girling represents myths not as merely conservative, but as "authentic responses to social change" (x) and "when new crises appear, new myths appear" (3). Nor do myths merely trap one in passivity toward what has happened: "Myths are an emotional response to structural conditions; but those who are motivated by myths can change conditions. Solidarity, awe, destiny are abstract terms. But in the form of myths they tell a story to be *enacted:* a mission, a confrontation, a prediction" (4).

Just how the enactments function is clarified later in Girling's analysis:

> The inspirational character of myths is evident in turbulent times. It is this that enables believers to adapt to, and even to shape, the "reality" of powerful, impersonal forces at work in society, in these ways: (1) they are able to *cope* with the existential condition of suffering, which becomes patently more acute in periods of crisis, and thus, by extension, with the problem of evil in the world; (2) they feel they *belong* to a community ("we" against "they"), providing shelter against present dangers—a community in which their place is recognized; (3) they are inspired by myth to create a *good* community, that is, to establish appropriate norms of conduct and the motivation for action to achieve them. Myths, in other words, provide both meaning and identity; myths are an emotional fulfillment of personality. (170)

In this sense, writes Robert Hughes, "a myth is a story that speaks of meaning and purpose, and for that reason it speaks truth to those who take it seriously.

[. . . O]ur national myths are the means by which we affirm the meaning of the United States" (2003: 2).

Although the emphasis here has been on myths as social-change agents—precisely because their conservative aspects are so frequently overstated—it is, of course, also extremely important to reexamine founding events expressed in such important arenas as Girling studies in the United States, Germany, and Great Britain. Burton Mack refers to the importance of the Bible in early American history, for instance, where it was often treated as a charter for the nation (1995: 2). Mack points out that "Social formation and mythmaking are group activities that go together, each stimulating the other in a kind of dynamic feedback system. Both speed up when new groups form in times of social disintegration and cultural change" (11).

What happens is less the fabricating of national stories from scratch as *re-shaping* of important religious or political materials to meet functional needs that arise at a later date than that of the original source materials. The situation is well described by Bernard Batto (1992), who demonstrates repeatedly that in spite of the recent theological claims that Judaism and Christianity are nonmythical because they are based upon strictly historical events, versions of these in the Hebrew Bible underwent constant revisions throughout its periods of formation over several hundred years. This is the normal way that adaptations and change of early ideological, political, or religious fundamentals for use in a later period occur.

In the context of millennia of theological-mythological overlay, Mack has to develop the technique of (neutral) *redescription* of the earlier materials, just to begin to be able to view it in adequate historical perspective. This task is a primary requisite of The Jesus Seminar of Santa Rosa, California, founded by Robert W. Funk, in its ambitious attempt to treat primitive Christian materials from a strictly historical, rather than a believing-theological, approach.

Another way of regarding social function concerns attention to the people for whom particular mythic materials were designed: another volume in this Greenwood series discusses how wonder/fairy tales were originally the creation of women resisting the social pressures of male ideals forced upon them; they were "refined discourse as a means through which women imagined their lives might be improved"—a situation that changed after 1700 in Europe to enforce the strictly-male-patriarchal code of *civilité* (proper behavior). Only after the 1730s when chapbooks of the tales were adapted for children and widely distributed did they become seen as didactic, addressing social obligations, inspiring good behavior in schools, and modeling how upper-class children should behave (Zipes 1994: 23–33).

And finally, we may approach the *function* of myths in terms of the ways their primary *use* has been identified in various periods of study. Russell T. McCutcheon lists seven such ways, which are merely listed here:

1. Prescientific explanations of natural phenomena
2. Tales of heroes
3. Expression of mythopoeic mentality
4. Social dreaming (Freud's treatment of dreams as disguised expressions of antisocial but completely natural desires and wishes)
5. Expressions of the collective unconscious
6. Structuralism (myths as structured public evidence of the order of human cognition itself; the message of a myth results from how its elements relate to each other as part of a coherent structure)
7. Myths as truth (especially as "veiled, deep truths," which cannot be simply expressed because they are so extraordinary) (2000: 193–98)

Obviously these "uses" or "functions" are not limited—as functionalism was originally (and called, properly, sociofunctionalism)—to *social* matters such as determining succession of leadership, organizing work groups, or forming the basis for traffic laws. They range from cosmological functions— explaining natural phenomena—to psychological functions—"expressions of the collective unconscious"—but they refer more broadly and pervasively to the psychologizing of much popular treatments of myth, as in the writings of Jean Shinoda Bolen or in Joseph Campbell's insistence upon the *individual's* appropriation of mythic perspectives.

Their use as models of possible behavior and character also has psychological overtones, but then so did Plato's desire to control the myths students in his model society would be exposed to, which means that pedagogical aspects are involved. The element of "social dreaming" or utopian thought is certainly related to the last item, "myth as truth," or a variant of that, "mythopoeic mentality," a term now used freely in the men's movement to indicate receptivity to revising interpretations of myths that have reinforced patriarchal social values.

Mythopoeic is a term that occurs frequently in literary studies, where it often refers to the sort of transformations of mythological materials and motifs that we have explored earlier in this chapter. It is as well a matter of looking toward creativity of expression as one polishes one's literary productions, as caught nicely by Julian Barnes, author of a fabulously mythopoetic account of versions of Noah's Flood: "For the point is this: not that the myth refers us back to some original event which has been fancifully transcribed as it passed through the collective memory; but that it refers us forward to something that will happen, that must happen. Myth will become reality, however skeptical we might be" (1990: 181).

CONTEMPORARY USES OF MYTHS AND THE CONCEPT OF MYTHOS

Already in 1946, according to the *Oxford English Dictionary,* George Orwell referred to "the Russian mythos." This term has had various associations ever since: it has referred to a particular organization of thought concerned with violence in the American West (*OED;* about 1974) or to "the complex of beliefs and attitudes, or patterns of meaning, that are characteristic of a given group, society, or culture" (*Wordsmyth: The Educational Dictionary-Thesarus,* online).

The Oxford Dictionary of Foreign Words and Phrases agrees with the mid-twentieth-century use of the term for "a traditional or recurrent narrative theme or pattern; a standard plot in literature," but in a usage note suggests that "*Mythos* and its Latin derivative *mythus,* [are] both now used solely in literary contexts." This would certainly fit literary critic Northrop Frye's position, "myth always means, first and primarily, *mythos,* story, plot, narrative" (1990: 3), or within a Shakespearean play, "the *mythos,* the total story being told" (8).

But while compiling references for several years now, I have found mythos used frequently in a much more generalized sense *outside* purely literary contexts, so that the entry in *Webster's Unabridged Dictionary* (3rd ed., online), "pattern of meaning and valuation expressive of the basic truths and enduring apprehensions of a people's historic experience characteristically expressed through a medium of high symbolism (as poetry art, or drama)," seems more accurate. In a similar vein, the *American Heritage Dictionary* (3rd ed.) suggests: "the pattern of basic values and attitudes of a people, characteristically transmitted through myths and the arts," and *Encarta World English Dictionary* has "**set of attitudes,** the interrelated set of beliefs, attitudes, and values held by a society or cultural group."

In *Deep Space and Sacred Time:* Star Trek *in the American Mythos,* Wagner and Lundeen conceive of mythos as "a people's deep stories—the narratives that structure their world view and that give form and meaning to the disconnected data of everyday life" (1998: 3). They suggest further that *The Cosby Show* helped "to construct an implicit mythos about race and social mobility in America during the 1980s (just as *Amos 'n' Andy* expressed an entirely different mythology of race for radio audiences forty years earlier)" (4).

Reference here to "worldview" strikes me as important—but refers to a concept that can be stretched infinitely until it defines too much to be useful.

Wagner and Lundeen are correct in suggesting that "The whole mythos of a culture cannot be found in any one place, but there is scarcely anywhere that it is not manifested in some way." We are talking about inclusive symbols such as The American West or The Frontier or Our Puritan Past that have historical referents as well as mythological elaborations, just what Rushing and Frentz refer to as "a cultural myth," that is to say, not a falsehood or stereotype (as in "it's just a myth that ___"), but as representing "a narrative whole which the critic reconstructs from singular texts often separated in time and genre but tied together by a single, unifying theme" (1991, 1993: 399).

Such an underlying theme can be identified in "the British imperial *mythos*" (Bradshaw 1991: 169); it can also have temporal references, as in several dissertation titles such as Allen-Richard Emerson, "Paradigms of Uncertainty: A Postmodernist Mythos (Thomas Pynchon, Virginia Woolf)" and Grace Stewart, *A New "Mythos": The Novel of the Artist as Heroine, 1877–1977*.

Something of this sense is found in cinema as well: Lawrence and Jewett point out how the movie *Death Wish* transformed the original novel from its pacific message to "a mythic prism throwing a golden aura onto the path of violence" (2002: 108). One can think of the *Star Wars* mythos, or that of the *Matrix* trilogy: in each case the mythos was created at a specific time, which Richard Slotkin has called "national mythology." Lawrence and Jewett note that Slotkin "shows how the historical experience of a nation provides metaphors and stories that assume mythic proportions in literature and art, so that the resulting myth exercises a reciprocal pressure on succeeding generations" (2002: 233; Hughes [2003] gives historical depth to fundamental national myths central to the American worldview).

I have also found that the contemporary use of mythos provides a basis for typifying a person or group: "the anti-gay mythos of the American Boy Scouts"; "the Pentagon's mythos of military supremacy"; "the mythos of the Masonic Orders"; even "the Christian mythos of suffering." In this context I am quite impressed by Jorge Huerta's *Chicano Drama: Performance, Society, and Myth*. The initial definition of mythos (Sp. *mitos*) is instructive: "A mythos, by definition means that a group of people, a culture, depends on myths which help them to explain the inexplicable, what some would call the supernatural. A mythos also gives a people a place in a cosmos, describing and recalling their ancestors, giving them a 'from the beginning,' as it were. For the believers these myths are no longer myths but doctrine. To the outside, however, that doctrine is just another myth" (2000: 15).

The dramatists Huerta studies have complex backgrounds in Mexico— and especially in the pre-Mexican Aztec and other Native American myth traditions. He sees them as attempting to develop and portray "an emerging

Chicano mythos" (19). "The problem," he writes, "when inventing a mythos, is that you are compressing time. Myths are created through generations of story-telling and cultural logic which gives those stories mythic significance, not through plays or murals on barrio walls. And yet, that is what the Chicana and Chicano writers and artists, composers, and poets began to do in the 1960s: create or re-create a Chicano mythos based on Mexican and pre-Columbian heroes and myths" (19).

Huerta recognizes that: "These theatre artists are reaching an ever-widening audience with their tales of myth, mystery, redemption, and damnation as they continue to express a mythos that gives their audiences an identity in a country [the United States] that tries to erase that identity" (192).

Obviously there are correlations of ideology and mythos here. What I found fascinating was the description of the enhancement of self-conscious political agency by developing mythological imagery, symbolism, and story. Reflecting back upon some of the movements within second-wave feminism in the years after the sixties, I recall similar attempts to craft "a feminist mythos," one that would honor long-ignored feminine symbols and images and perhaps just possibly overturn the patriarchal, masculine propensity toward violence as the main way of sustaining a society (see the previous discussion of Whitmer 1997).

Mythologies are tarred with the dark brush of conservatism along with other chartering materials. But the self-conscious attempt to change a social situation that Huerta's dramatists portray should remind us that myths are always being revisioned, allegorized, and set into different contexts. Marina Warner's observations are instructive and, I think, hopeful:

> A myth is a kind of story told in public, which people tell one another; [myths] wear an air of ancient wisdom, but that is part of their seductive charm. [...] Myths offer a lens which can be used to see human identity in its social and cultural context—they can lock us up in stock reactions, bigotry and fear, but they're not immutable, and by unpacking them, these stories can lead to others. Myths convey values and expectations which are always evolving, in the process of being formed, but—and this is fortunate—never set so hard they cannot be changed again, and newly told stories can be more helpful than repeating old ones. (1994: 19)

I conclude by mentioning another shading of the term *mythos:* that of identifying the "geographical genius" of a place. Information about a multimedia exhibition, *The Edge of Enchantment,* at the Heye Center in New York in December 2002, refers to the curator and photographer capturing for the exhibit the "personality" of small contemporary Native communities near Oaxaca, Mexico: "The exhibition centers on the *encantos,* or enchantments, of each individual community. As physical spaces of mystery and power that lead to an unknown world, these enchanted places are integrally woven into the story of each hamlet, village, or town, and inform the identity, beliefs, and dreams of each community" (González 2003: 1, 3).

I suppose one might say that the *genius* (Latin for nurturing spirit) of a place *leads to* a mythos, and formally that may be the correct developmental derivation. But I think anyone who has been truly awed by this sort of local spirit (for me it was especially at Delphi in Greece, the ancient underground tombs in Egypt, and repeatedly at the rims of the Grand Canyon) senses that, yes, these encantos are real and have mythic reality that the television soaps will never touch.

WORKS CITED

Anatol, Giselle Liza, ed. 2003. *Reading Harry Potter: Critical Essays.* Westport, CT: Praeger-Greenwood.

Asprin, Robert Lynn. 2002a. *Hit or Myth.* New York: Ace-Penguin Putnam.

———. 2002b. *Myth-Ing Persons.* New York: Ace-Penguin Putnam.

———. 2002c. *M.Y.T.H. Inc. Link.* New York: Ace-Penguin Putnam.

Barnes, Julian. 1990. *A History of the World in Ten and a Half Chapters.* New York: Random House.

Batto, Bernard F. 1992. *Slaying the Dragon: Mythmaking in the Biblical Tradition.* Louisville, KY: Westminster/John Knox.

Belli, Angela. 1969. *Ancient Greek Myths and Modern Drama: A Study in Continuity.* New York: New York UP.

Bolen, Jean Shinoda. 1984. *Goddesses in Everywoman: A New Psychology of Women.* San Francisco: Harper and Row.

———. 1989. *Gods in Everyman: A New Psychology of Men's Lives and Loves.* San Francisco: Harper and Row.

Bradley, Marion Zimmer. 1982. *The Mists of Avalon.* New York: Del Rey-Ballantine.

Bradshaw, Graham. 1991. "Mythos, Ethos, and the Heart of Conrad's Darkness." *English Studies: A Journal of English Language and Literature* 72 (2): 160–72.

Brunel, Pierre, ed. 1996. *Companion to Literary Myths, Heroes, and Archetypes.* Trans. Wendy Allatson, Judith Hayward, and Trista Selous. New York: Routledge.

Campbell, Joseph. 1968. *The Hero with a Thousand Faces.* 2nd ed. Bollingen ser. 17. Princeton, NJ: Princeton UP.

Chevalier, Jean, and Alain Gheerbrant. 1994. *A Dictionary of Symbols.* Trans. John Buchanan-Brown. Cambridge, MA: Blackwell.

Cohen, Patricia. 2003. "The Phenomenology of Harry, or the Critique of Pure Potter." *New York Times,* 19 July, on-line version.

Cohen, Paula Marantz. 2001. *Silent Film and the Triumph of the American Myth.* New York: Oxford UP.

Cousineau, Phil. 2001. *Once and Future Myths: The Power of Ancient Stories in Modern Times.* Berkeley, CA: Conari.

Doss, Erika. 2002. "Believing in Elvis: Popular Piety in Material Culture." In *Practicing Religion in the Age of the Media: Explorations in Media, Religion, and Culture,* ed. Stewart M. Hoover and Lynn Schofield Clark, 63–86. New York: Columbia UP.

Doty, William G. 2000. *Mythography: The Study of Myths and Rituals.* Revised 2nd ed. Tuscaloosa: U of Alabama P.

Dove, Rita. 1995. *Mother Love: Poems.* New York: Norton.

Emerson, Allen-Richard. 1996. "Paradigms of Uncertainty: A Postmodernist Mythos (Thomas Pynchon, Virginia Woolf)." Ph.D. diss., U of Wisconsin–Madison.

Feder, Lillian. 1971. *Ancient Myth in Modern Poetry.* Princeton, NJ: Princeton UP.

Ferrell, William K. 2000. *Literature and Film as Modern Mythology.* Westport, CT: Praeger-Greenwood.

Frye, Northrop. 1990. *Myth and Metaphor: Selected Essays, 1974–1988.* Ed. Robert D. Denham. Charlottesville: UP of Virginia.

Girling, John. 1993. *Myths and Politics in Western Societies: Evaluating the Crisis of Modernity in the United States, Germany, and Great Britain.* New Brunswick, NJ: Transaction.

González, Alicia María. 2003. Introduction to feature on The Edge of Enchantment: Sovereignty and Ceremony in Hualulco, México exhibit at the Museum of the American Indian. *American Indian* 3 (4): 1–3.

Gregory, Chris. 2000. Star Trek: *Parallel Narratives.* New York: St. Martin's.

Grimes, Katherine. 2002. "Harry Potter: Fairy Tale Prince, Real Boy, and Archetypal Hero." In Whited 2002: 89–122.

Guilbert, Georges-Claude. 2002. *Madonna as Postmodern Myth: How One Star's Self-Construction Rewrites Sex, Gender, Hollywood, and the American Dream.* Jefferson, NC: McFarland.

Harris, Neil. 1985. "Who Owns Our Myth? Heroism and Copyright in an Age of Mass Culture." *Social Research* 52 (2): 242–48.

Heilman, Elizabeth E. 2003. *Harry Potter's World: Multidisciplinary Critical Perspectives.* Garland Ref. Lib. of Soc. Sci. Pedagogy and Pop. Culture. New York: RoutledgeFalmer.

Holtsmark, Erling B. 2001. "The *Katabasis* Theme in Modern Cinema." In Winkler 2001: 23–50.

Huerta, Jorge. 2000. *Chicano Drama: Performance, Society, and Myth.* Cambridge Stu. in Amer. Theatre and Drama. New York: Cambridge UP.

Hughes, Robert T. 2003. *Myths America Lives By.* Urbana: U of Illinois P.

Jewett, Robert, and John Shelton Lawrence. 2003. *Captain America and the Crusade against Evil.* Grand Rapids: Eerdmans.

Kern, Edmund. 2003. *The Wisdom of Harry Potter.* Amherst, NY: Prometheus.

Kossman, Nina. 2001. *Gods and Mortals: Modern Poems on Classical Myths.* New York: Oxford UP.

Kuschke, Ilja. 2001. Review of Winkler 2001. *Bryn Mawr Classical Review* 12 (13) (available online at a number of sites).

Lawrence, John Shelton, and Robert Jewett. 2002. *The Myth of the American Superhero.* Grand Rapids: Eerdmans.

Lewis, C. S. 1956. *Till We Have Faces: A Myth Retold.* San Diego: Harcourt.

Lyon, David. 2000. *Jesus in Disneyland: Religion in Postmodern Times.* Malden, MA: Polity-Blackwell.

McCutcheon, Russell T. 2000. "Myth." In *Guide to the Study of Religion,* eds. Willi Braun and Russell T. McCutcheon, 193–98. New York: Cassell.

Mack, Burton L. 1995. *Who Wrote the New Testament? The Making of the Christian Myth.* San Francisco: HarperCollins.

Mackey-Kallis, Susan. 2001. *The Hero and the Perennial Journey Home in American Film.* Philadelphia: U of Pennsylvania P.

Madonna [Madonna Ciccone]. 1992. *Sex/Madonna.* Photo. Steven Meisel. Art dir. Fabien Baron. Ed. Glenn O'Brien. New York: Warner Bros.

Mathis, Andrew E. 2001. *The King Arthur Myth in Modern American Literature.* Jefferson, NC: McFarland.

May, Rollo. 1991. *The Cry for Myth.* New York: Norton.

Miles, Geoffrey, ed. 1999. *Classical Mythology in English Literature: A Critical Anthology.* New York: Routledge-Taylor and Francis.

Neumann, Erich. 1956. *Amor and Psyche: The Psychic Development of the Feminine. A Commentary on the Tale by Apuleius.* Trans. Ralph Manheim. Bollingen ser., 68. Princeton, NJ: Princeton UP.

Nye, Jody Lynn. 1999. *Mythology 101.* New York: Popular-Warner.

———. 2000. *Applied Mythology.* Atlanta: Meisha Merlin.

———. 2001. *Advanced Mythology.* Atlanta: Meisha Merlin.

Reid, Jane Davidson. 1993. *The Oxford Guide to Classical Mythology in the Arts, 1300–1990.* 2 vols. New York: Oxford UP.

Righter, William. 1975. *Myth and Literature.* Boston: Routledge & Kegan Paul.

Rushing, Janice Hocker, and Thomas S. Frentz. 1991, 1993. "Integrating Ideology and Archetype in Rhetorical Criticism." *The Quarterly Journal of Speech* 77 (4): 385–406; "Part II: A Case Study of *Jaws.*" 79 (1): 61–81.

Ruthven, K. K. 1976. *Myth.* The Critical Idiom, 31. London: Methuen.

Schmidt, Victoria Lynn. 2001. *45 Master Characters: Mythic Models for Creating Original Characters.* Cincinnati: Writer's Digest Books.

Stewart, Grace. 1981 [1977]. *A New "Mythos": The Novel of the Artist as Heroine, 1877–1977.* 2nd ed. Toronto: U of Toronto P.

Vogler, Christopher. 1998. *The Writer's Journey: Mythic Structure for Writers.* Studio City, CA: Wiese Productions.

Voytilla, Stuart. 1999. *Myth and the Movies: Discovering the Mythic Structure of 50 Unforgettable Films.* Studio City, CA: Wiese Productions.

Wagner, Jon, and Jan Lundeen. 1998. *Deep Space and Sacred Time:* Star Trek *in the American Mythos.* Westport, CT: Praeger-Greenwood.

Warner, Marina. 1994. *Six Myths of Our Time: Little Angels, Little Monsters, Beautiful Beasts, and More* (British title: *Managing Monsters: Six Myths of Our Time*). New York: Random House.

Whited, Lana A., ed. 2002. *The Ivory Tower and Harry Potter: Perspectives on a Literary Phenomenon.* Columbia: U of Missouri P.

Whited, Lana A., and M. Katherine Grimes. 2002. "What Would Harry Do? J. K. Rowling and Lawrence Kohlberg's Theories of Moral Development." In Whited 2002: 182–208.

Whitmer, Barbara. 1997. *The Violence Mythos.* SUNY Ser., The Margins of Literature. Albany: SUNY P.

Wilk, Stephen R. 2000. *Medusa: Solving the Mystery of the Gorgon.* New York: Oxford UP.

Winkler, Martin M., ed. 2001. *Classical Myth and Culture in the Cinema.* New York: Oxford UP.

Zink, Michel. 1996. "Arthur." In *Companion to Literary Myths, Heroes, and Archetypes,* ed. Pierre Brunel, trans. Wendy Allatson, Judith Hayward, and Trista Selous, 135–48. New York: Routledge.

Zipes, Jack. 1994. *Fairy Tale as Myth, Myth as Fairy Tale.* The Thomas Clark Lectures, 1993. Lexington: UP of Kentucky.

Bibliography

Only items cited in the Works Cited portions of each chapter that have broad relevance in the study of mythology are included here. In addition, several other (mostly recent) titles can be profitably recommended for a general orientation that have not been cited previously. Collections of myths are cited in the Works Cited for chapter 3.

Anderson, Pamela Sue. 1998. *A Feminist Philosophy of Religion: The Rationality and Myths of Religious Belief.* Malden, MA: Blackwell.

Asimov, Isaac. 1961. *Words from the Myths.* New York: New American Library.

Baeten, Elizabeth M. 1996. *The Magic Mirror: Myth's Abiding Power.* Albany: SUNY P.

Bailey, Colin B. 1992. *The Loves of the Gods: Mythological Painting from Watteau to David.* New York: Rizzoli.

Barthes, Roland. 1972. *Mythologies.* Trans. Annette Lavers. New York: Hill and Wang.

Bloomberg, Kristin M. Mapel. 2001. *Tracing Arachne's Web: Myth and Feminist Fiction.* Gainesville: UP of Florida.

Boitani, Piero. 1994. *The Shadow of Ulysses: Figures of a Myth.* New York: Oxford UP.

Bolle, Kees. 1983. "Myths and Other Religious Texts." In *Contemporary Approaches to the Study of Religion. In Two Volumes,* ed. Frank Whaling, vol. 1: 297–363. Religion and Reason, 7. New York: Mouton.

Bolle, Kees W., Richard G. A. Buxton, and Jonathan Z. Smith. 1993. "Myth and Mythology." *The New Encyclopedia Britannica* 24: 715–32.

Bonnefoy, Yves, ed. 1991. *Mythologies.* Trans. various, under dir. of Wendy Doniger. 2 vols. Chicago: U of Chicago P.

Brunel, Pierre, ed. 1996. *Companion to Literary Myths, Heroes, and Archetypes*. Trans. Wendy Allatson, Judith Hayward, and Trista Selous. New York: Routledge.

Buxton, Richard, ed. 1999. *From Myth to Reason? Studies in the Development of Greek Thought*. New York: Oxford UP.

Calasso, Roberto. 2001. *Literature and the Gods*. New York: Knopf.

Campbell, Joseph. 1959. *Primitive Mythology*. Masks of God, 1. New York: Viking.

———. 1962. *Oriental Mythology*. Masks of God, 2. New York: Viking.

———. 1964. *Occidental Mythology*. Masks of God, 3. New York: Viking.

———. 1968. *Creative Mythology*. Masks of God, 4. New York: Viking.

———. 1968. *The Hero with a Thousand Faces*. 2nd ed. Bollingen ser., 17. Princeton, NJ: Princeton UP.

———. 1972. *Myths to Live By*. New York: Viking.

———, with Bill Moyers. 1988. *The Power of Myth*. Ed. Betty Sue Flowers. New York: Doubleday.

Chevalier, Jean, and Alain Gheerbrant. 1994. *A Dictionary of Symbols*. Trans. John Buchanan-Brown. Cambridge, MA: Blackwell.

Cohen, Percy S. 1969. "Theories of Myth." *Man* n.s. 4 (3): 337–53.

Coupe, Laurence. 1997. *Myth*. The New Crit. Idiom. New York: Routledge.

Derrida, Jacques. 1982 [1971]. "White Mythology: Metaphor in the Text of Philosophy." In *Margins of Philosophy*, trans. Alan Bass, 207–71. Chicago: U of Chicago P.

Detienne, Marcel. 1986. *The Creation of Mythology*. Trans. Margaret Cook. Chicago: U of Chicago P.

Doniger, Wendy. 1998. *The Implied Spider: Politics and Theology in Myth*. New York: Columbia UP.

Dorson, Richard M. 1973. "Mythology and Folklore." *Annual Review of Anthropology* 2: 107–26.

Doty, William G. 1995. "Silent Myths Singing in the Blood: The Sites of Production and Consumption of Myths in a 'Mythless' Society." In *Picturing Cultural Values in Postmodern America*, ed. W. Doty, 187–220. Tuscaloosa: U of Alabama P.

———. 1999. "Exploring Politico-Historical Communication of Mythologies." *Bulletin of the Council of Societies for the Study of Religion* 28 (1): 9–16.

———. 2000. *Mythography: The Study of Myths and Rituals*. Revised 2nd ed. Tuscaloosa: U of Alabama P.

Downing, Christine R., ed. 1991. *Mirrors of the Self: Archetypal Images That Shape Your Life*. A New Consciousness Reader. Los Angeles: Tarcher.

Dundes, Alan, ed. 1984. *Sacred Narrative: Readings in the Theory of Myth*. Berkeley: U of California P.

———, ed. 1988. *The Flood Myth*. Berkeley: U of California P.

Eliade, Mircea. 1960. *Myths, Dreams, and Mysteries: The Encounter between Contemporary Faiths and Archaic Reality*. Trans. Philip Mairet. London: Collins.

———. 1963. *Myth and Reality*. Trans. Willard R. Trask. New York: Harper and Row.

Ellwood, Robert. 1999. *The Politics of Myth: A Study of C. G. Jung, Mircea Eliade, and Joseph Campbell*. Albany: SUNY P.

Feldman, Burton, and Robert D. Richardson. 1972. *The Rise of Modern Mythology 1680–1860.* Bloomington: Indiana UP.

Ferrell, William K. 2000. *Literature and Film as Modern Mythology.* Westport, CT: Praeger-Greenwood.

Flood, Christopher G. 1996. *Political Myth: A Theoretical Introduction.* Theorists of Myth ser. New York: Garland.

Frye, Northrop. 1990. *Myth and Metaphor: Selected Essays, 1974–1988.* Ed. Robert D. Denham. Charlottesville: UP of Virginia.

Galinsky, G. Karl. 1972. *The Herakles Theme: The Adaptations of the Hero in Literature from Homer to the Twentieth Century.* Totowa, NJ: Rowman and Littlefield.

Gould, Eric. 1981. *Mythical Intentions in Modern Literature.* Princeton, NJ: Princeton UP.

Hatab, Lawrence J. 1990. *Myth and Philosophy: A Contest of Truths.* La Salle, IL: Open Court.

Highet, Gilbert. 1949. *The Classical Tradition: Greek and Roman Influences on Western Literature.* New York: Oxford UP.

Hillman, James. 1989. *A Blue Fire: Selected Writings by James Hillman.* Intro. and ed. Thomas Moore. New York: Harper and Row.

Hofmann, Michael, and James Lasdun, eds. *After Ovid: New Metamorphoses.* New York: Noonday-Farrar, Straus and Giroux.

Hollis, James. 1995. *Tracking the Gods: The Place of Myth in Modern Life.* Stud. in Jungian Psych. by Jungian Analysts, 68. Toronto: Inner City.

Hynes, William J., and William G. Doty, eds. 1993. *Mythical Trickster Figures: Contours, Contexts, and Criticisms.* Tuscaloosa: U of Alabama P.

Jackson, Michael. 2002. *The Politics of Storytelling: Violence, Transgression, and Intersubjectivity.* Copenhagen: Museum Tusculanum P at the U of Copenhagen.

Jordan, Michael. 1993. *Myths of the World: A Thematic Encyclopedia.* London: Kyle Cathie.

Keuren, Frances Van. 1991. *Guide to Research in Classical Art and Mythology.* Chicago: American Library Assoc.

Knapp, Bettina L. 1997. *Women in Myth.* Albany: SUNY P.

Kossman, Nina. 2001. *Gods and Mortals: Modern Poems on Classical Myths.* New York: Oxford UP.

Larrington, Carolyne, ed. 1992. *The Feminist Companion to Mythology.* London: Pandora-HarperCollins.

Lawrence, John Shelton, and Robert Jewett. 2002. *The Myth of the American Superhero.* Grand Rapids: Eerdmans.

Leeming, David Adams. 1973. *Mythology: The Voyage of the Hero.* Philadelphia: Lippincott (3rd ed. 1998, Oxford UP).

———. 1990. *The World of Myth: An Anthology.* New York: Oxford UP.

———. 1998. *Mythology: The Voyage of the Hero.* 3rd ed. New York: Oxford UP.

Leeming, David. 2002. *Myth: A Biography of Belief.* New York: Oxford UP.

Lincoln, Bruce. 1999. *Theorizing Myth: Narrative, Ideology, and Scholarship.* Chicago: U of Chicago P.

Mackey-Kallis, Susan. 2001. *The Hero and the Perennial Journey Home in American Film.* Philadelphia: U of Pennsylvania P.

Malinowski, Bronislaw. 1991. *Malinowski and the Work of Myth.* Sel. and intro. Ivan Strenski. Mythos ser. Princeton, NJ: Princeton UP.

Manganaro, Marc. 1992. *Myth, Rhetoric, and the Voice of Authority: A Critique of Frazer, Eliot, Frye, and Campbell.* New Haven: Yale UP.

Maranda, Pierre, ed. 1967. *Mythology: Selected Readings.* Baltimore: Penguin.

McCutcheon, Russell T. 2000. "Myth." In *Guide to the Study of Religion,* ed. Willi Braun and Russell T. McCutcheon, 190–208. New York: Cassell.

Mercatante, Anthony S. 1978. *Good and Evil: Mythology and Folklore.* New York: Harper and Row.

Moddelmog, Debra A. 1993. *Readers and Mythic Signs: The Oedipus Myth in Twentieth Century Fiction.* Carbondale: Southern Illinois UP.

Murray, Henry A., ed. 1968 [1959]. *Myth and Mythmaking.* Boston: Beacon.

Noel, Daniel C. 1986. *Approaching Earth: A Search for the Mythic Significance of the Space Age.* Amity, NY: Amity House.

Oden, Robert A., Jr., and Fritz Graf. 1992. "Myth and Mythology." *Anchor Bible Dictionary* IV: 946–65.

O'Flaherty, Wendy Doniger. 1988. *Other Peoples' Myths: The Cave of Echoes.* New York: Macmillan.

Patton, Laurie, and Wendy Doniger, eds. 1996. *Myth and Method.* Charlottesville: UP of Virginia.

Reesman, Jeanne Campbell, ed. 2001. *Trickster Lives: Culture and Myth in American Fiction.* Athens: U of Georgia P.

Reid, Jane Davidson. 1993. *The Oxford Guide to Classical Mythology in the Arts, 1300–1990.* 2 vols. New York: Oxford UP.

Righter, William. 1975. *Myth and Literature.* London: Routledge and Kegan Paul.

Robertson, James Oliver. 1980. *American Myth, American Reality.* New York: Wang-Farrar, Straus and Giroux.

Rosenberg, Donna. 1994. *World Mythology: An Anthology of the Great Myths and Epics.* 2nd ed. Lincolnwood, IL: NTC.

Rowland, Robert C. 1990. "On Mythic Criticism." *Communication Studies* 41 (2): 101–16.

Russell, Ford. 1998. *Northrop Frye on Myth.* Theorists of Myth ser. New York: Garland.

Ruthven, K. I. 1972. *Myth.* Crit. Idiom, 31. London: Methuen.

Scarborough, Milton. 1994. *Myth and Modernity: Postcritical Reflections.* Albany: SUNY P.

Schilbrack, Kevin, ed. 2002. *Thinking through Myths: Philosophical Perspectives.* New York: Routledge-Taylor and Francis.

Schrempp, Gregory. 1997. "Comparative Mythology." *Folklore: An Encyclopedia* I: 135–40.

Schrempp, Gregory, and William Hansen, eds. 2002. *Myth: A New Symposium.* Bloomington: Indiana UP.

Sebeok, Thomas A., ed. 1958. *Myth: A Symposium.* Bloomington: Indiana UP.

Segal, Robert A., ed. 1995. *Theories of Myths: From Ancient Israel and Greece to Freud, Jung, Campbell, and Lévi-Strauss.* 6 vols. New York: Garland.

———. 1999. *Theorizing about Myth.* Amherst: U of Massachusetts P.

Shackel, Paul A. ed. 2001. *Myth, Memory, and the Making of the American Landscape.* Gainesville: UP of Florida.

Sienkewicz, Thomas J. 1996. *World Mythology: An Annotated Guide to Collections and Anthologies.* Lanham, MD: Scarecrow; Pasadena and Englewood Cliffs, NJ: Salem.

Simpkinson, Charles, and Anne Simpkinson, eds. 1993. *Sacred Stories: A Celebration of the Power of Stories to Transform and Heal.* San Francisco: HarperCollins.

Slochower, Harry. 1970. *Mythopoesis: Mythic Forms in the Literary Classics.* Detroit: Wayne State UP.

Strenski, Ivan. 1987. *Four Theories of Myth in Twentieth-Century History: Cassirer, Eliade, Lévi-Strauss, and Malinowski.* Iowa City: U of Iowa P.

Thompson, Stith. 1946. *The Folktale.* New York: Holt, Rinehart and Winston.

Turner, Victor. 1968. "Myth and Symbol." *International Encyclopedia of the Social Sciences* 10: 576–82.

Veyne, Paul. 1988 [1983]. *Did the Greeks Believe in Their Myths? An Essay on the Constitutive Imagination.* Trans. Paula Wissig. Chicago: U of Chicago P.

Vickery, John B., ed. 1966. *Myth and Literature: Contemporary Theory and Practice.* Lincoln: U of Nebraska P.

Von Hendy, Andrew. 2002. *The Modern Construction of Myth.* Bloomington: Indiana UP.

Wagner, Jon, and Jan Lundeen. 1998. *Deep Space and Sacred Time:* Star Trek *in the American Mythos.* Westport, CT: Praeger-Greenwood.

Warner, Marina. 1994. *Six Myths of Our Time: Little Angels, Little Monsters, Beautiful Beasts, and More.* New York: Random House.

Weigle, Marta. 1982. *Spiders and Spinsters: Women and Mythology.* Albuquerque: U of New Mexico P.

Westbrook, Deeanne. 1996. *Ground Rules: Baseball and Myth.* Urbana: U of Illinois P.

White, John H. 1972. *Mythology in the Modern Novel: A Study of Prefigurative Techniques.* Princeton, NJ: Princeton UP.

Whitmer, Barbara. 1997. *The Violence Mythos.* SUNY Ser., The Margins of Literature. Albany: SUNY P.

Woodford, Susan. 2003. *Images of Myths in Classical Antiquity.* New York: Cambridge UP.

Young, Jonathan. 2001. *SAGA: Best New Writings on Mythology.* Vol. 2. Ashland, OR: White Cloud.

Internet and Other Electronic Resources

Although there are wonders of information stored on the Internet/World Wide Web, the simplest search engine can produce almost overwhelming numbers of citations ("hits"). When I started looking more seriously at the Harry Potter phenomenon, for instance, the search engine Google brought me more than five million citations. The clever Internet user realizes quickly that the various search engines prioritize citations by one or another method: frequency of citation by other users, for instance, or the most recent entries listed first. Hence if one uses a "smart search" with multiple criteria for searching, the hits dwindle down fairly rapidly after satisfying *all* the search criteria. These systems are precisely analogous to bibliographic database search software at libraries.

My first advice, then, is to learn how to use the search tools such as Google or Yahoo efficiently—help files provide instruction on how to do the most efficient searches. But also any larger library has a Reference specialist (today often named Information Services specialist) who can have you running smart searches very rapidly. Failing such a resource, I suggest use of the *Librarians' Index to the Internet,* for librarian-tested sites of greatest usefulness—certainly not the largest sets of citations, but citations carefully selected by librarians whose business is helping people do research.

Because URLs change frequently on the Web, I have supplied in this chapter names of the Web sites and given their electronic addresses in Works Cited for this segment of the book. None of the search engines will have trouble searching for such a title as "Librarians' Index to the Internet." For an evaluative overview of the more than 800,000 search engines, you cannot do better than to access "The Major Search Engines and Directories" on the SearchEngineWatch.com site.

Another approach involves using the collections of materials that the major search engines have already established within their files: a Google search for "myth," for instance, takes you to that engine's Web Directory that drills down through Arts > Literature > Myths and Folktales > Myths. This will give you hundreds of hits arranged by cultural group as well as type of materials ("sacred texts—myths and sagas," "world mythology," "gods, heroes, and myth").

Where World Wide Web access is not available, the *Books in Print* Subject Guide is quite useful (especially in its CD-ROM or on-line version). Or online, the Library of Congress Web site provides 1270 references to publications on myth and mythology in its collection. Also on-line or from the Modern Language Association International Bibliography on Silver Platter CD-ROMs, this frequently updated resource is helpful as well for finding the most recent publications, including reviews, on a desired subject.

Hardly to be ignored are the services provided by commercial bookstores on-line. Amazon.com, for instance, provides a huge bibliography of myth-related volumes it hopes to entice you to purchase from them. Northern Light found 21,492 items for "myth, mythology." It is distinctive in rating its hits in terms of percentage of relevance—it hopes you will use its system to purchase reprints of relevant articles.

With respect to recommending Internet sites themselves, I begin with *Myth*ing Links* (www.mythinglinks.org) and include *The Voice of the Shuttle,* not because both are produced within the geographic reach of metropolitan Santa Barbara, but because the first, begun in 1998 when its author, Kathleen Jenks, was a faculty member at Pacifica Graduate Institute, is one of the smartest sites on myth I know, and because the second, produced at the University of California/Santa Barbara, is one of the best sites in the world on the humanities as a whole.

For the study of mythology, *Myth*ing Links* is truly an astonishing resource, beautifully illustrated, with excellent evaluations of the Internet links that it organizes. In addition to the traditional A–Z geographical area outline, there is a raft of well-organized themes, subindexed to geographical areas. These include Creation Myths (three divisions, with literally hundreds of links), Arthurian Themes, Old Europe, Pan-Slavic Traditions and Beliefs, Rituals of Puberty, Trickster, Crones and Sages, and Air, Wind, and Sky Goddesses and Gods. Especially if you are just beginning such research, don't miss Jenks's General Reference Page, with its "Reference Resources and On-Line Texts." Teachers of all levels will appreciate her "Teaching Mythology, Folklore, and the Arts." Jenks also has links to sites dealing with contemporary politics globally and to ecological sites.

Begun in 1994, *The Voice of the Shuttle: Web Page for Humanities Research* is maintained by Alan Liu. This site has extremely valuable general links at its Humanities Metapages and Portals page and Humanities Texts Archives (on-line resources; see also *Project Gutenberg* or the *Electronic Text Center* at the University of Virginia). Mythology is located in the Classics section and has only a hypertext version of *Bulfinch's Mythology* by Bob Fisher and a Cyber-Latin link, but search "Myth" to reach 33 excellent links to mythological matters in a large number of disciplines in the humanities and social sciences.

There are a number of different approaches to information on other on-line resources: Christopher B. Siren's *Myths and Legends* is with Jenks's *Myth*ing Links* one the largest collections of connections to specific cultural areas by geographic location, although it does indeed begin with a more general set of links to site-of-the-week pages, encyclopedias, collections, and some visual resources. Carlos Parada's *Genealogical Guide to Greek Mythology* has been brought usefully on-line in *Greek Mythology Link,* a fabulous place to find entries on individual Greek figures and sites of Classical interest, including very good bibliographies, both ancient and modern. The Thematic Index is augmented by access to many sorts of tables, maps, and illustrations (see reference to the CD-ROM version later; a downloadable Adobe Acrobat [pdf] file can be purchased, although it omits images) as well as internal links to other materials on the CD. *The History Net's Ancient/Classical History* page on "Mythology Encyclopedias" is useful to find additional resources.

Multicultural in orientation, *Mythology, Folklore, and a little bit of Religion* by Sarah Craig, and Philip Burns's *General Folklore and Mythology* are some of the most inclusive collections of links, along with Siren's mentioned in the previous paragraph. All three are well organized and extremely broad in scope.

Encyclopedia Mythica, an extensive dictionary begun in 1995, has over 6,000 brief entries on gods and goddesses from all over the world and is searchable by region or type; it has links to related resources. Texts on-line are links pointed to: "Folklore and Mythology: Electronic Texts at the University of Pittsburgh." "Classical Myth: The Ancient Sources" lists both texts and sources for Greek and Roman mythology.

The Internet Sacred Text Archive brings one to hundreds of ancient texts as well as more contemporary religious texts (it is also available on CD-ROM). One figure alone, Herakles (the Roman Hercules), has many resources for study under "Hercules: Greece's Greatest Hero" (why a site would use the Roman term for "Greece's Greatest Hero" escapes me!). Of course, one can always use a search engine for a specific figure or even culture, but these collections of links can save a great deal of research time because they have already eliminated some of the misleading links. You won't find a link to the notorious sex club, Plato's Cave, in any of these, for example.

The Joseph Campbell Foundation's *Gems of the Net* has the usual links to A–Z culture areas (although not listed alphabetically) as well as E-Texts, Civilization and Cities, Women, Language, and Archaeology, among others. You must register as an Associate (no charge) to use the service. A standard reference text in religious studies for world mythologies, Mircea Eliade's *From Primitive to Zen,* is available on-line at http://alexm.here.ru/mirrors/www. enteract.com/jwalz/Eliade/.

Imagery is available from *Mythmedia: Mythology in Western Art,* from Haifa, Israel, but even with a broadband (data-rich, high-speed) connection, I find the images stream in very slowly. *World Myths and Legends in Art* from The Minneapolis Institute of Arts features its extensive collection and is designed for easy access to school pupils and teachers. The *Endicott Studio for Mythic Arts* brings contemporary art and literature on-line, along with monthly journal essays on various topics. A search at the *National Gallery of Art* brings up 767 illustrations, arranged alphabetically by artist, but searchable; go to The Collection, search by site ("myth" = 38 pages, "mythology" = 91 pages). *Brewer's Dictionary of Phrase and Fable,* taken from the 1898 edition of the book of this title is available from Bartleby.com, a source for many titles of classic literature as well as searchable reference volumes.

Within the world of classical studies, *The Perseus Project* at Tufts University is simply outstanding, providing original language texts as well as translations. Special "Exhibits" change frequently; the main portal will most likely be "Classics"; that leads to 441 Greek, Latin, and English texts (nearly 31 million words), 56,652 images, and 83 secondary influences such as the marvelous *Beazley Archive Pottery Database,* Georg Autenrieth's *Homeric Dictionary,* and commentaries on many classical authors. This extensive project, based at Tufts University, has been supported by the Annenberg/CPB Project, Apple Computer, the Fund for the Improvement of Postsecondary Education, the Getty Grant Program, the National Endowment for the Arts, Boston University, Xerox Corporation, and other donors. The Project also has other major databases on, for instance, the English Renaissance and the History of London.

Four hundred and forty-one classical texts with user-provided commentary are available from *The Internet Classics Archive* posted by Daniel C. Stevenson. An interactive map of Greece is accessible at <Princeton.edu/ myth/old-index.html>. *Thesaurus Linguae Classicae* at the University of California/Irvine provides an extensive electronic data bank of ancient Greek literature from the eighth-century B.C.E. Homer to 600 C.E. The *Library of Congress* resources for Greek and Latin Classics are extensive; don't overlook their Internet Resources link.

The World Wide Web site *Greek Mythology Link* by Carlos Parada mentioned earlier is available on CD-ROM, updated to mirror the Web site as of the date of your purchase (the original 1993 print version, *Genealogical Guide to Greek Mythology,* is still being published). It features 1,430 pages, with 6,460 entries, and has 6,742 images. Ginette Paris's *Mythology: A CD-ROM,* vol. 1, Greek and Roman, is still in production, although a beta release as well as the Web version are extremely promising. The project began with extensive Canadian funding, including the Social Sciences and Humanities Research Council of Canada, and with international collaboration.

Begun in 1993, *Mythology* has some 25,000 pages of text from 70 academically pertinent authors providing information on divinities, heroes, sagas, concepts, themes, places, and lexicons, all supported by 50,000 pop-up definitions. A whole series of encyclopedias and classics textbooks are included (examples: all of H. J. Rose, *Handbook of Greek Mythology,* and Robert E. Bell, *Women of Classical Mythology*). Commentaries such as Walter Burkert's *Greek Religion* and Robert Graves's *The Greek Myths,* or Hamilton's *Mythology,* are included. Contemporary authors such as James Hillman and David Miller are included (and about 350 pages of my own writings). There are several interactive sections and animations, and the original contemporary graphics by Pierre Guimond are stunning. Without a doubt, this CD-ROM or Web site is like having a whole library in one's study

Other CD-ROMs include the Films for the Humanities and Sciences' *Mythology: The Great Myths of Greece and Rome,* featuring the voyages and activities of Ulysses (Odysseus), Jason and the Argonauts, Aeneas, and Hercules (Herakles). Macmillan's *Athena: Classical Mythology on CD-ROM* offers full-text translations of significant classical works and synopses of all classical myths, as well as epics, tragedies, and poems. At over $300 each, these may be a bit pricey for private purchase.

Who knows what pulls people into the study of mythology? Many a time I have had people tell me it was the high school text by Edith Hamilton, *Mythology,* which must have sold millions of copies by now. Others have cited a Disney movie or some other reference from a film. Today video/computer games are a likely source of influence, so the Microsoft Game Studios' *Age of Mythology* (2001) and its *The Titan Expansion* (2003) may well be the way new interest in classical mythology, at least, is stimulated—1,210,000 Internet citations as of April 2004 seem to indicate such interest indeed. Promotional materials inform us that "Taking on the role of one of nine ancient civilizations, players guide their people to greatness by commanding all aspects of their empire: gathering resources, raising massive armies, waging war against enemies, establishing profitable trade routes, building new settlements, enhancing production or military might with improvements, exploring new frontiers, and advancing through four distinct ages" (<http://www.microsoft.com/games/ageofmythology/>).

Gameplays include "God Powers—These rare and powerful gifts grant players the powers of the gods several times during each game." Sounds a bit like what the Greeks called *hybris*, the sort of human pride that usually led the heroes to their termination. But at least there's a wide range of travel opportunities: "The player will guide his forces everywhere ranging from the siege at Troy, to the pyramids in Egypt, to the snow covered mountains in the North, to the mythological underworld." The expansion adds "Atlantean mythology," and "A new victory condition. Gamers can create a Titan unit that dwarfs everyone else and employ it to wreak havoc and rain destruction on enemy civilizations."

Happy browsing!

WORKS CITED

Works Cited by Identified Author

Burns, Philip. *General Folklore and Mythology.* <http://www.pburns.com/myth gene.htm>

Craig, Sarah. *Mythology, Folklore, and a little bit of Religion.* <http://www.csm.edu/~bnagy/sarahsite/myths2.html>

Eliade, Mircea. *From Primitive to Zen.* <http://alexm.here.ru/mirrors/www.enter act.com/jwalz/Eliade/>

Gill, N. S. *The History Net's Ancient/Classical History.* <http://ancienthistory.about.com/mbody.htm>

Hamilton, Edith. 1942. *Mythology.* New York: Little, Brown-Time Warner.

Jenks, Kathleen. *Myth*ing Links.* <http://www.mythinglinks.org>

Liu, Alan. *The Voice of the Shuttle: Web Page for Humanities Research.* <http://vos.ucsb.edu/>

Parada, Carlos. *Greek Mythology Link.* <http://homepage.mac.com/cparada/GML/>

Paris, Ginette. Online version of CD-ROM *Mythology.* <http://www.mythology.org/>

Siren, Chris. *Myths and Legends.* <http://members.bellatlantic.net/~vze33 gpz/myth.html>

Stevenson, Daniel C. *Internet Classics Archive.* <http://classics.mit.edu/>

Works Cited by Name of Internet Site

Google. <*http://*www.google.com> [search engine]

Yahoo. <*http://*www.yahoo.com> [search engine]

Northern Light. <http://northernlight.com> [search engine]

Brewer's Dictionary of Phrase and Fable. <http://www.bartleby.com/81/> or <www.bibliomania.com/Reference/PhraseAndFable/>

Electronic Text Center. (The University of Virginia.) <http://etext.lib.virginia.edu/>

Encyclopedia Mythica. <http://www.pantheon.org/areas/>

Endicott Studio for Mythic Arts. <http://endicott-studio.com/>

Gems of the Net. (The Joseph Campbell Foundation.) <http://jcf.org/>

Internet Sacred Text Archive, The. <http://www.sacred-texts.com/>

Librarians' Index to the Internet. <http://www.lii.org>

Library of Congress. <http://www.loc.gov/> (Search, subject browse: myth, mythology.)

Mythmedia: Mythology in Western Art. (Haifa University.) <http:// http:// www-lib.haifa.ac.il/www/art/MYTHOLOGY_WESTART.HTML>

National Gallery of Art. <http://www.nga.gov>

Perseus Project, The. <http://www.perseus.tufts.edu/>

Project Gutenberg: Fine Literature Digitally Re-Produced. <http://promo.net/pg/>

World Myths and Legends in Art. (Minneapolis Institute of Arts.) <http://www.artsmia.org/world-myths>

Glossary

allegory A mode of interpretation, often moralistic in tone, in which items in a made-up story correspond to items in an earlier narrative. Fables often have allegorical elements.

apocalypse, apocalyptic The adjective refers to a type of eschatology, the projection of the "end" *(eschatos)* of all things (in both the sense of termination and goal). The literary expression, apocalypse, features elaborate descriptions of the supposed final times of the world and may predict new world beginnings. The biblical Ezekiel, Gospel of Mark, and Revelation all contain influential apocalyptic elements.

Apollodorus 180–120 B.C.E., Athenian grammarian, usually regarded as the author of one of the first major collections of Greek mythological stories, the *Bibliotheca/Library,* but that attribution is increasingly questioned today.

archetype A typical pattern of behavior or type of character that is widespread in a culture or perhaps universally.

Aristotle (in Greek transliteration, Aristoteles) 384–347 B.C.E., Greek philosopher, Plato's pupil until the latter's death; tutor of the son of Philip of Macedon, Alexander (the Great). Often considered the founder of the natural sciences, as opposed to Plato's founding of the humanities, especially philosophy.

Arthur, Arthurian Possibly King Arthur was a historical figure; Arthurian legends begin in the fifth and sixth centuries but really flourished in the twelfth and fifteenth; a romanticized court took on larger-than-life dimensions across European literature.

Barthes, Roland 1915–1980, French intellectual, brilliant analyst of culture and literature, especially well known for his semiotic literary analyses.

big bang A contemporary theory of the origination of the universe that suggests that an enormous explosion occurred about 10–20 billion years ago, flinging matter in all directions.

Buddhism The philosophy/religion represented by many groups, especially numerous in Asia, that profess varying forms of this doctrine, yet typically venerate the historical Buddha.

Campbell, Joseph 1904–1987, American myth and literature critic, who taught at Morningside College; most influential after his death, when the televised *The Power of Myth* interviews with William Moyers were rebroadcast many times.

Changing Woman The Navajo creative goddess with whom an adolescent woman identifies during her puberty ceremony, the Kinaaldá; partnered with the Sun.

charter A foundational idea, concept or plan. **Malinowski** suggested that instead of being trivial stories, myths represented functional charters for societies.

comparativism Several types of myth criticism that study parallels between myths of different independent groups.

cosmogony, cosmogonic The story generally accepted by a culture about the origins of things, especially the universe.

cosmology, cosmological The story generally accepted by a culture about the organization of the universe, typically in one or more levels of reality (worlds).

Coyote A prototypical trickster figure, especially in Native American Indian societies.

cultural studies Within academic areas such as American studies, interdisciplinary studies, or pop culture studies, attention to social causes and contexts of themes, images, myths.

demythologize, demythify Initially used mid-twentieth century to refer to getting "behind" the narrative details of a myth to indicate its existential meanings; now more generally refers to showing how a myth has rational or ideological aspects.

Dreamtime Especially Australian, a primordial time when the Ancestors established the features of the land.

Durkheim, Émile 1858–1917, French sociological theorist and analyst, extremely influential in the construction of modern sociology and anthropology.

earth-diver A sky being cast down from the heavens, rescued by birds who form a protective mat upon which the being is carried; then becomes the magical creator/creatrix of our planet's substance.

earth mother See **Gaia**.

Eliade, Mircea Influential historian of religion in Europe and at the University of Chicago; emphasized that performances of religious myths and rituals reinstate vital powers present in archaic beginnings.

emergence myths One of the many versions of origin or creation stories, in which the first people are said to have moved upward toward the present plane of existence through a series of previous worlds.

epic Long involved accounts, originally sung or chanted, of heroic figures and their companions.

eschatology See **apocalyptic**.

etiology Explanation of how something originated; sometimes used to suggest that myths have little other meaning or function.

etymology Derivation of words, either in terms of earliest meanings or in terms of how those change through historical usage.

euhemerism An assumption that myths refer not to historical realities but to the misplaced status of earlier figures who were elevated to the rank of deity.

fabula/fable The Romans chose *fabula* because the Greek *mythos* had become associated with trivial stories, and it exists in European languages in that sense; what is today formally named in English *fable* refers to moralistic stories with animal actors, such as those of Aesop or Jean de la Fontaine.

fertility myth A type of myth that emphasizes the rather magical growth of crops and animals, thanks to the power of sacred figures and ritual activities.

folklore, folkloristics Traditional beliefs, tales, myths, and practices of a people, mostly transmitted orally; the study of such is folklore studies or folkloristics.

Frazer, Sir James 1854–1941, British anthropologist who fantasized on the importance of magic, religion, and science in the development of human thought. See: ***Golden Bough, The.***

Freud, Sigmund 1904–1939, Austrian creator of psychoanalysis; his theories of the unconscious and the symbolism found, for instance, in dreams, vastly influenced much of twentieth-century intellectual life.

Frye, Northrop 1912–1991, Canadian literary theorist and analyst who developed extensive analysis for all of world literature; he proposed that four basic literary genres were associated with the four seasons of weather.

functionalist Looking at how materials such as myths actually exert influence on social groups, as opposed to views of such materials as purely imaginative, poetic in origin.

Gaia Ancient Greek Earth Goddess, one of the primordial deities who procreated the heavens and the seas and was the mother of a number of divine offspring.

genre Type of artistic material, such as literature or painting; example: the genre of musical comedy or of heroic epic.

Gilgamesh The Sumerian *Epic of Gilgamesh* is probably the oldest written story, about the adventures of the historical king of Uruk (somewhere between 2750 and 2500 B.C.E.), Gilgamesh, and his close friend and companion, Enkidu.

Golden Bough, The James Frazer's multivolume collection of world mythology (1 volume published in 1890 was expanded to 13 by 1915), extremely influential initially, but now increasingly seen as loaded with ideological influences of his own day, rather than accurately representing the myths he adduces.

Greco-Roman Greek and Roman culture in the Hellenistic period, ca. 700 B.C.E.–395 C.E.

hermeneutics The formal principles by which interpretation (primarily of literature or scriptures) proceeds.

Hesiod (Greek transliteration Hesiodos) Eighth-century B.C.E. poet who formalized several early Greek accounts of the beginning and ordering of the universe and gods in his *Theogony.*

hieros gamos The Sacred Marriage of the king and queen, or of the queen and her consort, their sexual union symbolizing the periodic renewal of the rich fertility of the land and its crops.

Hinduism A diverse body of religion, philosophy, and cultural practice native to and predominant in India, characterized by a belief in psychic reincarnation and a supreme being of many forms and natures. It considers opposing theories as aspects of one eternal truth and hopes for future liberation from earthly evils.

Homer (Greek transliteration Homeros) Greatly revered Greek poet/performer considered to be the main impulse behind both *Iliad* and *Odyssey*, although probably less an individual than a "movement" of bardic creators and performers. The *Homeric Hymns* of the seventh and sixth centuries B.C.E. were probably written by his followers.

Hopi Native American Indian people, most of whom still live in ancient pueblos (towns) in what is now Arizona.

iconography Analysis of images as they are established in a work or culture, e.g., "the iconography of *Star Wars.*"

ideology Underlying principles or impulses generating social formations; for example, a myth of violence may promote an ideology that gives high priority to warfare.

Inuit A member of any of the Eskimo peoples of North America and especially of Arctic Canada and Greenland.

Jung, Carl G. 1875–1961, Swiss psychologist, who was a member of Freud's Vienna circle but revolted against his authoritarian stand on the sexual nature of psychological problems and founded his own analytical psychology oriented to the soul (psyche) of the individual and the culture.

Krishna In Hinduism, the eighth and principal avatar (manifestation) of Vishnu, often depicted as a handsome young man playing a flute and adored by a host of young women.

legend An unverified story handed down from earlier times, especially one popularly believed to have some specific historical origins.

Lévi-Strauss, Claude 1908–, French social anthropologist who thought the structure of mythological expressions was perhaps more important than what is usually treated as their content.

logos *Word* in Greek, but historically it came to be contrasted to *mythos,* which also meant *word.* In philosophical use, logos came to be associated with rational reasoning, myth more with passing along traditional narratives, often about deities or heroes.

Malinowski, Bronislaw 1884–1941, Polish-born British cultural anthropologist known as the founder of **functionalism;** argued for hands-on field ethnographic experience.

Manu A great sage of India, who about 1500 B.C.E. developed the *Laws of Manu* that long had an influence.

marriage, sacred See **hieros gamos.**

Mesopotamia The ancient region of southwest Asia between the Tigris and Euphrates rivers in what is today Iraq, the home of a number of early civilizations, including Sumer, Akkad, Babylonia, and Assyria.

metamorphosis Transformation, as when a woman (Daphne) turns into a laurel tree to escape her pursuer Apollo.

monomyth A particular perspective thought to inform a large body of opinion or literature; e.g., the heroic monomyth.

myth-and-ritual school A perspective emphasizing the dominance of rituals over myths—which are then considered to be merely accompaniments to rituals.

mytheme An easily identifiable segment or theme of a complex myth (often interchangeable with *mythologem*).

mythicity What makes a myth a myth—not easily identified, but generally easily recognizable by a familiar tone or mode of storytelling or characterization or reference to figures of a mythical pantheon or primal events.

mythoclast Someone who regards myths negatively.

myth of mythlessness The sense in our scientific age that we have grown "beyond" mythological values or expressions.

mythography Earlier used to name archaic collections of mythological accounts and genealogies, primarily Greek; more recently used to refer to the analysis of myths.

mythologem A mythical unit or theme or figure.

mythology, comparative See **comparativism.**

mythology, world An inclusive reference to the many different types of mythologies found among the cultures of our planet.

mythopoesis The creative "making" *(poesis)* of myths, often in terms of reinventing earlier themes or mythological materials and themes in literature.

mythos Originally, *word,* then the words of myths, as opposed to those of logical or scientific expressions. At present it also serves as a sort of shorthand for worldview or perspective, such as "The mythos of the perfect barbecue."

mythostory, individual An automythological story that one tells to indicate how someone has become his or her own unique person; personal self-history.

narrativity Something that has the quality of narration, as contrasted with poetry or prose discourse.

Navajo Native American Indian people of the Southwestern United States.

nether world See **underworld.**

Oedipus complex In Freudian psychoanalysis, a subconscious sexual desire in a child, especially a male child, for the parent of the opposite sex.

Olympus, -ians Mount Olympus is the highest mountain in Greece; Olympians: the early organization of the deities thought to dwell there.

origin myths Accounts of the beginnings of things, often, in the case of cosmology, the creation of humankind or the world.

pantheon A circular temple in Rome, completed in 27 B.C.E., that was dedicated to all the gods; subsequently a general reference to a people's ranking of deities.

phenomenology Originally a philosophical movement that sought to study the actual "phenomenon" of something by bracketing one's own experience, and hence avoiding perceptual assumptions of the culture brought to the analysis.

Plato (Greek transliteration Platon) ca. 407–399 B.C.E., foundational Greek philosopher, whose philosophy was developed from that of his master, Socrates.

polysemy, polysemantic Having many possible meanings.

polyvocal Speaking variously to different interpreters.

postmodern Recognition that many of the traditional assumptions of Western culture are less "universal" or "absolute" than social constructions that have ideological implications; rejection of many Master Narratives in favor of a much more ad hoc orientation to cultural mores and values.

primal Something first in time; original; primeval; or something valued as primary.

primary myth A master, dominant myth of a society or individual that has influences across the culture, for instance, the importance of the Constitution to American values.

Prometheus, -ean One of the primal Greek Titans, considered to have brought culture (symbolized by control of fire) to humankind; the adjective is usually applied to some enormously important or difficult task.

Proteus, protean An old man of the sea who was a watchman for Poseidon and possessed the gifts of prophecy and transformation; the adjective is applied to a person or project that can take on many different forms of appearance.

protomyth An earliest version of a tradition or myth that strongly influences its transformations.

Ragnarök In Norse mythology, the final destruction of the gods in a great battle against the powers of evil—to be followed by a new era.

reference myth A particular myth or set of practices studied in a critical analysis.

rite of passage A ritual intended to guide and facilitate transitions between stages of life development.

ritualization An emphasis upon the *processual,* performative dynamics of a ritual happening; contrasted to *ritualizing,* making up a ritual.

romantic An emphasis upon feeling, folk-culture, nature.

saga Elaborate and dramatic narrative of the adventures or journeys of a heroic figure or group.

semiotic Sign-ificant, meaning-bearing; semiotics is the science of analyzing how signs and words have reference to things.

shaman/seer In contrast to the priest, the conservative ritual leader, the shaman flies beyond the traditional boundaries to reach (or "see") spirits, and subsequently to heal souls ceremoniously and dramatically.

socially constructed Current opinion that societies are more or less created by historical or commercial pressures, rather than being self-consciously and rationally constituted.

structuralism A twentieth-century method of analyzing social products on the analogy of linguistics, by projecting depth meanings (paradigms) and structures "behind" their surfaces (syntagms).

theogony See **Hesiod.**

theomachia A battle of the gods or other mythological figures, especially in the earliest times.

trickster A figure who operates by skillfully manipulating situations, deceiving people, or just getting the best bargains; Hermes was the prototypical Greek trickster, although many mythological stories involve various types of trickery played by the gods. See also **Coyote.**

underworld A concept of a lower world (hence "nether land") beneath the surface of the earth, often considered to be the place for afterlives of the dead.

vestal virgin Young woman dedicated to the innermost temple of Rome; she was immediately thrust out if she became pregnant.

Vishnu One of the principal Hindu deities, worshiped as the protector and preserver of worlds, and often conceived as a member of the triad including also Brahma and Shiva.

world mythology See **mythology, world.**

Index

About the Author

WILLIAM G. DOTY is Professor Emeritus of Humanities and Religious Studies at the University of Alabama, Tuscaloosa. His many books include *Myths of Masculinity* (1933), *Mythography: The Study of Myths and Rituals* (1986, 2000), *Contemporary New Testament Interpretation* (1972), *Picturing Cultural Values in Postmodern America* (1995), and *Mythical Trickster Figures: Contours, Contexts, and Criticisms* (1993).